50 Years of Christmas Letters

The Life and Times of a Lucky Man

50 Years of Christmas Letters

The Life and Times of a Lucky Man

Jack Pendray

Dedication

To Linda, my wife, my life. It has been said of me that I am lucky in the big things and unlucky in the small things, because I control the small things. In marriage, the biggest of things, I hit the undeserved jackpot.

Acknowledgments

I could fill another book with acknowledgments of all the fine folks who have redirected my pinballing peregrinations (one of my favorite words from junior high school) through life, but, rest easy, I won't. Instead, I'll try to thank those who were also involved in getting this book done.

Linda: My wife of 54 years-and-counting to whom this book is dedicated, was also a contributor, first draft editor, critic, and moderator of my wildest writings (you should see some of my drafts...no, bad idea!). Since my first reaction to most suggestions is usually an emphatic *no*, Linda knows to give me an idea, ignore the rejection, and then wait until I sheepishly crawl back and agree what a good idea it is. Imagine 54 years of putting up with me! Our friends call her Saint Linda.

Mike, Steve, Andy, and Sean: My three sons and nephew who got me started writing so I wouldn't go nuts during the Covid sequestrations. They surely rue the day they came up with that idea.

Liz Coursen: My publisher/editor/whip-cracker who had the vision, talent, and stubbornness to turn 50 years of my scribblings into a reasonably coherent book.

Paul Huck: A lifelong friend, contributor, draft reader, critic, and cheerleader for the book, Paul also wrote the Foreword. When Liz told me that the book needed a Foreword written by someone who has known me a long time and will say nice things about me, I was stumped. That phrase is an oxymoron, so I concentrated on the "known-me-a-long-time" part and contacted Paul. Paul's first question was, "Do I have to say nice things about you?" I gave him a full release to tell the truth, so he agreed to write it.

Caleb Estes, Ron Pantello, Tom Black, Tim Abbott, Frank Willingham, Susan Breese Bowers, Tom Prebianca, Bobby Victor, and some other members of my Ching Tang high school fraternity and my Sigma Nu college fraternity groups: They read the drafts of recently written pieces and gave me the huge encouragement of saying they were "readable."

Everyone else who was involved but not mentioned: In the interest of protecting many of my friends from public scorn of being associated with this book, and in recognition of the short-term memory problems of this old geezer, I left you out of this page. Beware, you are probably mentioned elsewhere in the book, sorry.

Table of Contents

Foreword

—Paul C. Huck

As Jack's Acknowledgments correctly discloses, I accepted this assignment only on the condition that I was in no way expected, much less obligated, to say "nice things" about Jack. Of course, as you and I well know, saying nice things about Jack is a piece of cake. This Foreword, like Jack's book, is a labor of love.

Why me? Well, I have known my dear friend, and sometimes mentor, since 1952, when we spent countless hours aimlessly rambling around Coral Gables and Coconut Grove, Florida. We spent our formative years together from junior high to the University of Florida. One gets to know best friends, and more importantly lean on them, during that challenging period. But then our paths parted, as Jack went off to pursue his dream, beginning with the U.S. Air Force, at Stanford University. Our paths crossed only sporadically over the next several decades. Yet, Jack thoughtfully always kept in touch, often through his well-crafted, oft wine-induced (according to Jack) holiday missives which serve as the backbone of this book.

So, of course, I know Jack pretty well, about as well as anyone, outside of his family (who were disqualified from writing this Foreword because of that saying "nice things" about Jack notion). Or at least I thought I knew Jack well. That was until I read his book, a very personal, revealing, all-encompassing account of his journey to this point. From the beginning, I knew Jack as a thoughtful, generous, talented and caring human being, with a subtle, yet endearing sense of humor. His story is a testament to a lifetime of those traits, revealed only if you read between the lines because Jack could never be mistaken for a self-promoter. As I now know, Jack is much more than that young friend I knew back when. His academic and professional accomplishments are exceptional. However, because of his self-deprecating humor and honest humility, they were unknown to me. To our old Gables gang, Jack was always just "one of the guys." Yes, we all knew that Jack was smarter and more conscientious than the rest of us, but little did we know then that Jack was so intelligent, and would grow into such an accomplished professional. His diverse, successful career is enviable, to say the least. Jack, you fooled us all.

Foreword

However, Jack's academic and professional accomplishments are not what make Jack so special, though he surely is the most accomplished, though sincerely humble, graduate of our old gang. No, his human, personal traits set Jack apart then and now. It's clear to me that in the unforgiving, competitive world of business enterprise, Jack succeeded because of his talent, people skills, character and commitment to doing things the right way. It is particularly revealing that I have never heard Jack utter a mean-spirited comment about another (though he has had ample reason and occasion to do so). Jack is uncompromisingly honest and fair, generous almost to a fault, optimistic, yet a realist, and genuinely caring of others. And, of course, we all know that Jack is just fun to be around.

But I digress; enough about Jack. About his book. I am dumbfounded by the thought that Jack would even consider writing such a profoundly revealing, personal account of his first eighty years. Such openness is a quality not often associated with males of our generation. And Jack has skillfully laid out his life's globe-trotting journey as he lived it. Thoughtful, creative, structured, wide-ranging, sincere, guileless, considerate of others, with a healthy dose of humor, mostly self-effacing.

Read carefully to appreciate that Jack has cast three overarching themes weaving together the various chapters of his journey: love of family, loyalty to friends and commitment to honest endeavor.

I thoroughly enjoyed Jack's well-written journal, especially the parts of which I was not aware. It was an eye-opening pleasure to travel with Jack through those diverse chapters of his eighty years. I look forward to traveling with him through the next chapters.

Jack's life story reminds me, as if I need reminding, why I am so proud and thankful to call Jack Pendray my dear friend. I am confident that you are equally proud and thankful to call him husband, father, grandfather, uncle, cousin and friend.

Introduction

Sneakily hidden amongst the 50 years of alcohol-fueled Christmas letters that tell the story of my family, you will find my autobiography. Most autobiographies are about how people made things happen. Mine is about how things happened to me while I pinballed my way through life, bouncing off individuals who usually propelled me in an improved direction. The family, friends, and work associates behind these deflections, both mentioned and unsung, are the heroes of this story of my life.

For Christmas of 2019 our "boys" (the youngest being 44, but always our boys to me, consisting of our three sons: Mike, Steve, and Andy, and my nephew, Sean) gave Linda and me a subscription to the StoryWorth website. On this website, your family poses questions for you to answer online, and the website sends a new question at regular intervals. My first reaction was, "Oh crap, they've given us a bunch of work to do to respond to silly questions." Nevertheless, being the team player that I am (not!), I joined Linda in responding to the first several questions with a short paragraph. Example: What were your grandparents like? To which I supplied a small paragraph showing that I had little idea of what my grandparents were like.

Then Covid-19 arrived, followed soon thereafter by personal sequestration. After deducing through serious experimentation that I could neither eat nor drink my way out of this situation, my responses to the StoryWorth questions grew in length until the boys regretted ever having started the whole thing. Example: What were your jobs like? To which I convincingly demonstrated my inability to hold a job by cranking out 23 pages about my 11 jobs. Moreover, I went back to all the previous questions and elaborated on the most boring of items in great detail. Payback to the boys!

Now, they should have known better since I have embarrassed them for 50 years with an annual Christmas letter in which they are reluctant featured persons. Composing this annual letter is accompanied by serious experimentation with adult beverages, or I would never have done it. To rub it in to the boys, Linda has diligently maintained albums of the original letters for each, and recently presented them their copies for safe-hiding in their own homes. Payback squared!

When one of my least-sane friends told me that he also had saved all of our Christmas letters in an album, I began to think, which was a rare and painful experience, "Maybe I could combine the booze-inspired Christmas letters with the Covid-inspired StoryWorth responses to produce a durable book that could haunt the boys to the end of their days, and haunt their progeny beyond that." Payback cubed! So there, now you know more than you ever wanted to know about how a book like this one comes about.

The story follows the evolution of the Pendray family through Christmas letters, interleaved with my autobiographical snippets. When our first son, Mike, was 3 months old, we moved to France. Since this was in 1970, it was the era of primitive French communications, so Christmas letters were our attempt to apprise our family and friends about our lives in the far-away Old World. When we returned to the U.S., I discovered that the letters were so annoying to the recipients that I made it an annual tradition. The book uses these letters as the backbone upon which to add other annoying autobiographical stories.

50 Years of Christmas Letters

Amongst my personal musings, you will find some articles that are not purely autobiographical, but contain some of my random thoughts. There is a document of very unfunny, biased personal opinions of little value. There is a list of books which impressed me because I understood them; consequently, it's a short list. For those who enjoy virtual lurking by Goggle Maps street view, you'll find a list of all my neighborhoods that have been relieved to see me leave.

While the Christmas letters are accurate reproductions of the originals which were written contemporaneously in their year of production, my life stories have all been written in 2020 based mostly on memory. Consequently, some are from vivid memories and probably quite accurate, some are from fuzzy memories, and a few could even be creations of my deteriorating mind, so don't take any of them too seriously. Nevertheless, these are my honest perceptions of what happened, to the best of my flawed ability.

I hope you enjoy reading about my life as much as I have enjoyed living it.

—Jack Pendray

The 1970s

50 Years of Christmas Letters

CHRISTMAS 1971

Hello out there,

I've always hated this type of
thing as being very impersonal, but we
have enjoyed those "missives" we have
received, so thought I would prepare
one. Here it is.

It's been a year and a half since
Linda, Michael and Jack moved into the
Middle Ages just south of Paris, France.
The strange thing is that we kinda like
it. Frenchmen are the nicest, rudest,
most independent, sheepish, backward,
advanced, educated illiterates living
with one foot firmly in 1800 (Napoleon
before Waterloo) and the other in 1980
(the Concorde SST). It's a challenge
just surviving in such an environment.
(I am into my second glass of wine and
already mellowing. Vive la France, and
the grapes). Actually, we came here for

11

one simple reason. We were stupid.
Think about it.... Would any
intelligent person move to a country
without knowing word one of the
language? (It took me half an hour to
get out of the subway the first time -- I
thought "sortie" was an Air Force
concept.) Linda spent her first three
days in France familiarizing herself with
French plumbing. (Some friends had some
medicine for diarrhea -- one spoonful
cured diarrhea, two cured constipation --
and they believe it! Middle Ages!)
Anyway, my American company took six
months to collapse and fired everybody
retroactively (simple, just bounce
paychecks.) We decided to stay and make
a go of it. Found a nice job with a
bunch of young French computer experts,
many educated in the states (PhD's, MS's,
and all that good stuff). This company
has been eaten by CGE: the 160th largest
company in the world. Behold! Pendray
works for a large organization at last.
Am working on a contract to improve the
telephone system in France by using
computer based line switching. The
telephone system in France is atrocious.
(Frenchmen refuse to do business over the
phone -- it's rude not to make a personal
appearance! Middle Ages!) There are
three govt agencies and four govt

dependent companies in the project. We
don't have a chance. Makes the Pentagon
look very, very efficient. Michael is a
mischievous, delightful, almost two-year-
old. He isn't really talking yet. Seems
to be studying the language problem.
Says some English words to the French and
some French words to us. (His study
seems to be as successful as some of his
old man's.) Linda got herself pregnant
again. We expect our Frenchman around
the end of January. We are torn to
choose names from among Pierre, Jacques,
Francois, Jean-Yves, etc., or an equally
confusing array of girls' names.
Probably stick to good old American names
like Luther, Clem, Oscar, Gertrude,
Matilda. (No offense meant to no one.)
We took a trip a month during the six
months around summer. Have seen a lot of
France and some of Europe. Linda's
eating that watermelon seed will slow us
down for a while. (They have only
natural childbirth here -- haven't
discovered the epidural! Middle Ages!)
Our French is progressing (we can now ask
for the toilette, for example). We have
met some delightful French, Belgians,
English, etc. and really enjoy the less
pressured life style, but we see an
American movie now and then and get
homesick. The breaking of the language

barrier is making everything more
enjoyable every day. Ya'll come see us.
The wines and cuisine really are all they
are cracked up to be, and we'd love to
share some of the great restaurants we've
discovered.

Bon Noël,

The Pendrays

CHRISTMAS 1972

Hello out there,

        Once again I take pen in hand to
compose the annual Pendray Christmas
blurb. (The pen is taken in the right
hand thereby leaving the left hand free
to grasp a goblet of fine French red
wine. This particular habit of right-
hand writing and left-hand sipping has
led to a disproportionately strong left
hand.) This is only the second year of
the "annual" message, but last year's
response was so overwhelmingly negative
that I decided to continue the effort to
ensure an indelible contact...We have
just returned from having a McDonald's
BIG MAC. The first French McDonald's has
been open 3 months and we go to watch the
French try to figure it all out. When
you consider that the average Frenchman
likes his food personalized and his meal

long, you can imagine what a McDonald's is like in Paris. The average service time is about 15 minutes in line plus an hour at the table eating. This place has got to go broke...We started this year with the addition of a new member to the family on Jan. 17. Stephen now makes it 3 to 1 in favor of the men. Linda had Stephen in the local French clinic, and the French believe in natural childbirth sans anesthesia. They treat childbirth somewhat like calving and invite the father, idle nurses, cleaning women, etc., to come spectate. Not a sterile procedure except that the doctor has some clean gloves, mask, boots, etc. I thought I would get sick and hovered near the door blending in quite well with the pale wall. In reality, I got so interested in the procedure that the doctor had to ask me to step out of his way a couple of times. Stephen was born doing the cord-around-the-neck trick, which gave me a start, but the doctor solved the problem quickly with his handy clamps and scissors. Quite an experience and I recommend it. (The French encourage children and we made $200 overall profit by having Stephen.)... Michael began school this year as the French allow one to start at age 2½. He attends a Catholic girls' school (boys

allowed in nursery school) for 4 mornings
a week and loves it. He is starting to
correct our French pronunciation. He is
talking in full sentences now, which is
late as he is 3, but in both languages...
Linda had nothing to do having only two
kids in a foreign land, so she enrolled
in a cooking class. A French lady
teaches it in her standard 4ft by 8ft
French kitchen so the class is limited to
only 6 students. Mme. Bergeaud actually
has one cupboard hanging outside her 5th-
floor window. Anyway, we are eating lots
of goodies... My business requires
traveling and I sometimes manage to take
Linda. She and the kids spent 6½ wks in
the States this summer while I spent the
same amount of time on airplanes. She
also took the kids to Miami for 4 days
and she and I got to Denver for a weekend
and visited lots of old friends out that
way. We have a great French student who
keeps the kids for us so we can get away
from time to time. We spent a spring
weekend in Amsterdam with the tulips, 4
days in London, and a week in Rome and
Pompeii this fall. My company has sent
me to San Francisco, L.A., N.Y.,
Minneapolis, D.C., Connecticut, Memphis,
Chattanooga, Miami (I have seen more of
the States from Paris that I ever did
from the U.S.), London, Munich, Nice,

Grenoble, and Torino. My job is great and the traveling tends to come in bunches with long family at-home periods in between. All you desk-bound technocrats eat your heart out... I must give one example of French life for this year: The French kids used to go to school on M, Tu, W, F, Sa, thereby destroying any possibility of a decent 2-day break in the week. There was a lot of fuss raised and the government tried a successful experiment in one city with a M-F school week. This year the govt, in response to public pressure, changed the school week for the entire nation. They now go M, T, T, F & S. Exchange Thurs for Weds?? Quite typical...

Smiling Stephen, vivacious Michael, busy Linda and happy Jack (could it be the wine?) send to one and all their warmest remembrances and wishes for a delightful 1973.

The Pendrays

The 1970s

50 Years of Christmas Letters

CHRISTMAS 1973

Hello out there,

For the third time, the flying feet of the various postal services are distributing the annual installment of the Pendray Pageant. For the third time, the vines of France (those of the region of Beaujolais to be precise) are serving as inspiration for the author. For the third time, many readers will abandon about right here.... We are still in France, which surprises us. We like it here, which surprises us. We plan to come home for good in the summer of 1975, which doesn't surprise us.... We are still continuing to do European things while we are here. We went skiing for a week in the Swiss Alps. Took Michael as there was a permanent kindergarten at the hotel. Jack's brother, Tom, and his wife came over for two weeks, and we made a

flying tour of western Europe. In ten
days we did Belgium, Germany, Italy,
Switzerland and France. In Nov. Jack
took his company (30 people) and their
families to Istanbul for a one-week
seminar on sales techniques. We spent a
weekend in London for Linda's birthday.
And Jack's business trips continue with
trips to Milan and Lisbon having been
introduced.... We had planned to move
back home last summer. In order to
prepare for this, Jack started phasing
out of long-term commitments at his job
around January. Jack was so successful
that he had no responsibilities by Feb.
Jack's boss got promoted upward in Feb.
Jack was the only man in the company
without long-term client responsibilities
(in other words, he was the only one
doing nothing and completely free). Thus
Jack was promoted in March and is now
President of his company. Jack and his
family didn't move home last summer....
The company isn't bankrupt yet. In fact
it is very profitable. This proves it
takes more than 10 months to see the
effects of a change in management.... In
July we moved to a house in Nanterre,
west of Paris. Nanterre is France's most
communist community. Imagine that, Mr.
Right-Wing himself in a communist
village! We like it. The people are

nice and the government services (which
are very important in France) are very
efficient and courteous. Kind of a model
village for the French Communists. Our
house was built in 1862 and gives us
problems all the time. The plumbing is
actually hand-molded lead piping with
soldered joints. The exposed wiring was
added after construction, as was the
john. We have a 12-foot wall all around,
but the neighbors in the adjacent high-
rise apts can still peer in on our bar-b-
q's in the 25ft by 25ft back yard. It is
comfortable and only ½hr from work for
Jack (last year he had a 1¼ hr journey
each direction). We have 5 bedrooms:
this gives us two guest rooms and a room
for our English student who helps Linda
with the kids. The guest rooms are for
you when you come to see us.... Michael
(almost 4) is now perfectly bilingual and
Stephen (almost 2) is just beginning to
talk (mostly English). They are fine,
healthy boys but are like night and day.
Michael is a thinker, learns by his
mistakes, and is naturally cautious.
Stephen is a bull in a china shop, never
learns, and is into everything. They are
both lots of fun and seem to enjoy
life.... Oh yeah, I almost forgot, we
added a new member to the family this
year - finally a female. She is a

Labrador Retriever called Kaki (after her color) and was a cute little puppy when we bought her. Now she knocks down the kids and the furniture by wagging her tail, but she is very gentle and loves the boys.... Linda's life is still hectic with two kids, a dog, an au pair, a husband, etc. She is still taking French cooking classes, and Jack has given up lunches to keep his weight down without missing her dinners. Between groceries, doctors (Stephen ate a bottle of aspirin and spent 24 hrs in the hospital; tonsils out for Michael in Oct.), cooking, business dinners (the boss's wife now), etc., she keeps from being bored.

We wish you all a most merry Christmas and a happy New Year with the hope that we may see each of you in the near future.

Bon Noël,

The Pendrays

The 1970s

50 Years of Christmas Letters

Interesting Happenings

Running Into the Fab Four

In early 1965, Alan Merten and I were bachelor roommates and we traveled to Nassau for a vacation from the Pentagon. We rented bikes and enjoyed exploring the back roads. On one deserted road we were cruising peacefully along when four guys on bikes appeared, coming from the other direction. They were swerving all over and acting crazy. We were unable to get out of their way fast enough and crashed into them, ending with all six of us in a pile on the road. Then some voices from the side of the road started yelling, and there appeared to be a small group camped out on the side of the road. On close observation, Al and I realized that we had just run into The Beatles, literally. We all introduced ourselves and they invited us to join the crew for a soft drink while they re-shot the scene for the movie *Help!* I recall that Ringo spent some time talking to us by the drink cooler. His accent was very difficult to understand, but he was pleasant, as they all were once they figured out what had happened.

I saw the movie later, but there was no bicycle escape scene. Al and I got left on the cutting room floor!

Becoming Legal in France

Sometime in 1971, I was to be interviewed by a French bureaucrat as the last step in getting my work permit, la Carte de Travail, to legally work in France (which I had been doing illegally for over a year). All of the French folks with whom I discussed this upcoming interview told me to be very wary of it, as the French were discouraging foreign workers, especially Americans, since de Gaulle had recently thrown the American-led NATO headquarters out of France. Moreover, French bureaucrats were known to be difficult and unfriendly. I was told it would be a real test of my French, which I was still learning, and that I would probably be rejected because of that. I applied myself assiduously to my French lessons-on-tape and was terrified at the prospect of the interview. On the appointed day, I arrived at the imposing 18th century French government building, and was let into a more imposing office with 20 ft ceilings. At the other end of the long office was a single desk at which an older French bureaucrat was seated. With great trepidation, I advanced to a respectful distance in front of the desk and said in a halting voice, "Bonjour, monsieur." He looked up with a scowl on his face and said, "Vous êtes Américain?," to which I fearfully responded, "Oui monsieur." At this, he jumped to his feet, rushed around to my side of the desk with his hand extended, and stated in perfect American English that he had served with General Patton in WW II and he loved Americans. We then had a half-hour conversation, all in English, about Patton and the war, and he showed me his photos from his time under Patton's command, including several photos of Patton. To conclude, he signed and stamped my papers, shook my hand again, and heartily welcomed me to France.

So much for difficult and unfriendly French bureaucrats! To this day, my French work associates from then are still incredulous.

Taking a Promotion in France

First, some background. In Jan of 1973, I had been working for TECSI, a French startup, for two years. TECSI had become a wholly owned subsidiary of Compagnie Générale d'Électricité (CGE), which was France's largest private enterprise and was unrelated to the American GE. Now, in France at that time the large companies and the government were staffed by the same folks who all came from several top universities, the "grandes écoles." Often, individuals from this coterie would move back and forth between senior government positions and company management, so I had the experience of working in a very small company that had very important French individuals in its upper chain of command. For instance, one of my bosses three levels up, whom I knew and with whom I attended meetings, Édouard Balladur, became Prime Minister of France from 1993 to 1995, and ran, unsuccessfully, to be President of France in 1995. (He was a nice guy and a very thoughtful and considerate leader.) The French founders of TECSI were all young graduates of the grandes écoles, and many of them had advanced degrees from America's best universities. (My MS in Computer Science from Stanford was my ticket into this group.) The founding president of TECSI, Jacques Bentz, was his year's top graduate of France's premier university, École Polytechnique, which was founded by Napoleon. (Jacques went on to become very successful and wealthy and was awarded the Legion of Honor, France's highest honor. We are still friends, and Linda and I dined with him three times during our visit to France in 2019. A great guy!)

The 1970s

Late in 1972, the coterie members at CGE decided that Jacques Bentz's success at TECSI merited a promotion into a higher position in a larger subsidiary, leaving the general manager position at TECSI open. TECSI had become a company of 30 people, but it punched way above its weight due to its consulting engagements with some of France's largest enterprises, banks, and government agencies. This was due to the terrific employees of TECSI, and also due to the influence and pull of CGE in France. Bentz sought out my counsel on who should replace him to run TECSI, and he said the higher-ups wanted to pick someone from inside TECSI. Together, we reviewed the list of talented engineers in the company and were somewhat frustrated that all were technically educated and not yet experienced enough in business for the job. Jacques asked what about me? While flattered, I said that I didn't think so. I pointed out that I had been a founding participant in two companies which both failed, that my mastery of the French language and culture was far from impressive, and that a French company having all French clients should be led by a French person. That was the end of that conversation.

Several days later, Jacques returned to continue the discussion. He said that he and the higher-ups agreed that no one in TECSI was qualified for the job, but they felt I was their best bet. With the understanding that I was perhaps the best of the poor alternatives, I reluctantly accepted. One hurdle remained, however. I had to have an interview with Bentz's boss's boss, a very senior CGE executive, and win his approval. Now, this man was Georges Besse, a leader known as a hard-nosed, hard-punching guy, who went on to become the CEO of several enterprises, the last one being Renault. (In 1986, he was assassinated near his Paris home by terrorists. George Besse's story is worth a Google.)

Anyway, the day arrived when I was to have my meeting with Besse, and I was having second thoughts about the job, and about the meeting with Besse. Taking the job could lead to yet another failure for me because I felt way over my head, it would delay our planned return to the U.S. by a couple of years, and what was I doing in a French company anyway? Nevertheless, I couldn't back out now, so Bentz's boss took me to M. Besse's enormous office, made the introductions, and left. Besse was friendly enough, but said something like, "They tell me they want to give you the TECSI job, but I'm not sure you are the right guy for it." I recall that he crossed his arms and leaned back in his chair, waiting for my defense of myself. I immediately agreed that I was not right for the job and repeated my litany of reasons why. Taken somewhat aback, Besse started pointing out the positive aspects of the job, praised TECSI and its success, assured me that he would help and protect me when I got into trouble, and asked me to accept the job. I thanked him for his support and took the job. I don't think I ever spoke with him again, as he soon moved on to run a government atomic energy agency.

First to CDG

In 1974, we were living outside Paris, and I made fairly frequent flights to the U.S. On one such flight back to Paris, they announced mid-flight that we were in a race with an Air France 747 flight to be the first commercial flight to land at the new airport in Roissy, France, baptized Charles de Gaulle (CDG). I was on TWA's Flight 2, a 747 from JFK to CDG. As often happened, there were some delays with the Air France takeoff, so our TWA flight had a lead in the race. We heard that the Air France flight was burning lots of fuel trying to catch us, because the Air France flight was supposed to land first at CDG, naturally. We were told that there were many dignitaries on the Air France plane and a large press corps was waiting to receive them at Roissy. We had the descendant of the Marquis de Lafayette on board our flight, and a smattering of business travelers like me, but a very light load for a 747. Our crew had prepared for a possible win by boarding lots of Taylor's New

York champagne and distributing it freely to the passengers. I would have much preferred the true champagne on an Air France plane. In any case, we won the race and the press corps had to settle for interviewing Lafayette's descendant and some bleary-eyed half-drunk business folks. I weaved and dodged and avoided the press, as it was 7 in the morning and I wanted to get home. I recently looked at the official history of CDG, and was pleasantly surprised to see that the success of the TWA flight was recorded correctly, without mention of the losing Air France flight. In fact, they imply there was no Air France flight, so it may have all been made up by TWA, the crew, or the other passengers, I'm not sure. I cut and pasted the salient section below, which refers to the official inauguration of the airport, now called Terminal 1, five days before our first flight arrived.

> Five days later, at 6:51 am on March 13th, the first commercial flight, a TWA B747 from New York's Kennedy Airport, landed at CDG with 60 passengers on board.

The small French company that I was managing at that time, TECSI, had two consulting projects involved with CDG. One was a computer system to automate the French customs process for commercial air freight, and the second was to automate the air freight process for Air France. So,

I thought it seemed fitting that I happened to be on the first commercial flight incoming to CDG.

Flying with Superman

On December 11 or 12, 1978, I was flying the BA Concorde from Washington to London. While in the Concorde waiting room at Dulles Airport, a strapping young man came in and sat down next to me. I looked over and he had a Superman emblem in the lapel of his suit coat (we all flew in suits back then). So, I snarkily said, "Are you Superman?" He looked me in the eye and coolly said, "Yes" and turned back to his reading. My thoughts started racing, thinking that I was seated next to, and going to fly with, a wacko. After a moment, he looked back and said that he should explain that he was on his way to the European premiere of *Superman: The Movie*, in which he played Superman, and introduced himself as Christopher Reeve. We had a brief conversation about the movie and the U.S. premier in Washington held on December 10th, and we were then called to board the Concorde.

When the plane reached Mach 2.2, I had a revelation, and got up and went back to Chris. I pointed out to him that he was surely the only Superman that had actually flown "faster than a speeding bullet." He thought that was pretty cool.

35

We later saw Chris give the Valedictory at Andy's UVA graduation in 1998. He was in a wheelchair, and promised to return one day and give a presentation standing. He did not make it. A great loss.

Traveling with the Judge

In May/June of 2017, we traveled in France with one of my high school fraternity brothers and his wife, Paul and Donna Huck. We spent a week in Normandy, a few days in the Loire Valley, and ended with three days in Paris.

Meeting French Justice

Paul is a sitting Senior Federal District Judge and likes to meet other equivalent judges when he travels in foreign countries and asked if I would help him try to meet a French judge. Thinking it rather unlikely, I agreed to give it a shot when we went to see Notre Dame. So, with all four of us dressed in our scruffy tourist attire, we presented ourselves, unannounced, to the receptionist at the heavily guarded entrance to the Palais de Justice. In my rusty French, I attempted to explain our quest while Paul showed her his credentials through her window. She made a quick phone call and then directed us to go to the top floor of a staircase on our left. We were in! We climbed the several flights of stairs and were met by a factotum who apologized that M. Molins was not available, but that one of his five deputies would be glad to meet with us. We were introduced into the office of M. Olivier Christen, who greeted us warmly and in perfect English. I would guess he was in his late 40s, and he spent most of the next hour explaining how the French justice system functioned, comparing it with both the American and British systems in some detail. The differences are enormous! Here are a few examples:

- Nearing graduation from French law school, the students may compete to enter the judge/prosecutor career track, or stay on the lawyer track. Those chosen for the former will spend their career starting from law school as judges, advancing in status and position based on merit.

- Judges are considered to be civil servants working as representatives of the state.

- The judges in France are very active and participate in the trial process from their bench. They will interrogate witnesses, as well as manage the lawyers and proceedings.

- The judges are also the prosecutors in the trials, and will switch from role to role depending on the case. A judge will be behind the bench on one case, and be the prosecutor in another case.

- In their role as prosecutors, the "judges" lead the investigations of cases and direct the participation of the police. At the end of the investigation, the judge/prosecutor will give his opinion and make a recommendation to the trial judge, who is not bound by the recommendation.

- The courts in France are divided into civil, criminal, and administrative sections. The administrative courts supervise the government and handle complaints against the government.

It turns out that M. François Molins, who was not available to meet with us on no advance notice(!), was the Procurer de la République de Paris, probably the most powerful legal position in France. His job combines many of the powers held by our Attorney General and those of our U.S. Federal Courts. Le Ministère de la Justice in France has mainly an administrative role in support of the judicial system.

M. Olivier Christen, who spent so much time with us, is one of M. Molins' five deputies. Among M. Christen's duties is the responsibility for prosecuting acts of terrorism in France! It is in that role that he became so familiar with the U.S. and British legal systems, as he coordinates the French participation in the international fight against terrorism.

At the end of the meeting, Paul asked if he could visit a trial in process to experience that in France. M. Christen said that our timing was good, as there was an active terrorism trial in process in the palais. He personally led us through the layers of police protection, which parted for him like the sea did for Moses, and sat with us for a while to explain what was going on. We then stayed and watched the trial of some of the terrorists responsible for the supermarket killings related to the Charlie Hebdo incident, a major terrorism trial. When the court broke for lunch, Paul introduced himself to several of the lawyers involved in the case and informally interviewed them. When Paul asked the lead defense lawyer how the trial was going, he replied, "Pretty good, until that last witness." With that, we left to go see Notre Dame.

When we lived in France, I knew the legal system was quite different, but I never understood much of the French system. I used to say that the American legal system was developed by revolutionaries who defined a system to protect the people from the government, while Napoleon, the Emperor who succeeded the French revolution, defined a system to protect the government from the people. I see some of that in this experience.

Honoring Our Fallen

The highlight of the trip occurred on the U.S. Memorial Day, May 29th, at the U.S. Cemetery in Brittany, where two American flags fly over more than four thousand graves of American, and some German, war dead.

The cemetery's layout is designed as a military emblem, that of SHAEF—Supreme Headquarters Allied Expeditionary Forces—the armies under Gen. Dwight David Eisenhower's command from 1943 through the end of the war. It depicts a flaming sword backed by a shield. As the cemetery's superintendent, Bruce Malone, explained during our visit, the Memorial building and the two walls with the Tablets of the Missing that flank it make up the sword's hilt. Two paths that lead through the center of the cemetery and meet behind a cenotaph at its far end form the sword's blade. Two paths that lead back to the Tablets of the Missing make up the emblem's shield and the curved rows of graves are the sword's flames.

This can be seen in the layout from the cemetery's brochure:

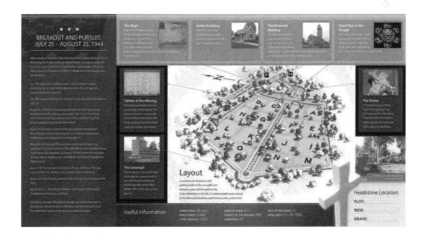

At 4 o'clock, Retreat was played, followed by a soulful and solemn version of Taps that seemed to envelop the thousands of graves. The cemetery was appropriately silent, with only the four of us and Bruce Malone present *in vivo*. Bruce gave us the honor of lowering and folding the two flags. The guys did one and the gals the other. Paul and Jack, the tough old vets, both had tears in their eyes.

CHRISTMAS 1974

Hello out there,

This makes four years in a row that we have turned out Pendray's Page of Instant Boredom. The number of returned Xmas cards marked "address correct - letter refused" seems to be decreasing, which encourages us to continue. This year's inspiration is a very old Chateauneuf-du-Pape (1973). As we are returning to the, as Michael calls it, Ninety States in 1975, it will be interesting to see if bourbon produces different Xmas letters than red wine.... We have had a very eventful year with lots of traveling and lots of visiting with friends. We spent 7 weeks in the US last summer and saw many friends and relatives. We managed to slip out on the kids for 10 days in Copenhagen and Stockholm and 3 days in Madrid. Also,

Jack's company spent 9 days, with
families (we left the kids again), in
Athens for their yearly retreat....
Speaking of Jack's company...it has
proven very resistant to management
influence as Jack has been president for
20 months and the company is still very
healthy. In fact, TECSI tripled in size
this year and is still very profitable.
A Spanish subsidiary will open in late
December and a Swedish one in early '75.
A Swiss activity is forecast for mid
'75. Jack's plan is simple: first
surround Europe, then.... The year
started with a bang. GSI, Jack's parent
company, acquired control of CITEL, a
computer-based hotel reservation company
in mid '73. After several months of
unsuccessfully trying to turn the company
around, GSI nominated Jack as president
in a move of absolute desperation. Jack
closed the company in four days. He now
has a reputation for being the American
who closed a European company the fastest
ever seen. We found jobs for everybody
and everyone lived happily forever
after.... Michael and Stephen are
progressing normally (we hope). They
both are spending their mornings at a
private school which we call "The Tower
of Babel." There are five children: 1
Mexican, 1 Dutch, 1 Portuguese, 2

Americans. They have a French teacher
and use French as the common language.
Michael told us one day, "Judith spoke to
me in Dutch and I answered in English,
now she speaks to me in French." Linda
finished her third French cooking course,
thereby exhausting the available
curriculum. Being bored, she signed up
for advanced French lessons and is now
learning to say things that Jack can't
understand. Jack's accent is improving;
people now say he sounds like a German
speaking French, not really a very good
thing to do in France.... Linda has been
kept busy this year with packing,
unpacking, driving to airports, etc.
Jack made 9 trips to the US plus many
others all over Europe. Linda has
received as houseguests some of Jack's
friends that Jack never saw. Our life
will settle down next year when we get
home, but it is necessary to prepare for
returning to the US.... Kaki, the dog,
is great and big and gentle (thank
goodness) except in greeting intruders
(thank goodness).... The French anecdote
this year is about the scandalous Post,
Telephone & Telegraph (PTT) in France.
There are three well-saturated phone
lines at Jack's office. TECSI needs, and
has asked for, 5 more lines. The PTT
responded that positively no lines will

be available before 1977, and that no one
knows what will happen after 1977. The
company may well spend $50,000 to move
into new offices in order to get 10
telephone lines. The PTT also cut
TESCI's leased lines to the computer
because it didn't receive a rapid
response to one of its letters. (The
lines still aren't reinstalled 6 months
later.) Other sidelights: we wait up to
an hour for a dial tone at our house,
and, lastly, we are in a postal strike
that has blocked all mail for the last
six weeks and no end is in sight....

Considering the state of the
economy of the Western world, we wish you
all a Merry Christmas and a full-time job
in 1975.

Bon Noel,

The Pendrays

The 1970s

50 Years of Christmas Letters

Hello out there,

Once again it's that time of year for
the Pendray poop-sheet of worthless information
and sincere Christmas wishes. The response to
last year's letter was mostly absolute silence,
which leads us to believe that our friends are
inured to the idea that I will write a Christmas
letter in spite of public opinion. This year it
is being composed in Virginia and is inspired by
Budweiser.

Most of you will receive this late, for
which we apologize, but we felt it would be unfair
to let everyone get their hopes up that we were
stopping the annual letter when, in fact, we were
only caught in the middle of moving. Our address
list is securely locked in storage until February,
so for most of you this is a wish for a Merry
Spring and a Happy Middle of the New Year.

We are home. In the U.S. In
Virginia. In Linda's parents' house for the
last five months. In a mess. Jack came up
with a brilliant plan to buy a big lot and put

49

a little house with a lot of add-ons on it. We bought the lot. The add-ons cost more than a big house, so we decided to abandon our construction plans. We just bought a finished tract house on a little lot. We now have a beautiful five-acre lot and a nice four-bedroom house. It's unfortunate that they are not in the same place. We are broke but secure; we can always farm the five acres if necessary. It's a hill so Jack is studying terraced farming.

The move from France was pretty easy, as moves go. We brought the kids over early and left them with Linda's sister. We then went back, packed, moved out and played tourist for two weeks in France and Germany. Second honeymoon! Linda reintegrated into American shopping and living without too much difficulty; it took her about 10 minutes to adjust. Prices in D.C have skyrocketed, but we compare to French prices and everything seems cheap. The only bad surprise was Linda's becoming the family chauffeur (chaffeuse?) to the screwy school schedules of the kids.

Jack's new job is a lot like his old job except that now he lives where he used to travel and travels where he used to live (clear?). He is with the same company (doesn't say much for them, does it?) and is looking for opportunities for his French company in America. He is also responsible for four small profit centers in Germany, France and Spain, which keeps him on the move. He has been 60% in Europe since July but should only be there 33% in 1976. It's not clear what his job is, but he should find something to do somewhere in his travels. As a side interest, his parent company put him on the board of one of their US subsidiaries which produces insulators for high voltage transmission lines. Talk about a useful board member!?

Credit establishment has been fun as no one is interested in contacting France to verify salary and employment. Most people just decide that Jack must be unemployed and refuse credit. The other half assume he is CIA and refuse everything. But by using his cool diplomatic style, he solved this problem through threatened law suits and obscene phone calls.

Michael was so excited about leaving France that he bust a gut. He had a successful appendectomy the first week of June right before going home. It was a confusing week for Linda as she was preparing to move and we were also keeping the two-year-old daughter of a friend who was in a hospital having quadruplets. (That's right, they have four healthy new ones.) What better time for an appendectomy? Michael was a real champ and took over his floor of the hospital without a contest.

Stephen is still quietly getting into everything. You can follow where he's been by the trail of innocent destruction. He is an effervescent fellow who will learn everything there is to learn by trying everything there is to try. Michael reasons through things, Stephen takes them apart and looks at the pieces.

Both boys are losing their French very rapidly. In fact, Stephen's is already gone. He just grins and says "oui" to everything. Michael refuses to speak French with us ... our awful accents hurt his ears.

The dog, Kaki, likes the States. She can swim and run and bark and be a general wet, fast, loud nuisance. She set a world record on her trip from France to the U.S. Fourteen hours without going to the bathroom! What training! She was busy for two hours after being let out of her travel cage.

As you can see, we had our usual dull, uneventful, unenjoyable year; however, we did have one amusing moment. This year's story is on the U.S. Customs people. Our shipment was inspected in Baltimore and, as usual, Jack had improperly understood the customs procedures and improperly declared the shipment. U.S. Customs sent us a bill of over $700 for a long list of smuggled items including such valuable possessions as: 12 jars of mustard, 2 bottles of Worcestershire sauce, one 14-year-old bike bought in the U.S., one case of wine (AHA!), various canned vegetables, etc. Sleep well, America, your Customs Service is ferreting out those dangerous smugglers! (P.S. They settled for $60 from a very embarrassed Jack Pendray.)

If we get mortgage credit, our new address will be 2753 Viking Drive, Herndon, Virginia, after February. Y'all come see us.

Happy Holidays,

The Pendrays

The 1970s

50 Years of Christmas Letters

Saturdays as a Child

The Saturday all-day sessions at the movie theater are one of the best memories of my childhood. Before we moved to FL when I was 7, it was at the Riviera Theatre in North Chattanooga, to which my brother, Tom, and I could easily walk. It has since been torn down and replaced by a strip mall called "The Corner at Riverview." For 10 cents we had a full day of entertainment with our friends. In Miami, Tom and I would usually take the bus to the Coconut Grove Theater. We each had a quarter to spend, which covered the bus fare, a box of rock candy bought at Liles Drug Store in The Grove, and the movie. We were ardent Gene Autry fans, and we each had Gene Autry outfits that we wore around the neighborhood. On rare occasions, we would go to downtown Miami's Olympia Theater to see a live show. I recall one time when Lash LaRue was there with his bull whip. Lash later taught Harrison Ford how to use the bull whip for his "Indiana Jones" movies. After we moved to Coral Gables, on Saturdays I caught the Industrial Section bus to Miracle Mile in the Gables, where I met up with friends and we all went to the Coral Theater. This lasted through junior high, and even included girls in the gang. There was some hanky-panky in that dark theater!

Me at age 10

CHRISTMAS 1976

Hello out there,

      Yes, it's that time of year again when
Pendray's Penance arrives in your mailbox. This
year's Christmas letter will be worse than ever in
line with past tradition. Jack Daniel's black
label is guiding my thoughts so don't be surprised
at anything.... Last Christmas was spent in Miami
and Chattanooga visiting Jack's family members.
This year we stay in Virginia with Linda's
folks.... We occupied our tract home in
February. The architecture is Virginia Blah but
it has a wooded backyard which we fenced in for
Kaki (and she patrols it regularly). After living
in French concrete construction, we had quite a
surprise. The invention of the quarter-inch-thick
bearing wall will surely go down in scientific
history as an American breakthrough.... Virginia
is quite changed from 1969. Now that we can drink
(after 1969), there are good dinner theaters and
restaurants for consenting adults. We rarely get
into Washington. We have our little country club
and follow the life of any middle-class Republican
(an endangered species?). We love it. We have
made contact with only about 1/3 of our old

57

friends in Virginia but we are looking forward to
seeing the other 2/3 soon.... Jack still travels
a lot, spending about 30% of his time in Europe
and another 30% on the road in the U.S. This
gives him a chance to keep in touch with good
friends all over, but his dog bites him when he
comes home unannounced. 1977 should bring less of
Europe and more of home. The reason that Jack
spent so much time in Europe was to clean up
messes. The Spanish company that he started
failed (rats, wrong again) and the company which
he acquired in Munich was a catastrophe (rats,
wrong again). We are thankful that he works for a
big company rather than investing his own
money.... His American activities have not yet
produced any acquisitions, so there are no major
losses to report - yet. He has proposed two
acquisitions, one in Pittsburgh, to prove he is a
sincere businessman, and one in San Diego, to
prove he isn't _that_ sincere. The U.S. company
where he is a member of the board is proving
resistant to his management influence as it is
still profitable.... June brought us a sad event
as Jack's older brother, Tom, left this life. We
miss him.... July was a fun month for us.   We
had Jack's nephews, Larry and Sean, up from Miami
for the month. We had a ball all acting like
kids. There was a steam train ride to West
Virginia and lots of tennis, picnics and
roughhousing. Five men around the house weren't
enough for Linda, so she gave birth to Andrew
Scott on the 23rd of July. (Yes, she got herself
pregnant again!) We had natural childbirth again
and Jack didn't faint. Andrew was no more than
two minutes old when he peed all over the doctor,
nurses, parents. Could it be an expression of his
philosophy of life?... In September Jack's
parents came to Virginia to see the family. We

had some good times including evening cruises on
the Potomac in Linda's parents' boat. Washington
is really beautiful at night from the river....
Linda's dad retired (again!). This time he left
civil service. They have moved to a great spot
on the lower Potomac where we go mooch as often as
possible.... Linda hasn't done much traveling
this year what with 3 boys, and a dog, and house
and station wagon (oh yeah, no more Mercedes, we
got a Cutlass wagon - middle-class Republicans all
the way). We did both get to New York for several
days. Saw a play which was expensive and awful,
and Andre Previn in concert which was good. We
plan on going to San Diego and San Francisco in
early 77, so all you West Coasters beware....
Michael (6) is becoming quite a horseman on his
pony (would you believe Trigger?) and has
confiscated the skateboard which the boys gave
Jack for Father's Day. (Jack tried his skateboard
once, fell off, and it shot down the storm sewer.
Jack spent half a day retrieving it, much to the
amusement of the neighborhood kids, and retired
from skateboarding.) Michael played his first
soccer season and was pretty good for a first
grader.... Stephen is still in nursery school 3
days a week. He still has that infectious grin
which puts Andrew in hysterics.... This year the
joke is on us. After paying French taxes for five
years to support the development of the Concorde
SST, we come to the U.S. only to have it fly right
over our house. When the neighbors complain about
the noise, I offer them a glass of good Bordeaux.
Trade a French wine for a French whine...(Sorry
about that).

We wish you all a very merry Christmas
and a delirious 1977.

The Pendrays

The 1970s

Four Pendray Men: Jack and Mike, Tom and Sean, Christmas 1970

50 Years of Christmas Letters

Hello out there!

It's Christmas time again and here comes your very
own personal Xeroxed copy of the Pendray letter.
We know that this annual letter is getting
delivered because the number of Xmas cards to us
is dropping dramatically. The courage to continue
in the face of public outcry is provided by a
three-olive martini; so fasten your seat belts (or
stop right here, which I recommend)...Our year got
off to a shaky start when we lost our dog, Kaki,
on New Year's Eve to a hit-and-run, but we soon
acquired another one very similar (love those
Labradors), which we call Chelsea. This provided
Linda a 3-month-old dog to raise with her 6-month-
old baby. Now the dog is bigger than the baby,
but in size only...We still travel a lot. Linda
and Jack did San Francisco, San Diego and Los
Angeles in March and saw lots of relatives. Both
of us have more relatives in Southern Cal than
anywhere else (what's that saying about all kooks
migrating to So Cal?) and we enjoyed them all (the
relatives and the kooks)...In May we again stashed
the kids and dog with our long-suffering relatives

63

in Virginia (so that's why they moved to Virginia!) and set off for Europe. Jack's demanding job required that he and Linda attend a one-week seminar in Crete, Greece, followed by another week seminar in Corsica, France, with a weekend in Paris between. Being a loyal employee ready for any requirement of the job, Jack overcame Linda's resistance and they went. It was horrible: nothing but sun, tennis, swimming, scores of dear old friends, drinking, eating, etc. We bore thru it as no sacrifice is too great for Jack's company...Coming home was uneventful except for reuniting with the family, taking delivery of the sailboat and preparing for the family's trip to Florida...Oh yes, we bought a sailboat in June which we park at Linda's parents' home on the lower Potomac. Knowing nothing about sailing, we thought it best to cut our teeth on something simple, so we got a 27-foot sloop that sleeps 6 and requires a crew of 2. We spent most of our summer weekends with Linda's parents and discovered two things: 1. Put Linda on a sailboat and you are guaranteed to get a thunderstorm within an hour and 2. Jack (the great sailor) doesn't know a darn thing about sailing. Consequently, there are only 2 people left in the family who like to sail: Jack, who is too stupid to know what a lousy sailor he is, and Andrew, who is too young to know what a lousy sailor Jack is...Jack's job took a turn for the worse in July. His company acquired Transcomm Data Systems in Pittsburgh, so now Jack has to work. After only two years' study, GSI insisted that Jack do something, so Jack recommended the purchase of a 20-person company which has the best leadership and personnel that he could find in two years of searching; and GSI, after thorough independent investigation (they aren't so dumb after all),

said yes. For the sake of Jack's job security,
let's all pray that Transcomm proves very
resistant to his management talent...In July the
whole family went to Florida for 2 weeks. It was
Jack's 20th high school reunion (everyone got
older, except Jack, of course), and we toured the
state to visit friends. We had a good visit with
Jack's folks and a great time overall...We find
that we have moved into the world's greatest
neighborhood. I think every American wishes that
all neighborhoods were like ours. Once again we
are lucky...Michael is in his 3rd season of soccer
and his first of basketball. He is good at it,
enjoys it, and does well in school besides (must
take after Linda)...Stephen started kindergarten
this year and will start sports soon. He also is
good at school and still has that lovable smile
and personality (must take after Linda)...Andrew
is a tiger! He is into everything: climbs, jumps,
slides, etc. He has four words to date: hot,
cold, Dada and uh-oh (this is the one that means
go find out what he has done -- must take after
Jack)...Linda still cooks great meals, gives love
to her children, has patience with her husband and
has started playing tennis (summer) and
racquetball (winter) to fill those long idle
hours??...Jack still travels a bunch but when he
is home, he's home. Lots of long weekends with
the family and home by 5 when he's in town. He
spent only 8 weeks in Europe this year (down from
12 last year), but gets around the US more than
ever. So far his bosses haven't developed a true
appreciation of his talents; therefore, he is
still employed by the same company...At this time
of year, one tends to count blessings. When we
count ours, we think of our friends all over the
world...After six olives (I become honest and open
when inebreetd, inebrateed--oh hell, smashed), let

us wish each and every one of our cherished
friends and relatives a merry Christmas and a 1978
as full of good fortune as our years have been.

The Pendrays

Hello Out There!

With the preceding extremely personal
salutation, I once again take pen and drink in
hands to prepare to bombard our dear friends
with the annual Pendray Page--In preparation
for writing, I reread all the precedent
Christmas letters to gather inspiration.
Unfortunately, I imbibe of Jack Daniel's
bourbon while doing this, which, after six
years' worth of letters, gets me off to a
roaring start. So, hold on, here we go--We
managed to spend a couple of weekends last
February skiing in Virginia (the cold, snowy
winter had its silver lining), and discovered
that Michael and Stephen take to skis like
Jack takes to sailing. Both boys (we left
Andrew with Linda's relatives) went down the
slopes like rockets (the ski patrol threatened
to tear up Michael's lift ticket if he didn't
slow down) and left their old parents in the

67

dust. We are going to take them (still without Andrew, the relatives get him again) to Vail for a week in December to show them some real ski country. Hope no one breaks anything--Jack's company (yes, the fools still haven't found him out yet) opened activities in Denver and Los Angeles this year, which gave him a reason to fly some more. He did over 150,000 air miles in '78, making 9 trips to Europe and about 40 US trips. Linda managed to join him on one of his jaunts to Paris, Deauville, and the south of Spain in May (it rained everywhere), but family duties kept her from doing much other traveling. She has given up on the hassle of tennis and racquetball (taking lessons, finding partners, reserving courts and hiring sitters) and, instead, peacefully jogs a mile or two before the rest of the family rises in the morning...Michael (8) and Stephen (6) are both doing well in school and we hope to inflict Andrew (2) on the school system next year (if we can ever toilet train him). Both older boys are good in math and reading. Our area is really into kids' sports and Michael plays soccer and basketball while Stephen plays soccer and baseball. Poor Jack is an assistant coach in soccer, basketball and baseball. (He got cut from everything as a kid; if you can't do it, coach it.)--Our neighborhood has a progressive dinner group with each course being consumed at a different house and with the men doing all the cooking. Needless to say, there is lots of drinking, and the walk from the main course to the

dessert is more like a stagger. It's fun and
Jack hasn't done too badly in his cooking
tasks--Last summer we had the daughter of one
of our French friends stay with us for six
weeks. It was a new experience for us to have
a teenage girl around the house, and we
enjoyed her very much. Andrew couldn't
pronounce her name, Emmanuelle, so he simply
called her Beup?--We managed to spend some
weekends down at Linda's parents (they keep
our boat as well as Andrew) but only made five
sailings this summer (now that Jack knows how,
he doesn't have time). Andrew caught his
first fish and loves boat rides (he's always
asking for a "boride an' fishin'"). He is
finally over the communication barrier (more
or less, everything's in present tense) and is
much less frustrated. He is obviously
destined to be an electrician as he has a
whole assortment of electrical apparatus that
he drags around the house, plugging into
whatever plug is handy. His assortment
includes three extension cords, one
nightlight, one wall lamp and one portable
humidifier. He hooks all these things
together, lays them out and plugs them in.
Lord knows how he does it, but everything
works. He has a great veneration for Linda;
when he awoke and saw the first snow of this
winter, he immediately said, "Mommy did
that."--We had season tickets to the Kennedy
Center and Wolf Trap Park this year, so we got
a little culture. Wolf Trap is an outdoor
theater and we got lawn seats (for the
unknowing, that means you take a picnic and

wine, sit on the grass, get snockered, and
listen to the music; some culture!)--We are
going to Miami for Christmas and New Year's,
and hope to see our friends down that way. We
wish you all a very merry Christmas and a new
year showered with blessings.

The Pendrays

CHRISTMAS 1979

Hello Out There!

Le Nouveau Beaujolais Est Arrivée! This is a wonderful French expression which means that the new Beaujolais wine is here and that the Christmas season is beginning in France. I have just finished a bottle of this in my hotel room in Paris and will now subject you to the annual Pendray Christmas letter...1979 has been rather uneventful for us so this letter may be short. All we did was raise kids, travel, move, change jobs and otherwise kill time...Jack gave a luncheon speech at his trade association's management conference last year and spent a half hour telling about his language faux pas in France. He set a new lower level for this type of meeting and was asked, by acclamation, never to speak again...December '78's skiing trip to Vail was perfect, and Michael and Stephen (Andrew was with Linda's parents) set outdoor downhill records by skiing faster than their father could slide downhill on his stomach. Linda gracefully skied down while pretending not to know this rabble. In Colorado we had a wonderful reunion of old Air Force comrades in computers. We will go back to Vail again this December for more skiing (and falling)...Jack journeyed to Venice in April for his company's annual management meeting. Linda couldn't make the trip, which took some of the fun out of it for Jack, but he survived anyway by overindulging in pasta and wine...We had season tickets to the Kennedy Center and Wolf Trap again this year and enjoyed both. D.C. is becoming quite a center for performing arts...In June we attended a seminar in Marco Island, Fla., followed by a weekend in Miami - it was a wonderful vacation for the family...In August Jack's company finally began to get wise to him (after nine years), so he quit before they fired him. Drats! No more trips to Pittsburgh! He was unemployed for 20 hours before he was offered a job with another French company which has its U.S. operation in Boston. He now has an apartment in Boston, headquarters in Paris and a house and family in Virginia. Normal Pendray routine...Right after accepting the job in Boston, we moved. That's normal. We moved into the house right behind us. That's normal for Pendrays. We were bored, not having moved in 3 years...In October we went to Linda's homecoming (I won't say which one, but it was more than the 14th) at William & Mary. It was absolutely wonderful - 70-degree weather, fall colors, Linda's old friends, W & M preserving tradition by losing the football game royally. Jack "had a few" and went around reading name tags of strangers, saying "Charlie (or Bob or Doug)! Good to see you after all these years. How the heck are you?" A lot of people couldn't place him in the class of '64, but others did. Linda is still the youngest and prettiest of her class, and it was a pleasure seeing her old friends greeting her with warmth and respect...Michael got his braces this year and supports them well. He is the first kid in his class of 9-year-olds to achieve this epoch of teenage success. He is the leading student in his class and quite a mature young man... Stephen is still full of light and also a good student. Both he and Michael were soccer standouts. Basketball is just beginning...Andrew stared nursery school this year and the school is still standing. His teacher just bought the house next to us, which will be a problem for Andy as he thinks she lives at the school. After all, she's there when he arrives and there when he leaves...The

The 1970s

French air traffic controllers have found a new type of strike. They let the planes land, but not take off (this makes for crowded airports). Must save gas this way. If they don't let me take off Friday, Linda will have a wonderful party for 60 people on Saturday without me. Let's hope I make it...May Christmas and 1980 bring each and every one of you the ability to recognize and seize the love and joy that surrounds us all.

The Pendrays

50 Years of Christmas Letters

The 1980s

50 Years of Christmas Letters

Hello out there,

We are skiing in Vail as I write this tenth annual Christmas letter... There are only two appendages still functioning in my old body after two days of skiing: my writing hand (right) and my drinking hand (left). The left appendage was being properly utilized, so I decided to put the right appendage into service....We are at Vail for the third year and this year we brought Andrew for the first time. He fell at the Denver airport and hit his head on the concrete. His resulting black eye and bruise look like he's had one unbelievable ski disaster while still miles from the slopes. This may be our last year at Vail, thanks to rising costs, but we will certainly continue our family tradition of skiing, as nothing does more for the family spirit than watching Jack do his fantastic rump slide with full ski apparel....

Jack's company hadn't changed its name in over a year, so it did. He now works for SESA-Honeywell Communications, Inc. The name is bigger than the company, but Honeywell doesn't know that yet. They bought 49% of SESA's U.S. subsidiary and added their name. They even agreed to leave Jack in charge, which should indicate that now is a good time to sell your Honeywell stock. Jack's office building is in a park and includes a racquetball court, hot tub, and sauna. Now and then, he even works some....Linda went along on one of his business trips to California in November and saw how hard he works. She had a chance to visit her relatives out West and even took Jack along with her when he was awake.

50 Years of Christmas Letters

In San Francisco we visited old Virginia neighbors who had recently moved there and Jack even took a day off (how can one tell?)....The annual company seminar has changed a little now that Jack is no longer with GSI. Instead of Greece, Corsica or Istanbul, his company drove 3 hours to Berkeley Springs, West Virginia, for 4 days. At least he got to take the family. While there, the kids adopted old Fred (the snake) and the local night-robber raccoon, but Jack wouldn't let them come home with us....

      When asked what happened of note this year, Michael responded, "We got older." Tis true, Michael is 10 going on teenage, Stephen is 8 going on strong, Andrew is 4, going on and on and on. Michael is in the gifted and talented program at school (takes after Linda); Stephen won the citizenship award in his class (takes after Linda); Andrew still screams as he's dragged off to nursery school (who could he take after?). They are all tall (where did that come from?), smart (repeat), nice (Linda's side) and stubborn (guess who?). We are terribly proud parents....Linda is into jogging, tennis, garden club, coordinating the elementary school foreign language program, and raising kids (in reverse order). She does a great job of all of the above....We had season tickets to the Wolftrap Park for the performing arts and JFK Center balcony seats (you need binoculars to find the stage)....Last summer was just great -- lots of sun, tennis, sailing, water skiing and family. We spent many weekends at Linda's parents' place on the lower Potomac and even took friends along on several occasions. A good time was had by all thanks to the hospitality of the Lawrences....Jack's Dad and Mom and brother also visited this year and all made trips to the Lawrences with us....As you see, it was a very family year, and one which we enjoyed tremendously....

      From our family to you and yours, a wish for a very Merry Christmas and a New Year full of love and true friends.

Cheers,

      The Pendrays

The 1980s

50 Years of Christmas Letters

CHRISTMAS 1981

Hello Out There,

Golly! I have just reread the last 11 years of fantastic Christmas letters and don't know if I can do it again. (Any of you who has received any of these letters will probably consign this one immediately to the fire.) This one is being composed to the accompaniment of clinking ice cubes in a glass of olives (surrounded by gin)...Everyone is well and we had a good year and we wish you a Merry Christmas and good bye...(Just kidding folks, you don't get off that easy)...Last year this letter was composed in Vail. After paying the bills for that trip, it worked out that the cost per letter sent was around $30 so this year the letter is being written in beautiful Herndon. Not that we have abandoned skiing, but this year we are staying a little closer to home with a week (weak?) at Snowshoe, West Virginia, scheduled for the first week of

February. We couldn't get through a year without Jack's famous rump slide on the slopes...We did some traveling this year. In May, we (sans kids) went to New Orleans (famous as Linda's birthplace) for a convention. We arrived late and the hotel was overbooked so they gave us the governor's suite for a week. Had a ball. Love that city...We spent a month this winter in Paris in June and July (maximum temp one week was 55°). The whole troop went (excepting Chelsea who stayed with Linda's parents and lost many pounds chasing Bob on his tractor) for Jack's month-long work (work?) period at his headquarters in France. We spent two weeks in downtown Paris and two weeks in a rented house in a quaint suburb. The commute by subway and train brought back old memories for Jack. Many French friends were visited who feted us with long hours of eating and drinking and eating and drinking and etc. It was a fantastic time for us all and brought back France to Michael and Stephen. While in France we attended two superb weddings of our friends' children...Jack's travels continue, but at a much less hectic pace. He's home most of the time and the dog doesn't bite him anymore when he comes home... Linda is slowing down a little. Her 6:30 a.m. jog has degenerated into a walk, but since she walks faster than Jack jogs it's pretty good exercise. She is still managing the foreign language program for the elementary school and active in the PTA, garden club and

tennis.   With Andrew now in
kindergarten she can see the light at
the end of the tunnel...When we got back
from France in July, things were a
little slow, so we had five houseguests
in August. A delightful teenager, son of
French friends, spent a month with us as
well as Jack's nephews Larry and Sean
paying us a visit. While they were all
here, Jack's Dad and Penny came for a
week.   (We installed traffic lights in
the hallway.)   It was an active and
enjoyable period... Mom and brother,
Keith, also paid a visit.   Keith was on
his way to Seattle to be a professor
(he's a PhD, no less)...Michael is still
playing soccer and basketball as well as
being a good student (6th grade) and boy
scout...Stephen is into soccer and
bicycles (he is slowly rebuilding his
bike, piece by expensive piece.)   He won
the good citizenship award for 3rd grade
as he had done in 2nd grade...Andrew
started kindergarten this year.   After
the first day, he came home, said it was
fun, but he wasn't going back to school
as he "already knew all that
stuff"...Michael went to scout camp last
summer and Stephen went to soccer camp.
Shades of freedoms to come...Jack's
company is still moving forward (much to
everyone's surprise). They signed 6
million dollars of orders this year, so
next year they have to deliver.
Fortunately for Jack, he has a group of
very good people to do this as he
doesn't really understand what his
company does...We are still sailing
quite a bit so will leave you with a

sailor's wish for a Merry Christmas and
a New Year of fair winds to your back,
beautiful sunsets, and shipmates as
enjoyable as all of you, our beloved
friends and relatives.

The Pendrays

Happy Holidays

*Jack, Linda,
Michael,
Stephen,
& Andrew*

CHRISTMAS 1982

Hello Out There! Well, you almost got away without
Pendray's Perennial Page this year. Lying in the 82° balmy
breeze of Hawaii, Christmas seemed a long way off; however,
getting off the plane the next day into 8 inches of Virginia
snow and a 20° temperature woke me right up - get out the
letter or our friends will forgive you!...Writing facilities
this year provided by Papermate, and Jack Daniel's black
label...This is our 12th Christmas letter in a row and most
of them were even mailed around Christmas. If you missed
any prior version, then thank your lucky stars!, or send a
self-addressed envelope and $5,000 for reprints...Jack's job
(you mean he's still employed?!? Yes, but just barely)
still keeps him moving around. With the new airline
frequent traveler programs, his traveling is finally doing
someone some good. He got tickets for his mom to come up
from Miami and for Linda and her folks to go to Hawaii (he
went along also)...Skiing is still a family event. (Jack's
rump slide gets more impressive as his rump gets more
impressive.) It's a great way to get away with friends and
relatives in family groups. We got in several ski trips
last year to Bryce Mountain, Virginia, (small hill, small
drive) and a week's trip to Snowshoe, West Virginia, (big
mountain, big drive). We like Snowshoe so much that we

85

bought a condo there (yep, Jack still drinks and buys) for investment rentals. Now we pray for long, cold winters with lots of renting skiers... Some of our dearest neighbor friends moved away this year and we had six months of going-away parties while they tried to sell their house, buy a house, find a mortgage, etc. (have you tried moving lately? Don't!) Six months of going-away parties in this neighborhood can almost kill you, but we hung in till the bitter end. No sacrifice is too big for friends...Linda and Jack got to New Orleans again, and overate again. Love her birthplace...Summer got the family to Bethany Beach, MD, with our dinner group and families. Lots of long weekends at Linda's folks' place on the Potomac for sailing and eating and drinking, etc...Linda got tired of the hassle of organizing the elementary school foreign language program, so she became president of the PTO. Since the person who took over the foreign language program had an illness in the family and had to bow out at the last minute, Linda got to do that also anyway. For their anniversary, Jack gave her a cordless phone so she could permanently attach "her phone" to her head and go about her household life without being tethered. She's still doing tennis and is close to driving Jack off the courts (where he doesn't belong anyway)...Michael is bused to school this year since he started junior high. He is in a special program for smart kids and doing well. When he's not playing soccer or doing boy scouts or computer games, he's reading...Stephen is also pulling down those A's and B's this year, playing soccer, doing cub scouts, reading, and riding his Mongoose bicycle (for the uninitiated, a Mongoose is a small dirt bike at a very large price)...Andrew started first grade and soccer this year and is doing well at both (in spite of the fact that his dad is the soccer coach). He also has a dirt bike (selected on its esoteric merits by Stephen) and is getting into reading and computer games...Chelsea, the Labrador, spends most of her time trying to trick the boys into feeding her twice per mealtime, and is quite successful and, consequently, rotund...If you have trouble reading this letter all scrunched up like it is, it will help you understand what Congress is struggling with. You have just received a Merry Xmas ("MX") missive launched in dense pack.

We hope that this Christmas season finds each of you with good health, good friends and good cheer.

Merry Christmas and

Happy New Year

The Pendrays

 Happy Holidays

CHRISTMAS 1983

Hello Out There,

Greetings from Connecticut! As I take computer keyboard
and Gordon's London Dry Gin in hand to compose the much-
rejected annual Pendray page, I listen to the rain fall
on my temporary abode in Connecticut (I finally learned
how to spell it and soon I are one). On the road
again...You have probably noticed that the Xmas mailing
is all automated this year. Just what we needed to
increase the personal touch in this letter. In fact,
this entire letter is being produced without any human
intelligence being involved. The words flow straight
from the gin bottle into the microcomputer...Jack had a
great year job-wise; make that a good year; rather, a
so-so year; well, anyway, December was great. He had
three different jobs in 1983 (his competence finally
caught up with him). The company he was president of
closed up in March so he joined Computer Sciences
Corporation. Mistake! Lots of great people at CSC, but
that gov't contractor business isn't for Jack. So, a
friend recommended him to become a vice president at
Bunker Ramo. The friend then promptly quit his job as
president of Bunker Ramo, but Jack joined anyway and is

89

delighted. He is in charge of the telecommunications network that supplies a quotation service to stock brokers. (Based on his experience in the stock market, he is better off supplying a service than investing.)...We are moving into a new house in Trumbull, CT, (next to Bridgeport) and Linda loves it. She just says "I'll have this over there and that over there" and Jack writes checks and drives nails and writes checks and puts in molly bolts and writes checks, etc. Jack can't complain since he bought the house before Linda saw it (one of the few things where she trusts him because they have similar tastes). The house is a contemporary with a backyard that drops (not slopes) down to a creek. There will be a room for guests, so ya'll come visit...Linda had it easy this year since she is no longer PTO president. Well, not quite easy. In fact, the year was a zoo. Just keeping track of Jack's office number was a job. The telephone never stopped ringing (why can't women get a tennis game together without 87 phone calls?) (and the kids have started with the phone also) (ever see three sets of parentheses in a row?) (how about four?). Since she gave up PTO, she doubled up on tennis time and got to be pretty good (beats Jack now, big deal!). She drives all over God's country (is it a sign of old age when you can sell the station wagon? If so, bring it on)...The boys are fantastic. Moving is not easy, but they are taking it in stride. Jumping into the unknown is always frightening, but they are doing it with aplomb. They are all still playing soccer and enjoy it (even when they don't win)...Michael gave Jack some hand-me-down shoes he outgrew. They were too big for Jack! Michael was Senior Patrol Leader of the new neighborhood Boy Scout Troop and helped get the troop started. Stephen was one of the first scouts and is convinced he will beat

Michael to the Eagle award. Michael spent August in France with some of our ex-neighbors. It was not easy for him, but the experience added to his stature. He's still a leading student and a joy even though he has entered teenagehood...Stephen still charms everyone with his vivid imagination, grand smile, and easygoing manner. He also makes good grades, but his main love is still his 24" dirt bike...Andrew is still a big fellow for his age. He was the best kicker on his soccer team and earned the nickname "bigfoot" for his powerful kicks. He is doing well in school and is a ray of sunshine around home...As we move on to our new address (35 Tudor Lane, Trumbull, CT 06611) in January, thoughts of leaving all our wonderful friends in Virginia are sad ones, but, if our travels have taught us anything it's that the only sure thing is that there are many marvelous people everywhere. We look forward to adding the people of Connecticut to our list of treasured friends upon whom we inflict this letter each year...The ending joke this year is on Jack. He always admired the old Cadillac Seville ('76 to '79), but never could afford one. They finally became old enough to be within his means, so he bought a '79 Seville in November. It is in perfect condition and will probably remain so since Jack will not let the car out of the garage if it's snowing, raining, windy, too sunny, etc. The question is, will Jack walk to work in Conn. rather than get his car dirty? It's only 8 miles or so...May Christmas and the New Year bring you and yours the wisdom to recognize, accept, and enjoy the love and friendship that surrounds us all. **Merry Christmas and a very happy 1984.**

The Pendrays

My Junior High School Days

Ponce de Leon Junior High: A Changing Place

I've always felt that junior high school is the perfect name for the school for kids beginning teenagehood. It's not elementary kid stuff, and it's not higher education, but it's a changing place where kids change from being children to beginning to become adults. In my case, it was quite a change, from a small Catholic school, Sts. Peter & Paul in Miami, to a large public school, Ponce de Leon in Coral Gables. Academically, junior high is still like elementary school with a fixed curriculum and few electives. Socially, the world turns upside down. Guys go from seeking approval from the gang of guys, to seeking interest from the girls. From my uninformed viewpoint, it appears that girls go from being groups of giggling girls in public, to being groups of giggling girls in private, but what do I know (never much on this subject!).

Somewhat lost in my new world of kids who knew each other from local elementary schools, and living in a dysfunctional household dominated by a bi-polar mother, I became a disruptive and defiant class clown during my 7th and 8th grades at Ponce.

My Free Period

In the 8th grade, I had an English teacher who taught me most of the English that I have used to my benefit all of my life, Mrs. Mitchell. She was a red-headed disciplinarian who didn't put up with any nonsense, and she knew her English and how to teach it. In return for her teaching me invaluable knowledge, I was obnoxious. I recall one time, after I had mouthed off in class, she said, in front of the class, "Jack, you are a veritable font of worthless information." I took that as a high compliment. One day, I was mouthing off again about something that I don't recall, but it must have been pretty egregious as she threw me out of class and said not to come back until I was ready to apologize. Being a stubborn brat who had no inclination to apologize, I decided that I had a free period every day. Ponce had three main buildings, a gym, and some portables, so I would wander around campus during my "free period" and check things out. After about a week of this, I happened to wander straight into the Dean of Boys, Mr.

Elmer Day, who asked me what I was doing. I explained that Mrs. Mitchell had given me a free period, and that I was doing that. He thought that a bit unusual, so we went to see Mrs. Mitchell after the period was over and she explained to him what had actually happened. After threatening to expel me, which Mrs. Mitchell resisted, he negotiated a compromise in which Mrs. Mitchell and I jointly apologized. I figured out that I had screwed up big time, went back to class, and became a better student of hers. I can still diagram a sentence and recognize a dangling participle when I see one. Thanks, Mrs. Mitchell.

The IQ Test

I believe it was in the 8th grade when they administered an IQ test to all the 8th grade students in Ponce. After the test results came in, the principal, Mr. Jack Prance, called my mother in for a meeting. I wasn't invited, but I deduce from what my mother told me that Mr. Prance said something like, "We thought he was just stupid, but he has an IQ of 131. What the hell is wrong with him?" Hell, I thought I was just stupid, too, so it was a shock to all of us. At least I started paying more attention in class, knowing that I was supposed to able to understand the stuff.

Hard of Hearing

I was saying "What?" so often to my mother that she thought I might have a hearing problem. She took me to a fancy hearing doctor in downtown Miami, and he ran a bunch of tests. The results were alarming, so he recommended to my mother that I undergo a new treatment where he would stick needles of radium up my nose and in my ears to fix the problem by irradiation. My mother was not about to spend the type of money he wanted before checking with the school about the effects of my hearing problem there. In an interview with one of the school counselors who knew me well (I was pretty well known by the counselors!), she told Mom something like, "Oh, Jack doesn't have a hearing problem, he just wants attention." Mom gave me more attention, and I stopped saying, "What?"

So, the answer to the question is, "No, my mental strangeness was not caused by radiation treatments." I never had them.

Lettering in Sports

My older brother, Tom, was a good jock and had been on the first team in all the sports at Ponce the year before I went there. In order to win a big "P" letter, you had to be on the school team in at least two sports (maybe three), and Tommy proudly had a P on his letter sweater, of which I was always envious. So, when I got to Ponce, I wanted to letter, so I went out for every sports team. The problem is that I am an embarrassing athlete, with the hand-eye coordination of a bat. I made one team, softball I think, and sat on the bench for the season. In another sport, they cut me, but let me be a team manager off the field. One time I was whining to a friend that I wasn't going to letter, and that would be embarrassing after my brother's brilliant record. I saw one of the coaches nearby and hoped he heard me. Sure enough, when the letters were handed out, my name was called and I got one.

Knowing that all the real jocks knew that I hadn't earned it, I don't think I ever wore that letter, but I learned a lesson. I never again tried to reap a reward that I didn't deserve, which certainly limited my rewards.

My Buddies

Having my birthday in November, I was one of the youngest in my class, and, to top that, I was small and one of the runts of the class. (At 80, I have finally given up waiting for my growth spurt, since I have shrunk an inch or two in the last several years.) Consequently, some of my best buddies were one year behind me in school. Amongst the closest ones were Bobby Victor (neighbors and friends from the 5th grade on), Paul Huck, and Tommy Prebianca. In spite of our misspent youths, all of them became very successful solid citizens, Bob and Tom in sales and Paul in law. In high school, we were all members of the Ching Tang fraternity, which cemented our bonds for life.

Wandering Around Aimlessly

Paul, Tommy, Bobby, and I would spend many hours together in groups of two, three, or all four. Being 13, we were too old to ride childish bicycles, but too young to drive, so we would wander around aimlessly on foot. We covered miles and miles all around Coral Gables and Coconut Grove, looking for mischief or friends' houses to visit. Now, my stepfather, "Pop," was in charge of landscaping for the Florida Power and Light Company, which required him to drive around most of the day visiting the different FP&L facilities in south Florida. He drove a green 1950 Plymouth, which we affectionately called the Green Turtle. It was amazing how often the Green Turtle would appear and give us a lift right when we were running out of foot power.

The 1980s

Crockery Transporteurs

When Paul, Bobby, and I were not wandering around aimlessly, we were Crockery Transporteurs at La Casita Tea Room in Coconut Grove. The owners, Bob and Ellen Ousley, called us busboys, but we knew better. At that time, the early '50s, the restaurant consisted of two large screened-in rooms on the side of a small house that was converted into a dining room and commercial kitchen. La Casita was famous for "Mrs. Ousley's Black Bottom Pie," which always made a big hit when "Pie" was mistakenly left off of the typed and mimeographed menu (which happened more than once while I was there). It was a good job, with after-school and weekend hours, and our head busboy was another future Ching Tang member, Nick Torelli, who gave us the jobs. Eventually, Bobby moved on to Tyler's restaurant, and Paul and I were both fired, at different times, but it was good pocket money for us while it lasted. Vestiges of the old La Casita can still be found in the rooms of The Taurus Beer & Whiskey House in Coconut Grove.

50 Years of Christmas Letters

Hello Out There;

Hard to believe that this is the fourteenth consecutive edition of the infamous Pendray Christmas letter. That's enough to fill a respectable trash can, or start a fire. It used to be easier to do this because it was drafted in longhand, thusly freeing the left hand for frequently moving the glass of bourbon from the desk to the lips without interrupting the flow of writing. In the new age of composing the letter at the Apple keyboard, the task requires both hands which results in: type a word, take a drink; type a worb, tike a trink; anb sew ferth… We moved to Connecticut as planned last January, well, almost as planned. The plan was as follows: pack van on Monday and Tuesday, close on old house and drive to Connecticut on Wednesday, close on new house and unload van on Thursday, unpack on Friday. The actual execution was as follows: snow like hell on Sunday, shovel snow and pack van on Monday and Tuesday, snow like hell on Wednesday during closing on old house, spend Wednesday snowbound with friends (the Nilsens) near old house, drive to Connecticut on Thursday, close on new house and unload van on Friday, snow like hell on Saturday…We love our new house, and our bank account almost outlasted its needs, almost. We were fortunate enough to move from one great neighborhood to another. Marvelous new friends, just like our old ones…Jack's job let him spend more time at home than in the past, which was welcome due to the demands of the new house. We're finally just about settled in, and it only took a year… We joined a small Episcopal church just around the corner. It looks like a picture postcard New England church, all white with a steeple and 200 years of history. Michael and Stephen are both acolytes and Jack may be elected to the vestry next year. Wonders never cease!...We found the local theater in New Haven and got season tickets. It's good to be back in the swing of dinner and theater with friends. Jack sold the sailboat. Sob, sob…The boys are all doing well and adjusted to the new schools rapidly. Soccer is also big up here, and all three are still playing…Michael (9th grade) is still a good student and has honors courses in English and math. He is taller than Jack (what disrespect!) and still growing rapidly…Stephen (7th grade) is on the honor roll, plays drums in the band, and races his BMX bike on the Trumbull course. In his first year of BMX (bicycle motocross, for the uninitiated), he garnered several trophies and no bruises…Andrew (3rd grade) is our computer whiz. He taught himself how to program the Apple by reading the manuals, and is now the neighborhood consultant…Linda still does those two-mile walks every morning at 6:30 and has even convinced a neighbor to join her. The rest of the time, she drives the station wagon all over the state. We went to her Munich high school reunion this summer (it was held in Washington) and she saw a lot of friends from those days 20 years ago…Jack just kinda gets older. He now has some granny glasses for reading, and peers at the world over them. Still jogging when the weather is right, but the pace is slowing down…Chelsea, the Labrador, is still in search of more food…We did some family traveling this year. Several trips into New York with visitors, day trips to Mystic Seaport and the trolley car museum in Connecticut, and both summer vacation and Thanksgiving in Virginia with Linda's folks… As we prepare for our first Christmas in New England, our thoughts go out to all those friends in other places with whom we would like to be. Have a merry Christmas and may 1985 be the best year ever for each of you.

The Pendrays

50 Years of Christmas Letters

Hello out there;

This is the fifteenth edition of the dreaded Pendray Christmas letter. Each year, in search of inspiration, I reread all the previous letters while sipping on something. It goes like this: sip, read, sip, sip, read, sip, sip, sip, read, etc. I figure in a few more years the letter will finally disappear, since I will pass out before finishing the sip, read, etc., preparation phase. Sipping this year is from a well-aged 1984 "Nouveau Red" wine produced by the internationally acclaimed Ingleside Plantation winery in Oak Grove, Virginia (no kidding, folks), which is not far from Linda's parents' home. (On a recent tour, they recognized Linda's dad, which makes me think he isn't unknown there.)...Jack hadn't changed jobs in over a year, so he did so in January. An old friend and business associate was over for dinner and described the new venture he was starting. Jack volunteered. The old friend must have been more friend than businessman, because he accepted. In January, the two of them, with a secretary, a dog, a cat, a wish, and a prayer, opened for business in an old Victorian house in Wilton, CT. The old friend turned out to be a great businessman in spite of Jack, since they are now 12 people in the old house and they are doing gangbusters. The company, Vanguard Atlantic Ltd., provides strategic planning and merger and acquisition

105

services to companies in the computer services and communications industries. Jack loves it and has found his career (at the tender age of only 46!)...We did a lot of vacationing this year. In February, the family was joined by Jack's nephew from Miami, Sean, and spent four days skiing in Killington, VT (Jack's old rump slide continues to amuse the slopeside spectators), and visited with one of Jack's old roommates from California who lives nearby. It was great...April saw Linda and Jack off to the Virgin Islands to join old friends from Houston for 10 days of debauchery. The four of us rented a 38 ft. Pearson sloop and crewed ourselves around for 9 days, followed by 2 days in a hotel at St. Thomas. We denied ourselves nothing. It was stupendous!! July saw the whole family off again to Virginia and Florida. We spent some days with Linda's folks before catching the Auto-train to Fla. Five days in Disneyworld finally quenched our desire to do everything there, and we headed on to Miami to see Jack's family. From there we did several days in Fort Myers (where we eventually bought an investment house on a lake in Cape Coral; Linda's Uncle Frank has retired in that area and watches over it for us). Overnight in St. Pete gave us a grand reunion with a gang of Linda's parents' army buddies, then, back to Virginia for a day, and on home to Ct. Whew!...We just got back from a reunion of our old dinner group in Virginia. That group is certainly worth the trip...Linda's whole family is joining us for Christmas in Ct., then we all leave on Dec. 26 to spend several days with the Pendrays in Chattanooga. Our travel agent loves us, but next year will be quieter (Thank God!)...Jack and Linda still get out to the theater, with a couple of weekends with friends in New York and season tickets to the local New Haven theater. Jack has been known to catch a few winks during some of the less exciting performances...Mike is several inches taller than his dad, Steve is about even with his mom, and Andy looks like he's going to be the really big one. Must be a tall relative out there somewhere; please identify yourself...The boys are a never-ending source of joy and

106

pride for us...Mike played JV soccer this year at Trumbull High (proudly wears his letter jacket all the time), and continues to be a scholar while making it look easy. He took a week-long canoe trip in Canada this summer. They were so far in the boonies, the only sign of human life they saw was airplanes passing high overhead...Steve plays soccer, is first drummer in the concert band, worked all summer to purchase a beautiful (and expensive) BMX bicycle, and made straight A's the end of last year, to boot. Quite a young man!...Andy also does soccer and started baseball this year. He remains the undisputed computer-jock of the house, and teaches techniques to his gifted-and-talented class group. He had fun at science camp this summer, and also brings home the achievements in the grades category...Linda remains trim (much to the chagrin of ole Pudgy Pendray) by walking her couple of miles each day at the crack of dawn. She's looking forward (with mixed feelings) to Mike's reaching driving age in January so he can do some of the chauffeuring. Connecticut sure is spread out when you have to drive for the family. She got back into tennis after a lapse of two years, and the new tennis club she joined also provides aerobics. Some days, she feels like the zoo keeper, but the zoo runs smoothly because of her...Chelsea, the Labrador, is 9 years old and going strong. She constantly hassles Steve to take her on run-alongs with him on his bike or skateboard. The rest of the time is spent providing amusement, love, and affection for the family.

The wine's running low and the old fingers are getting stiff, so let us send, from our home to yours, the love and gratitude we feel all year for having such wonderful friends and relatives, but which we only manage to express at Christmas. Have a joyous Christmas and a marvelous 1986!

The Pendrays

50 Years of Christmas Letters

Getting to School

This is only interesting if you realize that all of the ways I went to school as a child would be considered dangerous by most parents today and not allowed. Too bad.

In the first and second grades in Chattanooga, I walked to Normal Park School with my older brother, Tommy, first from 1233 Worthington St., and then from 232 Jarnigan Ave. after we moved. We started in Chattanooga at 1006 Mississippi Ave., across the street from Normal Park School, but we had moved to Worthington before I started school. In Miami, Tommy and I caught public buses to Sts. Peter & Paul Catholic School, first from around 2945(?) SW 21st Terr (our first house in Miami after my parents' divorce), second from 2777(?) NW 21 Terr., in Allapattah, after Mom married Pop, and then from 5600 Le Jeune Rd. in Coral Gables. From Le Jeune Rd., I walked or rode my bike to Ponce de Leon Jr. High. I hitchhiked down Le Jeune to Coral Gables High for grades 9 to 12, often being picked up by Inky Philips, who became a college Sigma Nu fraternity brother and is still one of my closest lifelong friends.

Places Where I Have Lived

As a baby, I lived at 2152 SW 23rd Terr., Miami, FL (near Coconut Grove).

1006 Mississippi Ave., Chattanooga, TN—Ages 2 to 5?—Across the street from Normal Park Elementary.

1233 Worthington St., Chattanooga, TN—Ages 5 & 6?—On a steep hill. I remember when it rained, I would build mud dams on the curb to stop the water.

232 Jarnigan Ave., Chattanooga, TN—Ages 6 & 7? —Coal furnace in basement. Fish pond in back with a snake in it (once!). Remnants of pond still visible on Google Earth.

2945(?) SW 21st Terr., Miami, FL—A dump of a rental house on same street as Mom's sister, called "Sister" by all the family. I remember that a scorpion crawled out of the bathtub drain. Learned to ride a bicycle here.

2777(?) NW 21 Terr., Miami, FL—Moved into Pop's house after he married Mom. My younger brother, Keith, was born here.

5600 Le Jeune Rd., Coral Gables, FL—Moved here when I was in 5th grade. Lived here until college, so this is my home best remembered. Area was sparsely settled, so I ran free on my bike all day. This is the house in which I grew up. Lucky to be raised in Coral Gables in the '50s. Best of times.

Dorms, Sigma Nu house (2 1/2 years), and rentals for five years of college at UF in Gainesville. Great times! Fall 1957-June 62

739 Layne Ct., Palo Alto CA—Two years here while getting MS in Computer Science (#15!) at Stanford. Nice apt. shared with other guys. Studied hard, played hard. A great way to be an Air Force lieutenant. Made some friends for life: Dick Abbott, Al Merten, Klaus Pfitzner, John Morse, and Fikret Keskinel. June 1962-June 1964 (8 quarters)

4327(?) Americana Dr., Annandale, VA—Shared with Al Merten and later Carl Harris. Al and I were both at HQ USAF in the Pentagon and commuted. Met and dated Linda, who lived in next building. 1964-1965

Glass House, 3440 Roberts Lane, Arlington, VA— Followed Merten to this bachelor pad of 5 officers on the Potomac. Lived there less than a year. Our

112

wedding reception was held here. Terrific venue. 1966

Places we lived, Linda and I!

5550 Columbia Pike, Arlington, VA—Our first residence as a married couple. On the 9th floor of a huge high-rise. I took the bus down Columbia Pike to the Pentagon and Linda drove to Marshall High School in Falls Church. Oct. 1966-Fall 1967

7415 Brad St, Falls Church, VA—Our first house, a 3/1 California-style house (rare in VA). Had a party room with a bar with two basket chairs, all hanging from the ceiling. Mike was born while we were here. Fall 1967-April 1970

5 Allée de Norvège, Massy, France—Moved to a Ville Nouvelle, Massy. Had a 3rd floor walk-up apartment of 1,000 sq. feet, considered very spacious by French standards. Stephen was born at the Clinique de Massy down the street. Made some French friends for life: Picots and Fontignies. Lived here three years. May 1970-June 1973

14 Avenue de Rueil, Nanterre, France—Rented this 3-story house for two years after I became the boss of TECSI. Had a private back yard where Mike, Steve, and Kaki the Labrador could play, and I could bar-b-q. July 1973-June 1975

4112 Wynnwood Dr., Annandale, VA—After returning from France, this was Linda's folks' house where we lived for about six months while we looked for a place to live. Great time to get caught up with Bob and Gladdie Lawrence. Best in-laws ever!

2753 Viking Dr., Herndon, VA—A house in Fox Mill Estates development. Plenty of room and great neighborhood. The Gourmet Group was formed in this neighborhood, and those friends became family for the rest of our lives. Andrew was born soon after we arrived here. When we lost Kaki in 1977, we acquired Chelsea, another Lab. Feb. 1976-Sept. 1979

2651 Petersborough St., Herndon, VA—Moved into a larger house right behind our Viking Dr. house in Fox Mill. It was larger than we needed, so the living room was never furnished. There was one lounge chair in the living room, where Chelsea slept. More good memories acquired here. Sept. 1979-Feb. 1983

35 Tudor Lane, Trumbull, CT—Our largest house ever, 4,400 sq. ft., on a cul de sac. Sharp drop off in the back to a stream and woods. Had a 24' by 24' great room with bar and fireplace. We had a deck built on the back to cantilever out over the drop off, and had a glass hot tub room built on the back of the ground floor to overlook the valley. The boys all went to Trumbull High during our 13

years here. Terrific neighbors like the Homas, Jaffes, Hammers, Halabys, and Steins. Still in touch with all of them. Probably our best period together as a family before the guys started going off to college. Chelsea loved it to her last days. Feb. 1983-March 1997

Thrush Ridge Rd., Reston, VA—A marvelous townhouse on a lake in Reston. Huge party deck and comfortable screened porch overlooking our boat dock and the lake. Outstanding sunsets! We had the fastest pontoon boat on the no-engines-allowed lake. Our electric motor would do 6 knots! We lived a life of quiet leisure in the middle of booming Reston. March 1997-Sept. 2004

Dockside Pl., Sarasota, FL—A 3/2 condo on a canal in Harbour Towne on Siesta Key. Great place to live while we traveled between Reston and Perth, Australia. Kept it for 6 years as a guesthouse. Sold it for 2 1/2 times what it cost us, a stroke of great dumb luck. June 1999-Sept. 2005

Marine Parade, Cottesloe WA Australia—I got a gig teaching in the MBA program at the University of Western Australia, in Perth, in 1999. UWA was on the quarter system, and I taught every other quarter so we were half-time in Perth for three years. We rented several apartments and one house in Cottesloe, Perth's beach suburb, but our favorite was 116 Marine Parade, which we rented for at least half of the time we were there. We had two balconies overlooking the Indian Ocean, where we could fire up the barbie and toss back a few, which we often did. June 1999-June 2001

Riegels Landing Dr., Sarasota, FL—Living like the rich! On the Intracoastal Waterway, this 3/4, 3,900 sq ft house had it all: pool, spa, 2 docks, decks galore, huge guest rooms, open plan, etc. We spent 16 fabulous years of non-stop entertaining and fun in this house. Great neighbors included the Gutfreunds and the Gibsons, still frequently seen for dinners and parties. Summer 2000-Oct 2015

Chestnut Ridge Rd., Mills River, NC—Escape from the summer FL heat to Asheville, NC. This 2,200 sq ft house on top of a small mountain half-way between Asheville and Hendersonville was our summer home for 7 years. Great neighbors, frequent guests, and beautiful western NC made it wonderful. Sold it at a loss in current value, but it was still a great investment to us. July 2012-July 2019

Palmer Ranch, Sarasota, FL—Time to downsize and get away from the effects of salt water on a 35-year-old wooden house. This 3,200 sq ft house is perfect for us at this time of our lives. Separate master suite, three guest rooms, small pool, spa, and a large pond in the back. No stairs, and no wood to rot! Oct 2015-present

Hello out there!

(Oh no! the dreaded Pendray Xmas letter has managed to
sneak into the mailbox again. Would any sane person
believe that they have done this for 16 years straight
and are still at liberty?)   Once again, I take computer
and wine in hands to compose the annual edition of
Pendray pap. (I looked up "pap," it means undemanding
reading material; sounds like the word was invented for
this letter.)   The wine this year is the world-renowned
Chesapeake Blanc from the famous Ingleside Plantation
in downtown Oak Grove, Virginia.   (For those of you who
are not wine connoisseurs, this winery is located about
15 minutes from the place where Linda's folks lived up
until last Friday.   Yep, they sold their beautiful home
on the Potomac and set out for parts unknown, the first
such part being our home for the Xmas holidays)...We
had our usual year, not much happened, just took 4
vacations, built (had built, we ain't crazy) a new room
on the house, had season tickets to three different
theatres, got into New York several times for _real_
theatre, etc...Let's start with the best part, the

117

vacations. We spent Xmas in both Ct and Tenn. Traveled on the 25th, so we got two celebrations in the same day. Visited Jack's dad in Chattanooga. A great time!...The family went skiing for a week in February at Mt. Snow in Vermont. (Jack has discovered that, no matter what the age, he can still go <u>down</u>hill, even if on his rump.) The old folks don't even try to keep up with the youngsters anymore, and, worse, they go to bed earlier than the kids. Must be a major epoch there, somewhere...The two weeks around July 4th were spent in Virginia. Using Linda's parents' place as a base, we went to Williamsburg (where Linda relived her college days at William & Mary), Busch Gardens, and Water Country USA. Linda's sister, her kids, and her fiancé (now husband - welcome Gordon Harvey to the family, folks (psst, she done good)), joined us for a good time by all. At the end, we took Mike for tours of William & Mary and Univ. of Va. since he's getting ready for the college thing (Jack was ready to go back to college when he saw UVA, little does he know that they would call him sir)...Our last vacation was for Thanksgiving at the Lawrences' in Virginia. It was great, but very sad to realize that it was our last time at this wonderful home of fond memories for all of us...The new room on our house is for the hot tub. It's on the back of the house, perched above the dropoff to the creek (the kids call it <u>the</u> cliff). Connecticut is known for its rocks, and we found out why. It cost us a thousand to cut up one such rock so the foundation could be laid (is that a dirty word?). It's marvelous to sit in the hot tub and gaze at the snow...We changed allegiance in theatres this year, which is why we ended up with three subscriptions. The old one got too serious for us (we like fluff), so we changed. Next year will be simpler...We had block parties in May and

118

The 1980s

September on our cul-de-sac. Terrific
neighborhood...Took the gang to New York to see the
Radio City Music Hall Christmas special last year and
also to see Cats. Both were spectacular
shows...Linda's life is still dull and boring. With
only two tennis leagues (she almost beat Jack last time
they played, scared the H out of him), driving the boys
to their events, running a house of five people and one
always-hungry Labrador named Chelsea, going on business
trips with Jack from time-to-time, and other things,
what do you expect?.. Jack still travels some. Mostly
to Hartford, White Plains, and Philly, which gets him
home for dinner, but, now and then, he suffers a trip
to Los Angeles, Vail, West Palm, or Phoenix. Linda
went with him to Florida and Phoenix, to ease the
burden of his travels. His company opened an office in
New York City, but Jack still works in the Ct. office;
no major commute for him...The boys are all tall (where
from?) and get good grades (not from Jack)...Mike got
his driver's license this year. He's a good driver and
helps Linda with the errands. We bought a Subaru wagon
as a 3rd car, but Linda drives it the most. Mike plays
soccer and track at Trumbull High, but seems to spend
most of this time in college entrance tests this year,
and he's only a Junior...Steve still plays drums and
soccer well. His gang likes the new hot tub and stays
in it long enough to get dish-pan bodies. He won two
free tickets to the first two games of the World
Series, so he and Jack went and had a ball...Andy is in
Cub Scouts for his last year. In April, the pack went
to spend the night on the retired battleship
Massachusetts. Quite an experience. Them was big
boats!...Andy also plays soccer, and he's the in-house
computer whiz. He took a calligraphy course, and the
results are evident below...The bottle of Virginia wine

is about gone, so I'll end with this...Every year, we leave a little snack and beverage for Santa. This year, I think we'll leave a bottle of this Chesapeake Blanc with the following note: Yes, Santa Claus, there is a Virginia, and here's proof, in fact, about 24 proof, according to the label on the bottle.

The Pendrays

Merry Christmas

Trains and Planes

In the late 1700s and early 1800s, Richard Trevithick demonstrated the first use of transportation by steam propulsion in Camborne, Cornwall, England. He also developed the first high-pressure steam engine and later built the first working railway steam locomotive. At that time, almost all known Pendrays lived in and around Camborne, working the mines and family farms. Knowing how much togetherness was practiced by town folks back then, it doesn't take a large leap of imagination to wonder if steam, engineering, and transportation were planted in the Pendray gene pool in Camborne. They seem to be in mine.

What good luck for me to be born in the middle of the transfer of long-distance travel from trains to planes. I have been lucky enough to ride the rails in their heyday right after World War II, to ride in relatively early propeller passenger planes, and to ride in many jet planes, including a half-dozen transatlantic flights in the supersonic Concorde. While being an active participant in the technological revolution of computers, I was also a passive witness and beneficiary of an equally impressive revolution in passenger transportation technology.

Trains

When I was a wee lad, transportation and trains were almost synonymous. Moreover, living in Chattanooga, a city that railroads built, trains were everywhere. I vividly recall going to both the Louisville and Nashville (L&N) Railroad's Union Station and Southern Railway's Terminal Station for my father's business trips. Like all railroad towns, the two best hotels were next to the two train stations. When we took the family to Chattanooga in 1986, we stayed at the Hilton in Pullman cars on the rails in the Southern's Terminal Station, now a tourist site called The Chattanooga Choo Choo. We had dinner at the Read House Hotel, across from where the L&N's Union Station used to be. We also rode the third railroad in town, the Lookout Mountain Incline Railway, which had been a childhood special treat. My favorite station was the Union Station, because they had The General locomotive inside. The General is the locomotive that was stolen by

Yankee spies in Big Shanty, GA, outside Atlanta and chased by the Rebs all the way to Chattanooga, where the chase ended. The 1956 Disney movie *The Great Locomotive Chase* is a pretty good re-telling of the story. The first Medals of Honor were granted by Congress to Union military participants of the chase.

The General was loaned to Georgia for one of their celebrations, and they kept it! It is now back where the chase started in Big Shanty, which was renamed Kennesaw in about 1870. Linda and I visited The General in August of 2018.

"The General"—the Locomotive, Not the Guy

I have always been fascinated by trains, but I'm not sure why. Maybe it's their history as the symbol of the Industrial Revolution and the unifying knot of many countries, the U.S. being a prime example. Maybe it's the easily understandable and visible engineering that harnesses raw power—first steam, and now diesel and electric. Maybe it's the childhood memories of watching the sleeping towns of Georgia pass by outside my window as I traveled between Miami and Chattanooga. Most likely, it's because there is nothing to do on a passenger train other than relax and enjoy the ride. Whatever the cause, I have seldom passed up a chance to ride a train or visit a train museum, making me a certifiable train nut.

Planes

While I am far from being a pioneer in passenger flight, I have logged a few air miles in my life. When United and Continental merged, I became a Million-Miler, having over half a million actual flown miles on each airline. Whereas I am enthralled by the romance of the rails, I'm less enamored by the attractiveness of the air. With few exceptions, my flights were not for the fun of flying, but rather to go somewhere efficiently.

In the early '60s and '70s, flying by jet was almost fun. You see, airline fares were set by governments and trade associations, and the same fare applied to all airlines. A ticket from point A to point B would be honored by all airlines, and anyone could use a ticket, as the name was usually not checked. Not being able to compete on price, the airlines competed on service. If you were in the air for a couple of hours or more, you were served a full meal, often accompanied by a small packet of four cigarettes. The seats were comfortable, space was plenty, recline was significant, service was frequent, and the food was good. Ah, the good ole days. Then the industry was deregulated, and, except for the introduction of lie-flat seats in the upper classes of long flights, service has declined as fast as ticket prices have fallen. In today's dollars, an international round-trip coach ticket between New York and London in 1970 would cost $3,200 ($550 in 1970 dollars), about three times what a similar flight costs in 2020. We are flying cheaper, subject to being able to avoid the got-ya economy of airline ticketing, but with much less comfort.

I have had a few flights that seem worthy of mention. Elsewhere, I have recounted the stories of being on the first scheduled flight into the CDG airport in Paris, and of flying on the Concorde with Superman, Christopher Reeve. I have also flown on one of the early 747s with a cocktail lounge in the hump. That was cool. The first row of business class in the hump was my favorite seat on United's 747 when flying to Australia (before lie-flat seats). I loved the 747 until the airlines turned most of them into max capacity cattle cars. Now they are mostly gone.

When I retired from the corporate world in 1996, I had hundreds of thousands of frequent flyer miles. We used some to fly all the kids to Australia on business class, twice. We used a bunch for Linda and me to fly around the world via Australia on British Airways in first class. We flew Linda's parents from D.C. to Perth, Australia, and back in United's first class. They had never flown 1st, and it was a thrill for them.

A quick word on the supersonic Concorde. It was a small plane with two-and-two seating in seats about the size of a regular coach seat. I was very comfortable, but big guys had a hard time in the seats. The service was a cut above all the others that I have seen, and the plane was very quiet inside (but not outside!). The thing I enjoyed most about the flight was that I never had any jet lag. Something about doing that transatlantic flight in three hours made up for the time change. In order to get customers, both British Air and Air France started offering Concorde flights on one way with a business class round trip ticket. Since I usually

126

flew business class, this was great for me and explains why I flew the Concorde as much as I did.

I'll finish this blurb on planes by saying that I am glad that I am retired and don't have to fly for business nowadays. While I enjoy being able to fly in shorts and flip-flops after 40 years of flying in suits, I find flying now to be a hassle and very not-fun. Could be that is part of being a crotchety old man.

50 Years of Christmas Letters

Hello Out There...

Bloody Mary...yup, Bloody Mary...I know you're all wondering what serves as the liquid elixir liquor lubricant for the loquacious letter launcher this year...Bloody Mary.   (Reader 1, aside to Reader 2, "Good Lord, we're still on the Pendray mailing list."   R2, "Maybe we can get in th4e (the 4 is silent) FBI protected witness program next year)...It's year 17 for this very personal Xeroxed (do we say Cannoned, now?) letter.   In order to prepare for this each year, I reread the preceding letters.   That goes like this: read, read, read, sip; read, read, sip; read, sip, sip; read, sip, sip, sip; etc. on the sipping...We had a great year in '87.   Vintage stuff...In February, we went on the annual skiing trip to Vermont.   Stephen showed us all how to ski, but Jack found it difficult to see with his face buried in the snow, as usual.   (R1, "A man his age shouldn't be skiing."   R2, "No problem, he doesn't.")...We did our usual theatres this year, with season tickets to two theatres, and a couple of trips to New York for plays. (R1, "Jack hasn't seen a performance in years." R2, "Maybe he's a sleep learner.")...In May, the big (rather, older) folks rented a sailboat in the Virgin Islands with the Guidos from Virginia and sailed away for a week.   Rained most of the time,

but a gin & tonic in the cabin tastes just like a gin & tonic on
deck. (R1, "Solved Linda's sunburn problem." R2, "Yeah, she
finally got to go on deck during the day.")...In May, Jack's high
school fraternity had a reunion in Miami. Thirty years' worth of
alumni got together for a weekend and all acted like they were 17
again. Jack loved it. (R1, "He never got beyond 17 anyway." R2,
"His body sure did.")...In August, his high school class had its 30-
year reunion. Only a Florida high school would have a reunion in
Miami in August, but they invented air conditioning since Jack was a
high schooler. It was a blast for Jack, and a drag for Linda (now
she knows what was meant by "for "better or worse," but wants to know
when the better starts)....We spent the July 4th vacation in Virginia
with Linda's sister and family. They bought a beautiful horse farm
in horse country outside Washington. It was so much fun, we went
back for Thanksgiving. They're coming to Connecticut for
Christmas. (R1, "Why go there?" R2, "The best defense is a good
offense.")...Linda's folks finally settled in Arizona after wandering
around most of the year. Something about sun and warmth. (R1, "Why
so far away from Jack?" R2, "Yes.")...Michael (18 next Jan.) is a
senior in high school and preparing for college next year. Between
college applications for six universities, ROTC scholarship
applications for the three services, and the National Merit
Scholarship application (he was one of eight semi-finalists from
Trumbull High), Mike has spent most of the Fall writing essays for
applications. A lot of his future will be decided in the next
months, and it looks promising. (R1, "How did Jack get into the
University of Florida, anyway?" R2, "No essay required.")...Stephen
(16 next Jan.) is in the 10th grade and had an active Fall. Steve
played drums in the high school band and was on the JV soccer team at
the same time. In spite of rushing from band to soccer, he held his
grades up. (R1, "What did Jack play in high school?" R2,
"Around.")...Andrew (11 last July) entered middle school (6th, 7th, &

8th grades) this year. Andy plays the trumpet, soccer, and writes poetry. A poem of his is on the back. (R1, "Did Jack understand this poem?" R2, "Yes, but only because he had access to the poet for questions.")...Linda is still busy running the family, or maybe we should say driving the family. Between driving to the store to replenish the supplies (they eat like an army), driving to pick up/drop off some kids, driving to tennis, etc., she's always on the move. (R1, "What does Jack contribute?" R2, "He drives her crazy.")...Jack got elected to the Trumbull Board of Tax Review this year. He ran unopposed, since no one wanted the job. (R1, "Why did he run for such a stupid job?" R2, "Yes.")...Chelsea the dog is 11 and grunts and groans a lot, but she jumps around like a puppy when there's food to be had...The joke this year is on Jack, again. He and his partner just published a book; Jack's first. In order to do so, they formed a publishing company. After the book was printed, they closed the publishing company. Anyone want a copy? There are plenty available. It's about strategic planning. As the kids would say: boring...We wish we could spend Christmas day with each of you, but only our love and thoughts must suffice.

Have a very Merry Christmas and Happy New Year.

The Pendrays

THE EYES

BY Andrew Pendray

THE EYES,

THOSE STRANGE, GREEN EYES,

WERE PEERING AT THE DEATH.

THE EYES,

THOSE STRANGE GREEN EYES,

HATED THE COLD.

THE EYES,

THOSE STRANGE, GREEN EYES,

WERE FULL OF SPRINGING LIFE,

WAITING FOR THEIR ONCE A YEAR CHANCE

TO LEAP OUT AND GRAB THE COLD,

TO SWALLOW IT WHOLE.

THEN THE GREEN POURED OUT

AND THE PUPILS WERE EMPTY.

THE WINTER FLOWED SLOWLY INTO

THE EYES.

THE GREEN HAD BROUGHT SPRING,

THE EYELIDS CLOSED IN WINTER.

133

50 Years of Christmas Letters

My High School Days

Coral Gables High: I Was Blessed

To have been a teenager in Coral Gables in the 1950s was a blessing. It was the best of times for the country and Miami. Coral Gables High was a new school, opened in 1950 and designed for south Florida before air conditioning, with lots of windows, open-air hallways, planted courtyards, and no access restrictions. Florida was still segregated, which was an unjust boon for white folks, but not for the blacks. Gables High students were drawn from all of southeastern Dade County, Coral Gables being the largest group. We probably had the wealthiest demographic of the five high schools in the Miami area. Nevertheless, we had a good representation of blue collar and even some farm families. To my memory, no one paid much attention to family wealth, even though differences were apparent by the fancy cars in the parking lot vs. those of us who hitchhiked, rode bikes, or took the bus to school. My class was the last class that went all four years to Gables High, making us the youngest class twice. Each class was almost a thousand students, so we were a big school. Lastly, Gables was a premier academic school and offered advanced courses in STEM and languages. Recognize that, in the '50s, the public schools in Miami were the best schools. If students went to private schools like Ransom or Everglades, one wondered what they had done wrong, or which judge sent them there!

Ching Tang

The social life at Gables was highly structured and very active. We had fraternities and service clubs for the boys and service clubs for the girls. All of the "in" group, e.g., jocks, good-lookers, politicians, etc., were in frats or clubs. Academic honors, drama, debate, and band all existed, but they were not the cool things. There were three levels of "cool" in the club structure, with four fraternities for the boys, and four service clubs for the girls at the top. Some would argue that there were only two at the top of each group, and I will talk of them.

The two fraternities were Tau Delta Tau (The Tau Delts, later changed to Stags as Florida outlawed Greek-letter high school fraternities, see: www.StagsClub.com) and Ching Tang (The Chinks, a normally pejorative nickname which we embraced proudly, see: www.ChingTang.com), and the two girls clubs were Junior Girls and Tallet, followed closely by Omega and Co-Eds. The Tau Delts were dominated by jocks and known as the tough guys, and Ching Tang, also with many jocks, was known as the "white shoe" guys who dressed well and courted the girls. My older brother, Tom, was a Tau Delt, and our first cousin, Jerry Degen, was a Chink. I really didn't fit well in either frat, as I was no jock and no ladies man. When I started at Gables, I was thirteen years old, 4' 11" tall and weighed maybe 120 pounds. My first semester, no frat rushed me. It was assumed by most folks, including me and my cousin, Jerry, that I would probably end up a Tau Delt because Tom was one. Cousin Jerry, who was a perfect Chink as a football starter and a ladies man, noticed that the Tau Delts didn't rush me, so he rushed me for Chinks the second semester. He pulled me aside and said, "You aren't a Tau Delt type, you should be a Chink."

My Ching Tang Rush Party at Crandon Park Beach, 1954.

I'm the little kid on the far right.

My cousin, Jerry Degen, presents my Ching Tang ring to me on my 15th birthday

Membership was by secret unanimous vote, and Jerry got me into Chinks, which I consider as one of the great favors done for me in my life.

Pledging Chinks was an arduous process, totally off limits nowadays. For six weeks, as a pledge you had to treat the brothers as gods, call them sir, do all of their chores, make single-handed paddles for them with which they paddled your butt, and then finish with "hell night." This latter was a several-hours long beating by paddles out in the woods somewhere, where you were covered with oil, given noxious concoctions to drink, and generally bullied. To call it hazing is a gross euphemism, as you were black and blue for a week after. It was inhuman torture and would not be tolerated by our children nor society today. If my cousin Jerry hadn't let them all know that anyone hurting me seriously would have to answer to him, I probably wouldn't have been able to take the punishment.

The Tau Delt initiation was similar, and this had been going on, and continued, for many years.

"Hell Night" Fall 1953

Jerry Degan '55, Barry Huff '55, Tom Adkisson '55
Mac McCraken '57. Jimmy Hall '56, Dave Taylor '54.
Don't be confused by the dates. Coral Gables High was a 4 year high school through the class of 1957.
McCracken was a freshman, Hall a sophmore, Degan, Huff, and Adkisson juniors, and Taylor a Senior.

Jerry Degen's Hell Night, 1953

Ching Tang was founded at Ponce de Leon High School in 1933, six years before I was born, and lasted until 1973, when the social norms changed and the fraternity voted to disband. It has been a special thing in my life, and the same is said by hundreds of other Chinks. Many of us are still in touch with the Chinks from our high school years, and we have had four reunions; 1987, 2001, 2006, and 2016, attended by hundreds of people. (I chaired the committee which organized the 2016 reunion.)

I'm not sure what made the bonds so tight, but here are a few of the possible reasons:

- The one-blackball membership elimination meant that everyone who was invited to join was liked by everyone already a member.

- The tortuous pledging system gave a strong bond of shared misery and accomplishment.

- In high school, Chinks was our main social activity. We partied together, double-dated together, gathered together in school at the "Chink Corner," sat together at tables at lunch and at school dances, exchanged the not-very-secret "Chink grip" handshake as we passed in the halls of Gables, confided in one another, helped one another, and even tended to date many of the same girls. We were also tolerant of each other's shortcomings, unusual in high school.

- We shared common enemies, mainly the Stags. (My brother Tom and I were considered strange because we got along well but were in the two different rival frats.)

Even today, I am in frequent contact with over a dozen Chinks, most of whom I have known for over 65 years. In Sarasota, we have a regional group that we call The West Coast Chinks, which still parties together, supports one another, and, sometimes, mourns together. I often see it mentioned in obituaries of one of the "brothers" that he was a member of Ching Tang. It should be in mine someday.

Girls

These are my perceptions of my youth, which, since they are mine, are reality to me. Many of them are probably misplaced, exaggerated, minimized, or just plain wrong, but it's what I have.

I grew up with boys, all boys. I had two brothers and nine cousins, all boys. A girl cousin came along later, but she was not a contemporary of mine as a youth. I had no friends to talk to who were girls. My mother was the only female who I knew well, and she was, at best, bi-polar, probably worse. Mom was negative, quick to criticize, slow to compliment, controlling, and manipulative. Consequently, I grew up knowing nothing of girls, but was very distrusting and somewhat fearful of women. My defense was to treat all girls like "one of the guys," because that was what I knew best.

Ignoring girls went fine until junior high and puberty, when my interest level increased significantly. Given my background, it is easy to imagine how successful I was in my attempts to attract interest from the other side, usually resulting in rejection and embarrassment, and reinforcing my preconceptions of distrust, dislike, and my own inadequacy. Nevertheless, between

143

Phyllis Kapp Dance Studio cotillion lessons and some mixers at Ponce de Leon Jr. High and the Coral Gables Country Club, I did develop enough social skills to keep trying.

High school was a dating disaster for me. I was in the "in" group, so there were many parties and dances that were in my calendar. I never had a girlfriend in high school; not until my second year at college did I think I had a girlfriend. I was popular enough to be named one of the "Tallet Boys" of one of the best girls' clubs, Tallet. They had six "Boys," one for each letter of their name. They were Talented, Athletic, Likeable, Leadership, and Thoughtful. And the "E" was me, which they made Efficient for my year. I was so clueless that I thought it was a high honor to be called efficient, as I was a geek before we knew what that was. Tallet was a service club, and they undertook service projects to do good. I have wondered if I was considered one of their projects, and they were each obligated to have two dates with me as a contribution. I did conclude that I was "Two-date Jack," and it was not difficult to understand. As an example of my dating skills, let me give you a story from two of my dates in high school.

But first, a little background is needed. One of Albert Einstein's gifts was the ability to explain very complex things that few people understood in such a manner that anyone could grasp the main idea. My senior year, I found a book he had written

144

on nuclear physics and relativity, which today would be called Nuclear Physics for Dummies. In the book, one of the things he explains is the basic concept of atomic and hydrogen bombs and how they are built and operate. I read the book and grasped most of what he said, thanks to his gift, and was fascinated by the bomb discussion. So, on one of my two-date dates with a Tallet girl, I got wound up and explained how to build fission and fusion atomic bombs. That must have been my second date with her, as next week I had a first date with another Tallet girl. On this date, while I was driving us down Biscayne Blvd. in Miami, I noticed that they were replacing the incandescent street lights with new mercury-vapor and sodium-vapor lights, and I pointed out that the mercury ones gave off the blue light, and the sodium ones gave off a yellow light. Then I caught myself, a bit too late, and said that I expected she wasn't too interested in streetlights and apologized. I'll never forget that she looked me straight in the eyes and said, "It's better than atomic bombs!" That is how I figured out that girls tell each other things that boys would never discuss. I think I was named "Efficient" soon thereafter.

Don't misunderstand me about opportunity. I had some dates with girls in high school where it appeared to me that they might have some interest in building a relationship. To my consternation, some of these girls were among the most attractive and most popular in the school. My reaction was usually to be terrified, feel in way over my head, be unable to talk about it, and simply avoid the girl thereafter. Several written entries in my high school annuals amount to girls asking, Where did you go and why? I guess the two-date model went both ways.

Education

I believe that school serves two purposes of equal importance. Firstly, school transfers academic knowledge to the students. Secondly, school provides a safe environment in which the students can learn non-academic knowledge about living life. The previous two sections are about the second purpose, and this section is about the first.

As I said earlier, Gables was a great academic school, probably the best in south Florida at the time. It was even reputed to be one of the top 10 public high schools in the country. In general, I took advantage of the STEM offerings and the English department, and avoided the rest when I could. I did manage to avoid taking a foreign language completely, but I have no memory as to why they let me do that.

In junior high, I was a disruptive and disobedient class clown, so I failed the standard math test given at the end of the eighth grade. Consequently, I started Gables in the remedial math course, led by "Ma" Murray, who saved me. She made math interesting and motivated me to apply myself. I liked it! At the end of the first semester, she put me back on the mainstream math program, but a semester behind. She encouraged me to go to summer school to catch up, which I did, at Jackson High School across town. Thanks, Ma Murray!

Gables was among the first to introduce advanced STEM courses, precursors of the advanced placement courses of today, and I took them all. I also loved English, and took a bunch of those, too. I also took typing, but that was because that class was where the girls were. Little did I imagine it would be one of my most used skills, as I spent my life in front of computer keyboards.

In summary, I did well academically in spite of my extreme social activity (see Ching Tang, above) and student government interests. I ran for student council Vice President, was thoroughly trounced, and was put on the student council cabinet as a consolation prize. I was the Assembly Chairman, in charge of the assignment of space in the auditorium, impressive! I was good at vice, and was the Vice President of both the National Honor Society and the Science and Math Honor Society.

Disappointments

The teenage years are full of disappointments for most folks, but two were of particular weight to me.

At the end of each year the high school annual had a section of superlatives which recognized the outstanding, or most popular, seniors. Many of my close friends received one; I didn't. Guess they didn't have one for Most Efficient!

On a more meaningful issue, I missed out on the Navy ROTC full scholarship. Several of us had passed the very competitive test, and the Navy sent a recommendation form on each candidate which could only be completed and signed by the principal, Mr. Rath. He gave great recs to all the others, but refused to complete or sign mine. I know, because the head of student affairs, Mr. Corcoran, filled it out for me and told me he was angry that Rath wouldn't. I must have still been disruptive and disobedient!

I got revenge on Mr. Rath ten years later. He was at our 10-year reunion, and I wanted to introduce my wife, Linda, to him. We went over and he looked somewhat askance at me. I introduced Linda to him and he asked what I was doing. I told him that I had completed my BES in nuclear engineering at Florida, gone to Stanford for an MS in Computer Science, and was a Captain in the USAF based at HQ USAF in the Pentagon. His jaw dropped and he blurted out, "I thought you'd be in jail!" Linda was stunned, but I just smiled! You see, Mr. Rath had, absolutely unintentionally, steered me onto the path that led to Stanford and computer science, an immeasurable boon to my life. Thank you, Mr. Rath.

50 Years of Christmas Letters

My College Social Life

Sigma Nu

My college social life revolved around my college fraternity, Sigma Nu. We were a large fraternity chapter, very large. In fact, we were the largest on campus, and, I think, the largest Sigma Nu chapter in the country. My pledge class in the fall of '57 was almost 100, and there were another hundred actives in the three upper years and grad school. If you have ever seen the movie *Animal House*, the resemblance is uncanny, and our nickname was "Sigma Zoo." As they said back then, we were "high spirited." But we also had a future governor and U.S. senator, Bob Graham, and many other future successful doctors, lawyers, engineers, businessmen, etc. It was a great group of guys, in a great time in history to be in college. I maintain that I learned more useful knowledge in Sigma Nu than I did in my classes. I was the House Manager my second year and Dining Room

Manager my third year, which paid my room and board and taught me a lot about business. I ran for president my fourth year, but was thoroughly beaten by Monty Trainer, who did a fabulous job as Commander, much better than I could have done.

My first year, I lived in the dorms. My second and third years, I lived in the fraternity house, where I had responsibilities. My fourth year, I joined with three other Sigma Nus and we rented a dilapidated two-story house on the other side of Gainesville from the fraternity house. Our bedroom had four mattresses on the floor, and no other furniture. We went to MLK Street, before it was called that, and bought cheap used furniture for the living room and study room. We lived in a very poor neighborhood, but they treated us as pariahs because we brought down the value of the other houses. (The house disappeared long ago, probably condemned.) We still ate most of our meals at the frat house, which is surely why we didn't burn the place down. Today, the four of us have just started doing weekly Zoom meetings with some others from our pledge class, and we remind one another of some of the stupid things we did in that house. We had a ball!

The Four Housemates:

Me, Inky Philips, Allin Crouch, and Frank Willingham

My fifth year, I lived in a rented garage apartment with another Sigma Nu, Jim Benedict, while I finished my last semester. It was very close to the frat house, so the apt. was mostly for sleeping and

153

studying. After graduating in February, I got a 4-month job at the nuclear engineering school, and moved back into the Sigma Nu house for the spring semester. I roomed with one of my fraternity little brothers, Phil Lazzara. Phil studied, and I went to work from 9 to 5 and partied the rest of the day. Phil was a good student, and he went on to become a prominent lawyer in Tampa, no thanks to me!

In summary, the social life was lots of 3.2% beer (everything else was illegal in the county), parties at the frat house on weekends, sports events, road trips to FSU to see the girls there (UF was two-thirds men, I believe), and the normal movies and other stuff. UF and Sigma Nu provided a safe place for us to do stupid things (and we sure did) without too much damage while we grew up to become adults.

Almost Famous in Gainesville

At the beginning of my fifth year at the University of Florida, fall of 1961, I had to have a professional photo made for some reason that I no longer recall. So, I put on my newly acquired sport coat and went to Gainesville's best photographer, who had his storefront studio downtown on one of the main streets of G'ville. He asked me to go sit on the stool in the studio while he finished some activity, so I took my pipe (yep, Mr. Cool smoked a pipe) and sat on the stool to wait. Soon, he appeared and said for me to freeze, he wanted to shoot me as I was.

He took some shots and I left, to return a week later to review the proofs and order perhaps 2 or 3 small pictures for whatever purpose I had. When I returned to see the proofs, I was stunned to see a 4 ft by 3 ft color portrait of myself in the middle of his storefront window, encased in a large, ornate gold-gilded frame. He liked the picture! For several months thereafter, when I walked around downtown Gainesville, I noticed folks staring at me and I could imagine they were thinking, "Where do I know him from?"

When my mother came for my graduation in February of '62, I took her to see the portrait, and it was still there. None of us could afford to buy it, so I have no idea what happened to it. All I have left of this episode is one little, beat-up half-tone copy. Here it is:

Home Life

Where do we live? Every time I went home from UF, I had to call Mom and Pop to find out where to go. After I went off to college, they became house flippers. They would buy a house, fix it up superficially, and sell it. It wasn't much of an issue for me because I went to summer school at UF my second summer, ROTC camp my third summer, and a Procter and Gamble internship in Cincinnati my fourth summer, leaving only my first summer at home. In a way, it was nice to be back in the Gables over that first summer, as I could finally get dates with the cool girls still in high school. When home, I usually worked at The Aluminum Box Shop, a job that Pop got me in high school, and which I continued for five years. There was an inter-fraternity drinking and partying group in Miami called Iron Eagles, and that wiped out some of my evenings. Carousing around with my fellow Ching Tang and Sigma Nu buddies filled the rest of my nights out. I also finally had some girlfriends during my college summers, but that's another story for another time.

50 Years of Christmas Letters

CHRISTMAS 1988

Hello Out There,

Question: "What gives them the courage to keep sending out the Pendray Christmas letter in spite of overwhelming public criticism and loss of friends?" This year's answer: Gin. (Someone told me that gin produces premature memory loss in older folks, but, since I can't remember who told me that, nor remember when, nor remember what evidence was used, I'm not worried about it.) This is the 18th annual infliction of this letter on our friends and no relief is in sight...1988 was a great year around the Pendray homestead, with one notable exception. On New Year's Eve, Jack's dad moved on to the next phase by leaving this world. He had 86 good years but his quality of life was deteriorating rapidly, so it was a very sad blessing for those who loved him. He died as he had lived, quietly and with consideration for those he loved...13 days later, his oldest grandchild, Mike, turned 18 and became an adult, and what a fine person to carry on the family name...Four days later, January 17th, Steve turned 16 and was overwhelmed by the strongest primordial instinct known to teenagers: the urge to DRIVE! He soon got his license, and we didn't see him for a while. Now, 11 months later, we see him a lot. "There is nowhere to go!" The trials of spending teenagerhood in Connecticut...In February, the family went off to observe Jack developing variations to the rump slide form of skiing: face slide, belly slide, etc. It's rather embarrassing, but he's good at signing the MasterCard slips...April saw the installation of air conditioning in the Pendray home, and what timing! The hottest Summer in history followed. The neighbors are now asking Jack for stock market timing advice. Little do they know that it was a gift from Linda's parents and Jack had nothing to do with the decision...Mike's graduation gift was a trip to Niagara Falls in April. We all went to see the frozen falls, and were impressed. Nature outdid herself on this one...In May, Jack & Linda set out for Florida and a cruise to Nassau on one of those LOVE BOATS, and they did...June saw Mike's graduation, with honors mind you, from high school...In July, the whole family went to Florida to participate in Mike's early orientation at UF. Jack kept saying, "This didn't used to be here" as we wandered around. On to Sanibel for a week, and then home to the heat of Connecticut...Andy turned 12 in July and passed his mother in height...August left us thanking Linda's folks for the air conditioning and sending Mike off to the UF...In September, the old folks (can't just say adults anymore), went to Virginia to see Jack's goddaughter, Tori Abbott, get married, and have a reunion with their old dinner group. When we got back, Jack bought a Jeep Cherokee, having finally admitted the need for a 4-wheel in Connecticut. Since he didn't sell any of the other cars, he now has more cars (4) than brains (?) or at-home drivers (3)...November saw Linda dodging jury duty in a murder trial in Bridgeport (a wise thing to do). We spent Thanksgiving in Virginia with Linda's sister. The gang is expected here for Christmas...Steve played varsity soccer this year, and is several inches taller than his dad. He did well on the PSAT tests (selection index of 197, for those who understand) and pulls down A- averages. Between dances, golf, hockey, soccer, etc., he keeps busy...Andy is still our resident computer guru. He started golf this year along with soccer and baseball...Linda still plays in two tennis leagues. She is on the town Library Board, and is in charge of Sunday school at our church...Jack is still plodding (that's one step below jogging), serves on the Vestry at church, and gets an occasional letter addressed "Honorable" since he's an elected official on the Board of Tax Review (little do they know!)...Chelsea (the Labrador dog) is twelve and going strong. Since she's not allowed to bark for food at the table, she has learned to cough at Jack instead. Strange dog! (fits right in)...This year's joke is on Mike. After all the work involved in completing college applications, he followed in his father's footsteps and went to the University of Florida. Since he went on a Merit Scholarship and an Army ROTC scholarship, he's making a profit. It's one of the few cases where a college student gets mail from his folks that says "Dear Son, Send money, Love, Mom & Dad."...May you all have a Merry Christmas and a marvelous new year, and keep a warm place in your heart for the Pendrays in cold Connecticut.

The Pendrays

162

My World War II Memories

Since I was born at the end of 1939, I do not have many memories of WW II, which was when I was in Chattanooga. I do remember we had a victory garden, because it was in the newspaper and I have seen that article. I also remember having recurring nightmares about Nazis. My dad was too young for WW I and too old for WW II, and he also worked for TVA, which was responsible for providing power to Oak Ridge, where they were helping build the atom bomb. Another memory I have is that our neighbor owned the Western Auto store in Chattanooga, so my brother and I got the first metal little red wagon in Chattanooga after the war. I remember that quite well.

50 Years of Christmas Letters

My Dad

Thomas nmn (Tom) Pendray, Jr. was born to Georgiana Winifred Smith (7/9/1872–6/3/1924) and Thomas nmn (Tom) Pendray (4/17/1864–7/24/1935) in Jamestown, ND, on April 20, 1901, and died in Chattanooga, TN, on January 1, 1988, at the age of 86. Dad was a first-generation-born American, his father having immigrated to the U.S. in 1872 as part of the mass exodus from Cornwall, England, after the mines petered out in the 1860s. The Pendrays in Cornwall were miners and farmers, and they were farmers in North Dakota, a difficult life. One day I asked my dad how he ever got to Miami, where he met my mom. He replied, "When I turned 21, I went as far from that damned farm as I could get without a passport." I guess he could have continued to Key West, but thankfully he stopped in Miami. Of his siblings, two of his brothers, Ed and Paul, moved to San Diego, CA, and another, Bill, joined the Army, where he made a career. The pattern of escape from the farm is clear. Only his sister, Frances, stayed in Jamestown, where she taught high school French until retirement. (When Linda and I were unpacking in our first apartment in France, Frances visited us. We fed her canned chili off TV trays, and were impressed that a Pendray could speak that strange, to us, language, French.) Dad, and probably Aunt Frances, graduated from the University of Jamestown (ND), two of the very few of my ancestors with college degrees.

I've often heard that my dad was involved in 1933 when an assassination attempt was made on the President-Elect Franklin Delano Roosevelt in Miami. The shooter missed FDR, but hit the Mayor of Chicago, Anton Cermak. Based on the *New York Daily News* article below, Dad gave blood for Mayor Cermak. There is also a *New York Times* article dated Feb 25 from which I infer that Dad probably gave the second transfusion, as an MD intern at Jackson Memorial Hospital gave him the first. Nice to know the lore is true.

Anton Cermak died on Mar 6, 1933, the date of the *New York Daily News* article which follows. In another reference, it said the transfusion from Dad happened on Thursday, Mar 2nd, which seems more probable.

> *DAILY NEWS*, MONDAY, MARCH 6, 1933 CERMAK GETS TRANSFUSION FOR STRENGTH Miami, March 6 UP). A

new blood transfusion was started for Mayor Cermak at 2:20 P.M. today for Mayor Anton Cermak. Physicians planned to give him a pint of blood. The blood was given by Thomas Pendray Jr., employee of the Florida Power and Light Company of which Joe H. Gill is president. Gill is the husband of one of Giuseppe Zangara's victims. Doctors said the transfusion was "just to give added strength that results when blood transfusions are made." The Mayor was reported "fairly quiet and comfortable." Alderman James Bowler said the chances for his recovery were "not so bright" as previously.

When I was five or six, my family rented a cabin on one of the TVA lakes in Tennessee. My dad took my older brother and me out for a ride in a rowboat. I was fearful that we would not be able to turn the boat around and get back to land, so I asked my dad if he was sure he could turn the boat. He reverse-rowed and did a 360-degree turn on the spot. I was so impressed, and he became my hero that day. He probably never remembered it, but I never forgot it.

I believe it was in driving to Chattanooga from Gainesville with Dad after my college graduation ceremony in February of 1962 that I learned what my native tongue is. During the drive through rural Georgia, we stopped at a gas station for gas and relief. I went inside and started chatting with the attendant while Dad did his turn at the relief aspect of the stop. Dad later joined us inside for a short time, then we hit the road again, gassed and relieved. It soon became apparent to me that Dad was unhappy about something, so I asked him what was wrong. He gently scolded me by saying it was not nice of me to make fun of southern people by mimicking their accent. Confused, I responded that I had done no such thing, but he belabored the subject by saying he could hardly understand the conversation between that attendant and me, our southern drawls were so thick. It was then that I realized that I had responded to a southern redneck in kind, because I are one! Having spent the ages of 2 to 7 in Chattanooga, that is where I learned to talk, and southern drawl is my native tongue. Many years later, this was confirmed by Linda at a cocktail party. She sidled over to me while I was in the middle of a conversation and asked me if I was talking to a southerner. I replied, "No." She then asked if I was talking about my days in Tennessee, to which I also said, "No." "Well then, stop drinking!" she said. It seems that those are the three times that I revert to my native tongue. Guess I better not drink and drive anywhere but

Tennessee, where they wouldn't know the difference.

When I was seven, my parents separated and my mother didn't allow me to see my dad for many years after that, so my memories are from under age 8 and over age 13.

My dad was a smart, kind, gentle, and likable guy who made the mistake of marrying an attractive, intelligent woman who was probably bi-polar, at best. He spent much time trying to shield my brother, Tom, and me from the damage caused by my mother, but lost the struggle and withdrew from the conflict to avoid my mother's putting us in the middle of the conflict as hostages. My mother influenced my opinion of my dad in my early years by attacking him on every occasion, but later in my childhood I understood where the problem really was and appreciated my father's patience and sacrifice to protect us as well as he could. As adults, we spent many good times together, and I developed enormous love and respect for my dad.

I was privileged to attend his retirement ceremony from TVA. I was stationed in the Pentagon and flew down to Chattanooga in my blue USAF Class A uniform with my silver lieutenant's bars and walked into his ceremony as a surprise guest. He got tears in his eyes. Naturally, I got to Chattanooga early so that I had time to get a lunch of Krystal burgers, a great memory of my early childhood when Dad took me there for 10-cent Krystal burgers and Double Cola. Krystal was founded in Chattanooga in 1932, and filed for bankruptcy in January of this year, 2020. Damn! Double Cola was founded as The Good Grape Company in Chattanooga in 1922, and is still headquartered there.

Dad and His Family in Early Good Times

Hello Out There:

Ole!...(That's what you say when drinking your second batch of frozen margaritas. Ole!)...Welcome to the nineteenth episode of the Pendray Pageant brought to you by tequila, triple sec, lime juice, and the modern marvels of personal computers, copiers, and a feat of the flying feet fleet (if one dares describes our postal service thusly)...Last Christmas saw us off on our annual trek into New York to see a play, "Into the Woods," with all of Linda's family (eleven in all). Same thing again this year to see "Phantom of the Opera" on Dec. 27th...Jack's cousin, Jay, and his wife, Anne, were considerate enough to buy and refurbish a large inn in Vermont so the Pendrays could have a great place to stay for skiing in February...Stephen was considering Boston University for college, so we took a weekend in Boston in March. He's since changed his mind, but we had a good time visiting old friends, BU, and the other sights of Boston...Jack and Linda did their biannual Virgin Islands sailing, drinking, relaxing, drinking, listening to Jimmy Buffet music, drinking, etc., thing in April. After Jack's visit, the natives were prepared for Hugo...Jack got down to Miami for his mother's birthday in May, always a good excuse for more drinking and eating...Jack surprised Linda with a red Honda Prelude this Spring. She looks pretty spiffy whipping around town in it (as do Mike and Steve, whenever they get a chance). Since Steve went away to prep school this year, this left Jack with 5 cars for 2 drivers (the sum of which approximates his IQ). He finally did sell two, including his precious 1979 Cadillac Seville (which was financing the dealer's service department). Now he drives the Jeep Cherokee (can a pickup truck with gun racks be far off?)...Jack's cousin, Jay, (remember?, the guy with the Vermont Inn that looks like Bob Newhart's, but has guests) had a family reunion in June. It was a gas! One of Jack's uncles would tell a family story, then the other uncle would say, "Do you want to hear the true story now?" Lots of stories in that family, whichever you believe...Linda's parents celebrated their 50th anniversary in July, so we all went out to Green Valley (that's south of Tucson) to help them. While we were there, it broke the records for the hottest day recorded, the most record-breaking days in a row, and the hottest week. Talk about your hot party, those Lawrences really put on a show! They rented a huge van, and we all went to the Grand Canyon where it was only 105. We spent three days there and saw the hole thing (punny, huh?)...Not having been to Paris in over 5 years, Jack wasn't sure if his French still worked when he went over in July. It did, because he was arguing with the taxi driver within 15 minutes of landing...The old half-century mark was passed by Jack in November, and he really took off! He went to Gainesville to celebrate with Mike, Miami to celebrate with Mom and Pop, back to Connecticut to celebrate with Linda, Steve, Andy, and the neighbors, and then he and Linda went to Virginia to celebrate with their gang down there. He's now 51, since he aged a year doing all that celebrating...We went back to Virginia to Linda's sister's for Thanksgiving...December 1st, Linda and Jack went to Gainesville to see Florida <u>almost</u> beat FSU in football. Jack's nephew, Sean, came over for the game, so it was a real Pendray affair. Sean is carrying on the tradition of his father at FSU, and Mike is doing the same at UF. Damn proud of them both...Linda is still doing the same things as last year, Trumbull Library Board, vice president of the town PTA, two tennis leagues, chairperson of the Sunday school; except now she gets back and forth in that red Honda...Mike is doing great at UF. Carrying a B+ average in engineering and he was just initiated into Sigma Nu Fraternity (yup, that's the same one Jack was in way back then)...Steve decided to get serious his senior year and went away to prep school. He chose Loomis Chaffee in Hartford (where many of the Rockefellers went). He is working very hard and got a B+ average his first term, a rare thing according to the school. He's already been accepted to Georgia Tech, but is far from a decision where he will go. His SATs were great at 1430, and his 750 in math even beat Mike!...Andy not only passed his mother in height this year, he passed his dad by three inches. At 13, he's 5' 10" and still growing. He's still our in-house computer wizard, but also plays soccer, basketball, and the trumpet...This year's joke is on Jack...Afraid that he would miss an important call (which he seldom gets), Jack, the electronic junky, had a phone installed in his Jeep. It's several months now, and he is still waiting. You now have your choice of not calling Jack at the office or not calling Jack in his car...May this Christmas bring you and your loved ones together, and may 1990 be a prosperous and happy new year.

The Pendrays

The 1980s

At Jay and Anne Degen's Village Country Inn, Manchester, VT

50 Years of Christmas Letters

The 1990s

50 Years of Christmas Letters

CHRISTMAS 1990

Hello Out There...

Twenty years of Christmas letters, a number larger than our remaining friends who read it... Once again I take computer and gin in hand: sip, hunt, peck, peck, sip, sip, peck, sip, sip, sip, sing, peck, dance, etc.; which all takes an ungodly amount of time, what with all the sipping, singing, and dancing...We have developed a concept of money around here called DM, which means Dad's Money, aka stupid investments. The boys spend DM fast, but are real tightwads with their own money, i.e., they get their brains from Linda and their avarice from Jack...This was a wonderful year around the Pendray household with exhilarating highs and soul-numbing lows - life at its utmost...An old friend of Jack's from Turkey visited with his daughter who was looking at MBA graduate schools - what a great thing to see dear old friends who have been separated by time and geography - she chose the University of Virginia, an excellent choice...In March, the first annual St. Patrick's drink-and-raise-hell party at the Pendrays'. The

179

dinner group from our days in Va. came up for St. Paddy's weekend, 12 houseguests for 3 days, good thing we all like each other. A blast was had by all, and a new tradition is created! The group dropped in on the next door neighbors, who promptly moved to Maryland. No cause-effect relationship, they say, but we miss them...April was a busy month for Steve and Jack as they visited Tulane, in New Orleans, Vanderbilt, in Nashville, and Virginia Tech, in Blacksburg (where the hell is Blacksburg?). During the same month, Jack slipped down to Gainesville to see Mike (where the hell is Gainesville?)...In June, one of the daughters of the Va. dinner group got married in Long Island, so we went over and did some carousing. Any excuse to party will do for this group, but this was a legitimate one and a real bash...In July we, less Mike, spent a week at Virginia Beach with the Va. dinner group and the rest of the old neighborhood from Va. Hell, we spent more time this year with our Va. dinner group than we did when we lived there! No better way to spend time!...This was the Summer From Hell for us in many ways. Steve had an eye "accident" (an euphemism for a fist fight), which resulted in four hours of (successful) eye surgery at Yale...Andy caught pneumonia (cured)...Mike had two bouts of surgery (both successful), one for a deviated septum and one for his broken hand caused by striking Andy on the hip in anger (Andy was not hurt, must be some justice there somewhere)...In August, we had Chelsea, our dog, put down, after almost 14 years of reciprocal love. Jack cried for three days, and we all still expect her to appear in the same old places. We even have to pick up dropped food off the floor nowadays. She raised three boys and did a great job!...One of the nice things about living in the Northeast is being invited to the Bar Mitzvahs of our Jewish friends' sons. We did two this year and enjoyed them enormously. The warmth and family tradition of the Jewish Temple are to be envied by us Christians...Jack is back on the European circuit. His company is starting up a European venture, so he spends 30% of his time there. He was fortunate enough to celebrate the monetary reunion of Germany with some dear German friends who had some East German guests...Jack also got a piece of The Wall for the mantle...As a reward for flying so much, the airlines give him frequent flyer points so he can fly some more for free. A game for masochists if there ever was one...Linda needed a few things to do on top of her two tennis leagues, library board, Sunday school leadership, and child rearing; so she started teaching four hours a week and became president of the town PTA. The rewards were quick, however, as she got to go to Indianapolis for the national PTA convention. Those PTA party animals, they sure know how to pick a resort convention site!..She also managed to slip off to spend a week with Jack in Europe in Oct. for their 24th anniversary. Jack worked all day, and she made evening plans all day for Jack. He damn near died, but the wine and old friends pulled him through. What a guy!...Mike changed majors at the University of Florida, from aeronautical eng to materials eng. With a grade point average of 3.3, he can do whatever he wants...Steve graduated from Loomis Chaffee prep school in Hartford in June, and his cousin Sean, from Miami, surprised him by appearing at his graduation. Steve picked Virginia Tech for college and has started in mechanical eng. He had a summer job with the Trumbull highway dept., leaning on a shovel and waving flags at motorists. Jack bought him a computer which never worked quite right, so Steve became a hacker out of necessity trying to get the thing to work...Andy went to soccer camp after the pneumonia was cured and then played on the Trumbull High 9th grade team. He broke six feet and 170 lbs at the tender age of 14, and won the nickname of "horse" on the soccer team. Good thing he looks a lot like Jack, or there would be a lot of explaining to do...Jack is now the smallest male family member and just calls his sons by the affectionate name of "Sir!"... Mike played the joke on his parents this year: he spent the summer jumping out of airplanes. The Army gave him some little parachute wings for his efforts. His folks were comfortable in the knowledge that the Army is very scrupulous about parachutes, until Mike told them that he had been skydiving the year before at the University of Florida to get used to the idea! Guess this goes in the category of "what you don't know can't bother you." From our home to yours, a wish that the recession may be mild, the war avoided, and the holidays joyful...

Merry Christmas and Happy New Year!

The Pendrays

The 1990s

50 Years of Christmas Letters

Family Vacations

As I recall, my family didn't take vacations when I was a child. In the summers, I remember that my older brother, Tommy, and I went by train to spend a month or so with our dad in Chattanooga. Those were good times, as we returned to the place where we had lived for several years and found some of our old friends to play with. Dad went to work every day, so we had unusual freedom. Dad taught us how to play tennis on the court at Riverside Park, a block from where he lived. The park and court are still there, not far from Normal Park School where I went to 1st and 2nd grade.

Another summer vacation memory is going to Camp Sawyer Boy Scout camp on West Summerland Key in the Florida Keys. The camp is still there almost 70 years later.

The road north from West Summerland Key went over the Bahia Honda Bridge, the tallest bridge in the Keys, now out of use but still there. Originally, the train went through the bridge structure, but the highway was built over the top of the old structure, leaving the tracks inside. I remember that a bunch of us walked the mile from the camp to the bridge and went up on the road, where we found a ladder over the side down to the tracks. Naturally, we climbed down and walked the tracks, watching the water rush under us. Scary, but thrilling, and stupid! But not as scary to me as the ghost stories the counselors told at night around the smoky (for mosquitoes) campfire.

The 1990s

Bahia Honda Bridge

50 Years of Christmas Letters

CHRISTMAS 1991

Hello Out There:

This year's blarney blurb is inspired by Powers Irish Whiskey, which brings out the Irish in me. The consequence of this is, since the Irish become rather long-winded when under the influence of booze, this Christmas letter will be approximately 37 pages long and require registration with the Food and Drug Administration as a potent sleeping drug. Since such registration takes a decade, this letter should arrive in time for the turn-of-the-century Christmas, when our President, William Kennedy Smith, will be locked in a struggle with the Chief Justice of the Supreme Court, Clarence Thomas, over whether all sexual acts will be performed in the presence of two or three witnesses. Only in America...Another ordinary year in the Pendray household, except that the "parental units" or simply "rents" (as they are affectionately

189

referred to by their "children units" or simply "ingrates") celebrated 25 years of marital (or is that spelled martial?) bliss. This event required much celebration and trumpeting, since no human knowing Jack would possibly believe that someone could tolerate him FOR 25 YEARS. To draw the world's attention to this magnificent achievement on the part of Linda, she arranged for several small, but expensive, activities. Included among these were a trip to Virginia to, jointly, celebrate the 25th of friends from our Virginia gang, a "love boat" cruise to celebrate, jointly, with friends from our Virginia gang (I'll return to this), a dinner in DC to celebrate, jointly a 25th, with Jack's old roommate from the Air Force, and a trip to San Francisco to visit friends and relatives. Jack has decided that if the 50th will be celebrated twice as much as the 25th was, he'll invite everyone for a quiet party to honor his 49th anniversary and his leaving the country...Did you ever take one of those real love boat cruises? We did. Went with three other couples from our Virginia gang, one of whom was doing the 25th anniversary bit too. It was drink, eat, drink, eat, sing, drink, eat, sing, dance, drink, sing, dance, drink, drink, gain weight, eat, etc. I'm not sure where we went, but we had a hell of a good time...More on the 25th anniversary. We discovered that three couples in our church had anniversaries on Oct. 15th, so we went out together to celebrate. Since then, we have discovered a fourth couple in our church with the same anniversary date. The interesting thing is that all the guys are named Jack. Out of 50 active families in our church, all of them in which the husband is named Jack were married on Oct. 15. Go figure...In March, we discovered that our two college-aged sons were experiencing Spring break at the same time, so we canceled our usual ski trip and rented a sail boat in the Virgin Islands. Jack wasn't sure of his new crew, but he went anyway. The first day, it blew 10 mph from the south, and everyone, but Jack, liked that. The next day, it was blowing 20 mph from the west, and everyone liked that. The third day, it was blowing 45 mph from the north, and only Jack liked that. In fact, several members of the crew practiced feeding the fish through direct overboard dissemination of previously ingested food articles. The next day, in a quiet harbor, Jack managed to run the boat into another. No damage, if you don't count the loss of Jack's ego and the crew's confidence. On the fourth day, Jack gave the helm to Mike while he went below to share some used beer with the fish. While he was below, the wind shifted 90 degrees, blew up to 40 mph, and took the boat off for a wild ride. From then on, Jack was not allowed to go below, so the beer supply lasted a lot longer. The rest of the trip was relatively uneventful, except that Mike's luggage disappeared, forever, on his trip home...Jack is now spending 50% of his time in Europe. 15 trips across the Atlantic to Paris this year, with 9 stops in Germany, 12 in Spain, and 1 in both England and Switzerland, ensures that he never knows where he is or what time it is. Finally, he has a reason...In July, the "parental units" went to upstate New York to join the Lawrence reunion of Linda's family. Linda's ability to drink and party is obviously an inherited trait...August saw the whole family at Beach Week in Virginia. This is now an annual tradition in which about 15 families from our old neighborhood go to Sandbridge, Virginia, for a week and try to drink all the beer in the Western Hemisphere. This year, we came close; next year is a sure thing...Thanksgiving was spent at Linda's sister's in Virginia. Her parents came from Arizona, and all the boys came from wherever they were. It was a real family gathering...Linda is still doing all those things like PTA President for the town, Sunday school chairman, tennis bum, teacher for GED students, wife, and mother. Other than that, she does nothing...Jack is still employed, which, considering his innate abilities and the state of the economy, is a miracle...Mike is now a legal drinker (with the emphasis on legal). He did ROTC Summer camp in Washington State before coming to the beach in Virginia. He is being initiated into the Tau Beta Pi engineering honorary at the U of Florida, and is pledge master for his fraternity next year...Steve is in his second year at Virginia Tech, and likes Mechanical Eng. He spent the summer leaning on a shovel for the town of Trumbull and has decided that that is not a career aspiration for him...Andy is a sophomore at Trumbull High. He played JV soccer and has five honors courses. He started guitar this year, so the "parental units" are hopeful that he will become a rich and famous rock star and shower them with much-deserved money and privilege...The joke this year was, as usual, on the "rents." After getting over the shock of Michael's jumping out of planes last year, Stephen calmly informed us that he had done it also. He's in the sky diving club at Virginia Tech! Oh well...

Wishing you and yours a very Merry Christmas and a prosperous New Year.

The Pendrays

CHRISTMAS 1992

Hello Out There:

Extending my life! That's what I've been doing all these years: extending my life. The latest scientific studies show that drinking wine is good for your health. I saw some of the results, but can't remember what the prescribed dosage was; it was either two glasses or two bottles a day. In order to be sure, I've chosen the higher dose, which leads to an extended life of which you don't remember much of (grammar conundrum of the year: is a prepositional phase that begins and ends in a preposition a dangling preposition?). This year's life extender is a fine Côtes du Rhône which was brought by a dinner guest as a gift, but I served a cheaper wine that night and sequestered this until I could drink all of it alone.

We're all fine and had a boring year and that's the end of this Christmas letter.

Have a good one.

The 1990s

Hah! You should be so lucky. This is edition number 22 and there will be no mercy!...Last year ended with a revisit to see the Phantom of the Opera with eleven family members. The reason we did a revisit is that two years ago we had a flat tire on our way and only saw half of it (the tire really wasn't flat, but Jack had messed up the valve and all the air escaped and so he changed a tire which really wasn't bad in the first place and that all took a lot of time). The show is much better when you see it from the beginning...Jack only went to Europe 13 times this year since he didn't go at all in Oct., Nov., and Dec. He also went to Miami 7 times to help his folks resettle into a retirement community. Other than his 7 trips to Virginia and some other trips, he was home a lot. He's turned into a football fan, which is a euphemism for couch potato*e* (I'm a Quayle Republican)...We're still active in our little church (a picture of which you will find on our Christmas card this year). Jack is on the Vestry, Linda runs the Sunday school, and Andy is an altar boy (please pray for this church!)...In between his travels, Jack organized a reunion for his Sigma Nu fraternity chapter at the University of Florida in April. Thirty-five geezers showed up and told Jack's oldest, Michael, who is also a Sigma Nu at Florida, some of their exploits in college. Fortunately, Jack never participated in any of these exploits and was held blameless by his contemporaries (if you believe that, I have some ocean-front property in Arizona for sale)....May saw Jack and Linda off to Linda's birthplace, New Orleans, for a convention. Good music, good food, good God what else is there?...May also took them to Charlottesville, Virginia, for the MBA graduation of their Turkish friends' daughter, Asli Keskinel. Sorry to see her go, as that means we will see less of her and her parents...May was also the month in which our ex-baby-sitter from France came to visit us (busy month, wasn't it?). Maryse brought along her husband, Dominique, but left her kids at home with our dear friends, her parents. Their visit was too short. (In its wisdom, the U. S. Customs searched and detained this dangerous schoolteacher mother of three for three hours. Welcome to America!)...In August, we did the usual Beach Week at Virginia's Sandbridge with our old(er) friends from Northern Virginia. (The older we get, the younger we act, so the way we're going, we'll soon be drinking our beer out of baby bottles.) Linda and Jack had to leave early to attend Jack's nephew's graduation at Florida State University. Well done, Sean!...Steve and Andy drove the family vehicle home from Sandbridge, and lost the top to the cartop carrier in the process. (How loud do you figure the music was in the car to not hear the top blow off?!)...In August, Linda joined Jack on one of his trips to Europe. We visited some old friends, drank wine on the Rhine and on the Seine, and relived some old times...September produced Linda's birthday. (I can't say which one is was, but it was a combination of the numerals zero and five.) Linda's sister, Susan, arranged a surprise party for Linda's sixty closest friends in Susan's horse barn in Virginia. Talk about a stomp'n party! Linda's folks came in from Arizona, and all her sons and nieces were there too. Jack arranged for some hands' free drink holders which said "Linda's Fabulous Fifties," which you'll see in the photo...In October, Jack had a business trip to Arizona, so Linda went along for dinner with her folks (frequent flyer awards inspire some strange doings)...Jack's Aunt Frances (his father's sister) also visited from North Dakota in October. It was her 82nd birthday, so we celebrated by driving to Anne and Jay (Jack's cousin from the other side of his family) Degen's wonderful inn in Manchester Village, Vermont, for the end of the foliage season and a marvelous birthday party...Thanksgiving saw the whole lot in Virginia. Linda's folks, as well as her two aunts, joined the rest of us. We all went to Gettysburg the day after to visit the most important battlefield of what one of Jack's uncles calls "The War of Northern Aggression."...Mike is in his fifth (and last!) year at Florida, headed for a degree in materials engineering with a minor in business. He hopes to drive a tank for the Army (five years of college for that?)...Stephen is a junior at Virginia Tech (would you believe "The Home of the Fighting Gobblers"? Yup, turkeys.), and is doing well in mechanical engineering...Andy is a junior at Trumbull High, doing well, playing soccer, and looking like he may be able to support his parents' retirement on his guitar playing ability. In August, the roads of Connecticut became unsafe. Andy completed one of the most important rights of passage of teenagehood: the passage to driverhood (and his parents' auto insurance passed to astronomicalhood)...The joke this year is, as usual, on Jack. Having made a tax-advantaged investment in a ski condo in West Virginia in the late seventies, Congress destroyed the value of his investment with the tax act of 1986. Since he can't deduct it and can't sell it, he now drives twelve hours to ski, rather than the three hours that would take him to the much better slopes of Vermont!

Wishing you and yours a very Merry Christmas and a prosperous New Year.

The Pendrays

CHRISTMAS 1993

*** Notice ***

The information contained herein has been determined to be of no material value to any living being and absolutely inconsequential to the functioning of the US Government; therefore, it would normally be classified Top Secret. However, since no politician has discovered any reason to conceal this information from the public, it will not be. Consequently, the classification of this document is:

*** Bottom Secret ***

For Noses Only

Burn Before Reading

CHRISTMAS 1993

Hello Out There...from in here,

Here being the inside of a 747 somewhere over The Pond. Having spent about 180 days on the road this year, that seems appropriate. This year's liquid inspiration is club soda (yup, as in water with bubbles!). Surrounded by folks drinking free booze and wine, I'm on club soda. No it's not my heart, it's my head. I'm on my punishment diet. I can eat whatever I want, but I can't drink any booze until I lose 10 pounds. That eliminates some calories, and provides one hell of a motivation!...The year started out, actually it was the rump of last year, with a wiggle. On Dec. 30, the whole gang went into New York and saw Miss Saigon. Jack had written for tickets a year in advance and got 11 front-row center seats. Well, this play starts out with about 30 beautiful, almost naked women rushing on stage, backing up to the lip of the stage, and shaking their spectacular fannies in the faces of the people in front-row center seats. Needless to say, we were all impressed and the boys all fell in love with people whose faces they were yet to see. Anyway, that's why I say the rump of last year started with a wiggle...Jack cashed out his partnership of eight years at Vanguard Atlantic in January and he moved his office into the basement and became a consultant (the euphemism for unemployed executive). In fact, he was having a ball, doing quite a bit of consulting, getting in shape, preparing to take a year off to write a book, fixing up the house, etc. He made the mistake of telling a headhunter (executive search person) that he was out of Vanguard, and had an interview the next week. The job involved international, software, and telecommunications, just the three things that Jack has spent his entire life screwing up. So anyway, he took the job as president of the European units of Cincinnati Bell Information Systems (CBIS). Once they found out that he was dumb enough to travel to all those places frequently, and they also developed an appreciation of his management skills, they added Mexico, Australia, and Japan to his duties in November. The idea is clearly that he will now spend so much time traveling that he will not be able to interfere with the good work that is being done by others. It's working; Jack is never anywhere! He has offices in his home, in Cincinnati, and in Brussels, all empty. He has quit tennis, quit the church vestry, quit his German class, quit taking care of the house, quit watching football, quit life...In Feb. we took the annual ski trip to embarrass Jack and justify, in our minds, the investment we made so many years ago in a ski condo in West Virginia. We accomplished the former easily, but not the latter. After the 1986 real-estate-investor-retroscrew tax act, there's no way to ever justify that investment. (And people wonder why we had the S&L problem after 1986! At a cost of only $300 billion to bail out the S&L's, Congress raised several tens of billions in taxes from real estate investors. "I'm from the government, and I'm here to help!") Steve did come over from Virginia Tech and join us, but Mike couldn't make it...March saw Jack's last meetings as the Chairman of the Trumbull Board of Tax Review, a political, elected job of six years. Between this experience and Bush's fine job as President and campaigner, Jack quit the Republican party and joined Perot's United We Stand. After Perot's performance on NAFTA, he quit that, too...In May, we had a wonderful event: one of the kids finally finished college! Mike graduated from the Univ. of Fla. in engineering with a minor in business, got commissioned as a 2nd Lieutenant in the Army, and reported for duty the next day at the UF ROTC unit, where he spent the summer doing Army things like stuffing letters in envelopes. At least he's getting paid and has a job, not true for all graduates. In Sept. he reported to Ft. Leonard Wood (affectionately called "Fort Lost in the Woods") in some unexplored and uninhabited part of Missouri. There, he went to basic engineering officer's school where they taught him four weeks' worth of material in only four months. (The Army is not like it was in the good old days. Mike had a private room with color TV, VCR, etc. When Linda sent him a package UPS, it appeared in his room. She asked Mike how that happened since he was in the field, and he replied that the maid must have let UPS in. THE MAID?!?! What ever happened to mud and pup tents?) He had Linda's Honda Prelude on loan, and spent every weekend discovering different parts of America. Now, he's on his way to Korea and will miss Christmas at home for the first time in his life, another page is turned in the book of life. Notice that he is going to the last hot spot left, Korea, at his own request. Pendrays ain't too bright, a family tradition...In June, the three boys all flew (those frequent flyer miles are good for something: send the kids away!) out to their grandparents' in Arizona. They picked up their deluxe van and headed out for parts unknown. From the Grand Canyon to Los Angeles, the van full of young

Pendrays rolled. Apparently they had a good time and collected no police reports (that we know of)...Aug. took us to Virginia Beach for the annual Beach Week. Mike and Steve couldn't make it, and Jack spent most of the time on the phone trying to lose a $50 million Dutch job for his new company. (Thanks to his having a good sales team there, they won the job anyway.) It was great spending the week with our dear friends from Virginia, in spite of miserable Jack and missing Mike and Steve...In Oct., Linda and Jack sneaked away for a long sailing weekend with their usual sailing partners, the Guidos. Jack left his computer at home and didn't check his messages, so he was able to enjoy the friendship, relaxation, and good times and didn't even ruin it for anyone else, either. We went to Oriental NC, where the sailing is great, and everything else is perfect, if you like boredom. At least we found one place where we know we don't want to retire, but it was a great way to get a week's vacation in four days...Nov. ended with the Thanksgiving family gathering at Linda's sister's horse farm in Virginia. Watching those folks work that farm made Jack realize that he has a lot of spare time! This time we got most everyone there, all the boys, Linda's parents, and all of Susie's family save Kelly. Too much to eat and too much football, but, then, that's Thanksgiving...Linda's pace is still crazy. In fact, she's so busy she doesn't even know that Jack is gone a lot. Got a second part-time teaching job this year and starting to add to the income tax problem with all this working for money. Still does two tennis groups, runs the church Sunday school, etc. She also applied to seven colleges this year. If those colleges only knew who was really doing the work, Andy wouldn't get accepted anywhere; however, due to her efforts, he's already been accepted at Georgia Tech and Univ. of Fla. (took each school two weeks to send back an acceptance, not bad.)...Andy is having a great senior year at Trumbull High. He worked hard last year and it paid off. He won the outstanding Junior English award, is a National Merit semi-finalist, ran on the cross-country team (he walks faster than Jack jogs), is humor editor of the newspaper, plays guitar in a band, and on and on...Steve is in his fourth year of (he hopes) a five-year mechanical engineering program. He's pulling down good grades now (which he needs to pull up that average after his Freshman Frolics) and may even have a chance to find a job in his chosen field next year (not an easy thing to do nowadays). He bought another car (that makes two, since he kept his other one too). Maybe you don't know about his first car, a Blazer. It didn't have a big enough engine for Steve so he paid a Blacksburg mechanic to put in a bigger one. The bigger engine never arrived, the mechanic couldn't get the old engine back in (swore it didn't fit!), and finally skipped town. Luckily for Steve, he went there the day after the mechanic skipped, gathered up his car, engine, and assorted piece-parts, and, somewhat embarrassed, took them to the local GM dealer for reassembly. Now, one year and several thousand dollars later, the car runs as good as when he first bought it. Wonder what plans he has for this second car he just bought, or if it's too late for him to switch majors to business...The joke this year is, as usual, on Jack. After eight years of making lots of money without working too hard, he is now doing the opposite. However, since Bill Clinton has convinced us all that anyone making enough money to send kids to college without getting in debt to the government is evil and should have their wealth confiscated through higher taxes, Jack is, much to his displeasure and for the first time in his life, PC (politically correct).

From our house to yours with love, Merry Christmas and Happy 1994!

The Pendrays

The 1990s

50 Years of Christmas Letters

My Grandparents

I didn't know my grandparents except for my maternal grandmother.

My dad's parents were in North Dakota and had died long before the time I got to ND after graduation from grad school at Stanford in 1964. I know they had a big farm in Jamestown, ND. My grandfather is reputed to have had the first farm tractor, steam powered, in ND, and he was also a state senator for a while. I know nothing of my paternal grandmother. I do know that farming in ND back then was not for wimps. My dad told me how they would have to go out in the winter looking for cows that had frozen to death. Not for wimps, not for me.

My maternal grandfather died when I was almost four, but I have a vague memory of visiting him in Miami when he was sick. My maternal grandmother, Meme, was always an old lady to me, as we moved back to Miami when I was 7 and she was 59 or 60. She lived alone. I grew up thinking that she was meddlesome and negative, and I attributed much of the Condon family turmoil to her. Much later in life, her sons, my uncles, let me know that she was an angel, but that Daddy Nick, my grandfather, was a real jerk. Guess I didn't really know my maternal grandmother well either.

My College Education

Majoring in Nuclear Engineering at UF

I had known since 8th grade that I wanted to be an engineer. My dad got his degree in chemistry at Jamestown (ND) University, but ended up doing electrical engineering work at Florida Power and Light in Miami, and then at TVA in Chattanooga. After my folks divorced, my mom returned from Chattanooga to Miami, where she dated, and later married, one of my dad's old roommates from their bachelor days in Miami. "Pop" was also doing electrical engineering work at FPL, so I grew up thinking that every home received three magazines a week, *Life*, *Colliers*, and *Electrical World*.

My senior year at Coral Gables High School, I read a book by Albert Einstein in which he explained nuclear physics and relativity on an elementary level. I was enthralled by the subject and decided that I wanted to be a nuclear engineer. When I got

213

to UF, I found out that the school only gave Master's degrees in nuclear engineering, but they were working on a new honors degree that would allow undergraduate engineering students to major in Nuclear Engineering. This degree was to be called a Bachelor in Engineering Sciences and was modeled on the PhD process. You had to apply at the end of the sophomore year of general engineering courses. If accepted, a committee of three faculty members was established to determine your curriculum, which could be whatever they decided. To graduate, you had to produce a thesis of original work and be verbally tested and approved by your committee. In my case, my committee chairman was the chairman of the department of nuclear engineering, and the other two members were the chairman of the physics department and the chairman of materials engineering. The curriculum they developed for me had me wandering all around taking courses. I had two years of chemistry, three years of physics, four years of math, two years of nuclear engineering, two years of electrical engineering, one year of chemical engineering, two years of materials engineering, and all this was on top of the basic liberal arts courses then required of all students at UF. I graduated with 160 semester hours of credits. I also think I was elected president of the engineering honor society because I knew so many of the engineering students, having been in classes with many of them. It certainly wasn't because I had the best grades, as I still continued my geek-who-parties frat life.

My thesis was directed by the materials engineering chairman, Dr. Frederick N. Rhines. (Rhines Hall near the Ben Hill Griffin football stadium is named after him. Also, Ben Hill Griffin III was a fellow Sigma Nu a couple years behind me.) Dr. Rhines wanted to determine if aluminum hardening could be induced by nuclear radiation. If it could, then one could mask sections or patterns with something such as lead, pass the masked metal piece through a radiation field, and end up with a piece of aluminum that was hard in some areas and malleable in others, e.g., malleable fold lines in an otherwise hardened piece of metal.

So, I took pieces of aluminum and stuck them into the UF's nuclear reactor for various amounts of time and then tested them for hardness. There was one inconvenience: the reactor was on one corner of the campus and the hardness testing machine was on the furthest other corner, and I had to get the radioactive metal samples back and forth in order to test the hardness. The metal samples were small, so I put them in a small lead "pig" after irradiation and carried them across campus. My trips looked like this: in front of me walked the department nuclear health physicist carrying a big sign that said, "Caution Radioactive Matter," followed by me carrying my 40-pound pig, with a similar sign on my back. Some students knew me as "the radioactive guy," and my ongoing difficulties in getting dates increased dramatically. Anyway, the project was successful in that it proved that radiation induces precipitation hardening in aluminum, and Dr. Rhines used it to apply for a federal grant to continue the investigation on a serious level. I don't know if he got the grant or not.

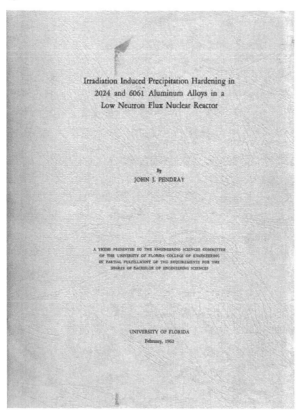

Irradiation Induced Precipitation Hardening in 2024 and 6061 Aluminum Alloys in a Low Neutron Flux Nuclear Reactor

By
JOHN J. PENDRAY

A THESIS PRESENTED TO THE ENGINEERING SCIENCES COMMITTEE OF THE UNIVERSITY OF FLORIDA COLLEGE OF ENGINEERING IN PARTIAL FULFILLMENT OF THE REQUIREMENTS FOR THE DEGREE OF BACHELOR OF ENGINEERING SCIENCES

UNIVERSITY OF FLORIDA
February, 1962

The 1990s

I received my BES in February of 1962. Much to the embarrassment of my committee, I graduated from the honors BES program without honors, probably the only person to ever do that. UF doesn't seem to give a degree in engineering sciences anymore, but they do offer a Bachelor's in nuclear engineering.

Epilogue: I graduated with an Air Force lieutenant's commission from ROTC, scheduled to enter on active duty in June of 1962, so I was offered a four-month job as a research assistant at the nuclear reactor facility. They gave me the job of determining if they could safely increase the power of the reactor from 10 KW to 100 KW. I spent four months taking measurements and making calculations of coolant water flow, radiation shielding, air evacuation, etc., and submitted my conclusion that they could increase the power. I was told that I was correct, and they had done it a month or so ago. You see, a nuclear reactor is one of the most highly instrumented devices on earth, so they had just slowly increased the power and closely watched all the meters for problems. There were none. That is what engineers do...calculations are for the mathematicians and physicists! I think my four months as a practicing nuclear engineer were not in vain however, as they used my study as part of the submission to get approval to operate the reactor at 100 KW.

Winning Respect in ROTC

Other than being a nuclear engineer, I really wanted to be a jet pilot, which is why I was in the four-year Air Force ROTC program, and not the Army program. Back then at UF, all healthy males did two years of mandatory ROTC, and we had no Navy program. Being a large school, the two ROTC programs each had over a thousand student cadets. My senior year, I was one of three Group Commanders in the Air Force ROTC, each Group having over 300 cadets. One weekend a year, we had the military ball, preceded by a formal military formation and march. Each Group Commander brought his (ROTC was all guys back then) date for the ball to the formation and introduced her to his group and she was presented with flowers and a cheer. I managed to persuade the Homecoming Queen, Karen Alfonso, to be my date for the ball, and my cadets were very impressed. Finally, I had won some respect from them!

Washing Out to Get to Stanford

In the summer between my 3rd and 4th years, I went to ROTC summer camp at Eglin AFB near Pensacola for a month. This was a kind of refined boot camp with lots of stress and activity. While there, they gave each of us a physical examination. They determined that I had nystagmus, a form of nervous eyeballs, and washed me out of flight

218

eligibility. I believe that I was just under a lot of stress and nervous. I was later re-tested by Navy ophthalmologists at Jacksonville NAS, who determined that I did not have any more nystagmus than the average person. They reported to the Air Force what the Navy regs said, i.e., my "minor nystagmus is not disqualifying for flight school." It seems that the Air Force regs say that any nystagmus is disqualifying, so I remained washed out. On hearing of this, the head of the AF ROTC at UF, Col. Vernon Smith, asked me to report to his office for a discussion. When he asked me what I was going to do, I said I was considering dropping out of AF ROTC and trying for Navy flight school after graduation. He asked if the Air Force sent me to graduate school, would I stay in the program. I said, "Yes, sir!" He knew that the AF had just increased its Air Force Institute of Technology (AFIT) program and was looking for STEM graduates to send to get Master's degrees, and he thought he could get me into the program. Bear in mind that Col. Smith was no normal person. For example, when Vice President Richard Nixon came to UF and was giving a speech to a packed auditorium, he looked down and saw Col. Smith in the audience. In the middle of the speech, he stopped and called out, "Is that you, Catfish?" Col. Smith responded, "Hi, Dick." Col. Vernon "Catfish" Smith was one of America's greatest athletes. A college hall of fame football player and All-American for Georgia, he was also the captain of the Dawgs' baseball and basketball teams. He was especially known for having scored all 15 points for Georgia in the first game played in Sanford Stadium when the Dawgs beat Yale in 1929 (worth a Google: Vernon Catfish Smith). With his support, I got into the AFIT program, a process which deserves another paragraph or two.

The application for the AFIT program was a normal military form with lots of items with three preferences, which were usually ignored by the military. On this form, they asked for three subjects in which you would like to get a Master's degree, three universities you would like to attend, and three areas of the country in which you would like to go to school. My choices for subjects, in order of preference, were: nuclear engineering, nuclear health physics, and electronic data processing. I knew something about the first two of these, but chose EDP out of desperation for a third choice and because it sounded new and cool (remember, this was 1960). My university choices were the USAF nuclear engineering school at Wright-Patterson AFB, GA Tech (where all southern engineers go after death, if they were good engineers!), and UF. My location choices were California (yeah, baby!), Colorado (learn to ski), and someplace else I forget.

The 1990s

When I got my orders, I was assigned to Stanford to get a Master's with a major in EDP. In disappointment and consternation, I took my orders to my committee chairman, the head of the nuclear engineering department (Google Dr. Robert Eugene Uhrig) and showed them to him. He smiled a bit quizzically (wondering how I got into Stanford, I imagine) and said congratulations. I then asked him if he had ever heard of this Stanford place (as I never had!). Without flinching, he reached over and flipped on the broadcast switch for the department intercom system and announced, "Hey everyone, listen up. The Air Force is sending Jack Pendray to Stanford for a Master's degree, and Jack wants to know if we have ever heard of Stanford." The laughter was heard all over the engineering building.

That's how getting washed out of flight school got me into Stanford, with the help of Catfish Smith and the USAF.

My First Computer Program–1961

Having listed EDP as my third choice on the AFIT application, I thought it would be wise to learn something about it in case that was what the USAF assigned to me. In the fall of 1961, my last semester as a student at UF, I found a graduate course in the Electrical Engineering Dept., EL580 Computer Principles. Having had two years of EE

221

classes, they let me enroll. The professor was Dr. W. Wesley Peterson, who had come from IBM and was an early computer scientist and great teacher. He later won the distinguished Japan Prize in 1999 for his work in computers.

UF had received one of the early IBM computers, an IBM 650, and that was our class machine. It was a revolving-drum-memory, vacuum tube machine that used 12-row/80-column IBM punched cards as its means of input and output. We programmed in Symbolic Optimal Assembly Program (SOAP), which was an assembler. It went like this: you punched your SOAP program into cards using a keypunch machine, the SOAP cards were then input to the 650 via a card reader, the assembler program translated the SOAP instructions into numerical instructions, and then punched out a new deck of cards. The new deck of cards, which we called the binary deck, was then input to the card reader and the loader software loaded the program and began execution. The results of the program were then punched out on cards. You took these output cards to a 407, which printed out the contents of the cards on paper.

My first program in SOAP was very complicated: the program added X to Y to get Z, and then punched out a card that would print out, "The answer is Z." In my test, I used X=2 and Y=3. I went through the process of assembling, punching out, loading, executing, and punching out my answer card. When I put the output card in the printer, it printed a line looking like a comic-book string of cuss words in strange and unusual special characters. Having no idea where to begin to debug my disaster, I sheepishly went to Dr. Peterson with my answer card and printout of coded foul language. He went to the printer and put my answer card in with the <u>correct</u> side up, and out printed, "The Answer is 5." So began my long life of programming screwups!

Stanford–1962-1964

When I got to Stanford in June of 1962, I was nonplussed to discover that I was enrolled in the math department and was working on a Master's in math, with some EDP courses along the way. Well, I was an engineer, not a mathematician, and math was just a tool that we used, not something we actually thought about. Here I was, enrolled in one of the toughest math programs in the world with nothing but geniuses around me. At Stanford, it was said that the chemists only talk to the physicists, the physicists only talk to the mathematicians, and the mathematicians only talk to God. I believed it, because I didn't understand any of the talk coming from my professors and fellow students.

My path to the Master's in math had a series of required math courses and a mandatory qualifying test that had to be passed. I started going to church often, but I still couldn't figure out what the mathematicians were discussing with God.

Fortunately, the math department had plans to spin off Computer Science as a separate department giving a Master's degree, and it was understood that I was there for that, if I could hang on. Long story made short, my transcript from Stanford is replete with D's in math courses and A's and B's in computer courses. I'm convinced the math professors had mercy on me because I was there for the Air Force; thanks, guys. I was still required to take the math qualifier test, but no longer had to pass it for the Master's in Computer Science. I was somewhat miffed about having to spend a half day taking this test when it was no longer a requirement. We all took the test in a monitored lecture hall, and I was one of the first to turn in my paper and leave. Later, I heard that some of the math majors who didn't know me mistook me for one of the Stanford math geniuses who had whizzed through the test. The folks who did know me knew that I didn't understand most of the questions, more or less have a clue on answers, and had left most of my paper blank. What no one knew, was that I didn't feel well because I was hung over from a great party the preceding night. Anyway, it didn't count anymore. Good thing, as I made a score of 1 (one) out of 100 on it! That test is not on the transcript; thanks, Stanford.

The Computer Science Department was created in 1963, I think, under the chairmanship of Dr. George Forsythe. Both Stanford and Wiki say that the CS department was created in 1965, but my degree says M.S., Computer Science, is signed by Forsythe as Chairman, and is dated June 14, 1964. Maybe this explains why, on my transcript, the department is first shown as 45 Mathematics, which is then lined out and replaced by 67 Computer Science. Moreover, in 2016 I received an invitation to the 50th anniversary of Computer Science at Stanford, which puts the foundation in 1966. I replied that they were off by a couple of years, as my degree was given in 1964. They responded that I was correct, the 1966 date is when the CS Dept. was transferred into the school of engineering, and, by the way, I had the 15th CS degree given by Stanford. As it took me two years to get my degree, I'm sure I knew all of the first 14 recipients of the Stanford CS degree. I think that's pretty cool!

The Computer Science Department did require an original thesis or project in order to receive the degree. Having been spun out of the math department and being led by mostly math professors, the department had a heavy emphasis on numerical analysis. I think in recognition of my lack of math skills, they let me team up with Dick Abbott to do a joint thesis. Dick was a mathematician and I was a programmer, so we developed a computer routine to do least-squares curve fitting using orthogonal polynomials, or something like that. Dick did the math and I did most of the programming. The requirement also included a one-on-one private Q&A session with an overseeing professor to verify that you knew what you were doing. My professor was Dr. Gene Golub, a world leading numerical analyst and a really good guy. Gene knew me well and realized that math was not a strong suit of mine, so his expectations were low. In our private session, I did manage to demonstrate that I understood the math underpinning our thesis, to which he blurted out in surprise something like, "I didn't think you'd know that at all." I owe it to Dick Abbott, who had spent hours explaining, teaching, and preparing me for my session with Gene. I no longer have a clue what an orthogonal polynomial is; sorry, Dick.

Learning COBOL–1964

Computers were initially oriented to scientific and mathematical uses, which partially explains Stanford's computer science department's coming from the math department. The most-used higher-level programming languages at Stanford were ALGOrithmic Language (Algol) and FORmula TRANslator (Fortran), both oriented to scientific computing. I wondered about using computers for business data processing, a subject little discussed in the CS department. So, I found a course in the MBA School at Stanford, BUS366 Intro to EDP, and met the professor, Dr. John Lubin, who was visiting at Stanford from Wharton to teach EDP to Stanford MBA students. He let me sign up for the course in my second year. The business school used an IBM 1401 computer and programmed it in Autocoder assembly language. It was a revelation to me. In business processing, one thought of records, files, and data movements, not in terms of formulas and computations. At the end of the course, in which I barely garnered a B, John offered me a 4-unit course of individual research under his tutelage. He knew that the CS department had a new Burroughs B5000 computer which came with a compiler for the COmmon Business-Oriented Language (COBOL) developed and pushed by the Air Force, Navy, DOD,

Burroughs, and many other organizations. He wanted me to learn COBOL and locate and exercise the COBOL compiler on the B5000. He had coordinated this with the CS department, so I had permission to use the B5000 for this purpose. Briefly, COBOL was designed around records, files, and data movement and manipulation. It was also supposed to look like English sentences, so it would be self-documenting if done properly. Naturally, computations were provided for, but it was designed for business use. In 1964, COBOL was beginning to be widely accepted by banks, businesses, and government, but I believe I may have been the first person in the CS department at Stanford to write and run a COBOL program there, and may have even been the first to use COBOL at Stanford. The COBOL compiler on the B5000 was relatively new, and Burroughs sent its compiler project leader to Stanford to talk to John and me about our experience and get feedback from me on bugs. I was somewhat of a heretic in the CS department: running COBOL, talking about records and files, and doing business data processing tests.

By 1970, COBOL was the most-used programming language in the world. Under the impulsion from the government and large businesses, it grew fast! Without John Lubin's support and guidance, I would have received a degree in computer science having scant understanding of business data processing, which is the main use of computers.

The Air Force let me stay at Stanford for eight consecutive quarters—two years—and I wandered over to the EE department for a course in computer hardware design, took a bunch of statistics and operations research courses, and even slipped in a quarter of German (got a C-) to see what a foreign language was like. In 18 years of education, I had never had a course in a foreign language. Talk about a STEM bias! I graduated from Stanford with 83 quarter units. My education was over; it was time to go to work.

50 Years of Christmas Letters

CHRISTMAS 1994

Hello Out There...,

It's time to wrap my arms around a bottle of wine, reach for the trusty computer keyboard, spill the wine into the keyboard, short out the whole darn system, go get another bottle of wine, and start over on the backup computer. This year's loquacious locution lubricant comes from a bottle labeled "Cheap Red Wine." This was a present from one of our friends who knew the true depth of Jack's sophisticated oenological knowledge. Jack even let it "mature" two years! I believe this is one of those "hearty, full bodied wines with a strong presence of the grape." Translation: it's so raw you can't talk for several hours after drinking it... As most of you know, the 1993 - 1994 Winter was the winter from hell! We had two feet of snow on our yard for over three months. Plow, plow, and plow. Since Jack's too cheap to pay for a plowing service, Andy got to spend most of his senior year of high school moving snow around (or so he says). Now that Andy is off at college, Jack finally contracted a plowing service (but don't tell Andy, it's a secret!)...Winter did manage to catch Jack good once. On one of his trips to Australia this year, he returned through D.C. in February. It being summer in Australia, he had all summer clothes. After he landed in D.C. for his connection to Connecticut, the airport closed for three days due to a blizzard. Thank goodness Linda's sister and husband live there. They took in the poor waif and fed and clothed him for three days...In March, some friends invited Linda and Jack to spend a long weekend with them in South Carolina. It was wonderful to have warm friends and a warm climate...In April we made a visit to three colleges so Andy could make his final decision. He had been accepted at many great schools, but narrowed it down to UVA, Duke, and UNC. So, Linda, Jack, and Andy set out to visit them. After three days of exhaustive investigation of the schools, faculty interviews, curricula analyses, etc., Andy announced his decision - UVA. When queried by Jack as to what was the key factor in this scientific analysis that persuaded him, Andy replied, "The girls at UVA are much prettier." Nice to know some basic values never change...June saw Andy's graduation from Trumbull High School, 12th out of 335. Trumbull has been good to us and our kids...After Andy's graduation, we all set out for a vacation in Australia. Mike was in Korea doing Army things in the mud (it turns out that Mike led a platoon that specialized in mine fields, laying mine fields and demining enemy mine fields!), and he took some leave and joined us. We spent 6 days in Sydney, 4 days in Cairns, and 5 days in Melbourne. From the Opera House in Sydney, to snorkeling the Great Barrier Reef off Cairns, to the Melbourne Zoo, it was terrific! The animals down under are very unique. One of Jack's Australian friends made a wonderful comment about the kangaroo: "Kinda makes you wonder who the hell designed that!"... We traveled business class on frequent flyer miles, so Steve had a steak between New Haven and Chicago, another between Chicago and LA, and two more between LA and Sydney - a four-steak flight - way to go, Steve!...In August, we kicked the birds out of the nest; Andy went off to UVA, Stephen returned for his final year at VA Tech, and Mike was in Korea. It took Jack about a half-hour to adjust to the quiet and order, but Linda took a lot longer, maybe a day...Being a National Merit Finalist and all, UVA invited Andy into an honors program called the Echols Scholars. In this program, he has no required courses and doesn't even have to declare a major. After he gets 120 credits, they graduate him with a BA in interdisciplinary studies. Even so, he expects that he will take a major. He's living in a heady atmosphere at UVA; all the Echols Scholars live together, and 6 of his 16 suite-mates were valedictorians...Steve is doing his final year (of five) in mechanical engineering at VA Tech. He is down to only one car and one credit card (with no balance owed!). Now he faces the really tough part of college nowadays, finding a job...Jack is still up in the air most of the time, sometimes in an airplane. Between his 10 trips to Europe, 3 to Australia, and 21 to Ohio (he works for Cincinnati Bell Information Systems), he managed to get to Florida 5 times and Virginia 13 times...After working in the mines (very punny!) a year in Korea, Mike returned to the U.S. in early Dec. He's off to Ft. Knox for the month of January, then on to Ft. Stewart in Savannah, GA. Lord knows what type of assignment he'll pull this time, but I'm sure it won't be boring...Speaking of bored, Linda just sits around the house bored all day waiting for Jack to call from wherever he is (yeah, right!). Other than trying to sell the house in Connecticut (we're trying to get back to Virginia now that the nest is empty), teach GED classes, play tennis, and run the Sunday school, she has nothing to do. Well, she has started to travel a little with Jack (a week with some of our best friends in London in Sept., a week in Virginia at Thanksgiving), but has a difficult time fitting it in to her schedule...The joke's on Jack again this year. In January, Jack's job went from "difficult but rewarding" to just difficult. The company "retired" their president who had hired Jack only seven months previously (could there be a cause-effect relationship here?) and brought in a turnaround specialist (read, bad dude) who came with a sidekick. Having been hired to be part of the solution to the company's problems, Jack was now part of the problem in the eyes of the new guys. Jack went from being empowered, to being guilty. Amazingly, he's still there, so the new guys must not be as bright as they are cracked up to be...

From our house to all of our dear friends that we have been fortunate enough to make over the years...

Merry Christmas and a Prosperous and Happy 1995!

The Pendrays

50 Years of Christmas Letters

Hello Out There...,

25 years of this abuse by mail! Yup, this is the Silver Anniversary of the Pendray Christmas letter. Our mailing list is so old that most of the folks receiving this letter no longer have any idea who we are, but they still write us "To Whom It May Concern" letters requesting us to remove them from the list. NOT ON YOUR LIFE!...Having drunk all the good wine in the cellar in anticipation of selling our house and moving back to Virginia, I'm reduced to jug wine, Almaden Mountain Burgundy in particular. Needless to say, the house didn't sell in the 15 months that we've been trying, so all we got from the process so far is an empty wine cellar. I'm told that jug wine will affect your vision but it hasn't bothered mine at all yet...Last Christmas, we all went to New York

for our annual theater, and drink and eat, and drink and eat, etc., night. Saw "Tommy", which sure was loud. How loud was it? Jack didn't even fall asleep, so that's loud...We spent New Year's Eve in Baltimore with some friends (are they really called Baltimorons?). Our friends are younger than we (yes, "we" is still correct, even if it does sound funny), so it was quite a trip to see us trying to stay alert until midnight...Jack still has the job where he travels. Doesn't do much else, but he sure does travel. 12 trips to Europe, 2 to Australia, 20 to Cincinnati (remember, he works for Cincinnati Bell), 13 to Virginia, 3 to Florida, and various trips to Dallas, Chicago, and some other places he can't remember. Linda says, "Jack is never anywhere." Jack's boss (another new one, third boss in 2 years. Guess they haven't identified the real problem, yet.) says that Jack is never where he should be. Jack never knows where the hell he is, so don't ask him...In Jan. and Feb., Jack spent five weeks in Melbourne, Australia. His mission was to secure the future of his company's operation there. He was so successful that they closed the office there and sent everyone home! Linda joined him for the last three weeks, and we spent three days in New Zealand on the return trip. In New Zealand, Jack decided to try driving on the "wrong" side of the road for the first time, so they went to the metropolis of Tauranga where he rented a car. After two days of fighting the traffic of Tauranga (five cars and several horses), he ventured onto the main road and drove all the way to Rotorua (which he thought was called Roto-Rooter and was a plumber's town) (why would anyone root for a roto anyway?). It was very impressive to see him screaming along the highway at speeds often approaching ten miles an hour, and on the wrong side! Australia and New Zealand are lovely countries, and remind one of the U.S. in the '50s: friendly and free...In April, Jack and Mike went to a fraternity reunion in Gainesville, Florida. Yup, both UF grads (go Gators, kick Nebraska's tail!) (Linda's Dad is a Nebraska alum, so we got a small family problem) and Sigma Nus. While there, they consumed no alcoholic beverages and told no exaggerated stories of their college days. (Yeah, right!)...In May, Steve graduated from Virginia Tech (way to go!), after only five years, and entered the ranks of the unemployed mechanical engineers. Since it's more fun to be unemployed in Colorado than in Connecticut, he went there. Nevertheless, he found a temp job and is now awaiting ski season...In June, Linda joined Jack on one of his European trips. In Paris, they went to a dinner of the founders of the company that Jack worked for 20 years ago. What a blast, and all in French! Jack kept saying things that made everyone laugh, even though he was serious. Guess his French is a little rusty....Linda has traveled about as much as Jack this year. Trips to London (twice), Geneva, Australia, New Zealand, Vermont (twice), New Hampshire, Arizona, Virginia (thrice), and Savannah...Savannah? That's where Mike is, in the Army. Actually, it's Hinesville, Georgia, of which Savannah is a suburb. Mike got his silver bar (1st Lt.) in May, and is in charge of the support platoon, which is the cooks, medics, and other very important folks if you're in the Army and want to eat and have your life saved on the battlefield...We went to Arizona in Oct. for a great time. Linda spent a week, and Jack spent four days. Took two train rides, including the one to the Grand Canyon. Had dinner in Tucson with Jack's commanding officer from the Pentagon in 1968, who remembered Jack as saying, "I'm going to be a roaring success or a roaring failure." At least we got the roar, the rest is still unclear...We're going to see Les Miserables on Dec 29. Jack and Linda have seen it once, but Jack didn't understand it and wants to see it again...Thanksgiving took us all to Virginia again. Four generations gathered, from Linda's parents to her niece's daughter...This year the joke is on both of us. In August, we drove Andy back to the Univ. of Va. for his second year. There was a "Music in the Mountains" weekend in Snowshoe, West Virginia, at the same time, so we went there first. Since it was West Virginia, we all wore our jeans and T-shirts. We sure stood out sitting in the middle of the black-tie crowd during the symphonies and six-course dinners, but that didn't stop us from having a great time and going to all of the events...

As we contemplate the end of another year (and the Mountain Burgundy sets in), we think of all of our blessings, and they all have names. To all of our blessings, far and near, we wish a

Merry Christmas and a Prosperous and Happy 1996!

The Pendrays

50 Years of Christmas Letters

ANNUAL REPORT FOR 1996
ON THE ACTIVITIES OF
THE PENDRAY GROUP

To our Stakeholders (i.e., those losing their shirts in our stock):

This was an exciting year for The Pendray Group (i.e., we scrambled around all year not knowing what we were doing), full of challenges (i.e., really bad problems) and opportunities (i.e., unpleasant events that surprised us completely). We responded by reengineering and restructuring (i.e., we hired some consultants on whom to blame it all), which produced a significant downsizing (i.e., we fired the least competent folks, which immediately precipitated the leaving of all of the most competent folks) and increased productivity (i.e., the remaining staff is working twice as hard to compensate for the 25% downsizing). We will start with an Executive Summary (i.e., for those who don't care enough to read our detailed obfuscations) for those who wish a brief review (i.e., those whose span of attention is under thirty milliseconds).

EXECUTIVE SUMMARY

Jack traveled around the world at 600 miles per hour while Linda stayed home. Then Jack traveled around the world at 600 miles per hour, often with Linda. Then Jack retired and traveled around the U.S. at 60 miles per hour (OK, more like 75) with Linda. Then Jack became a professor in Virginia while Linda stayed at home in Connecticut. In brief, a normal uneventful year.

CHRISTMAS 1996

Hello Out There...,

26 years of this letter and the craziness continues...This year's courage is provided by a 1992 Neethlingshof Pinotage from South Africa (a good friend of Jack's became a wine distributor of great South African wines, which made him a <u>very</u> good friend of Jack's!)....The year started as usual with Jack gone five days a week flying around trying to keep Cincinnati Bell Information Systems' (CBIS) international activities from making meaningful progress. Ten trips to Cincy, six to England, four to Holland and Switzerland, etc., and all in six months before he ran out of gas (not his plane, fortunately, just him. More later.)...On March 8th, Jack's mom quietly passed away after several years of debilitating illness. He was able to be there at the time, say good-bye, and share memories with Pop, his stepfather (92

and going strong), and brother Keith...Soon thereafter, Jack and Linda set out with friends from CT for a two-week sail in the Leeward and Windward islands of the Caribbean. They rented a crewed 50-ft ketch and went from Antigua to the Tobago Cays and back, 350 miles in ten days of sailing ain't bad. (Not being busily in charge telling everyone what to do, Jack actually got seasick twice! Linda (who barfs often on sailboats) felt sooo sorry for him!) It was a great trip with good friends and a good crew...In April, Jack and Linda went to Fla. for the annual Sigma Nu reunion and drinkfest. Mike was recognized as the outstanding young alumnus of Sigma Nu, which made his dad pretty proud. Then on to Miami to see relatives and friends...In June, Linda and Jack went to England to visit old friends from Virginia. Jack had been contacted on the Internet by a Pendray in Derby, England, who hailed from Cornwall, just like Jack's ancestors. He arranged a visit to Cornwall for Jack and Linda where they met other Pendray families. (No!, they weren't all in jails or asylums; in fact, they were warm, wonderful, bright folks.) Before the trip was over, they had traced the family tree to discover that they all had the same great-great-great grandfather. After England, Jack and Linda went to Switzerland to spend several days with old friends from CT who live in England and work for CBIS in Cincy (simple, huh?)....In July, CBIS had a bash in San Francisco, and Jack took Linda along. Love that City!...Also in July, Jack resigned from CBIS and retired on August 1st. He had done all the damage he could and was tired of looking at the world from 30 thousand feet. They gave him a warm send-off and he carries fond memories of his many friends at CBIS...August was spent by Jack catching up for three years of neglecting the house chores, but with a trip to North Carolina's beaches to join those Virginia friends who live in England (tough to follow this crowd around, ain't it?)...Also in August, we returned to our condo in Snowshoe, WV, (a very long-range investment - like never) for the Music in the Mountains. We went with friends from Virginia (who actually live in Virginia!) and wore the right clothes this year (see last year's letter about our blue jeans in the black tie crowd)...September was the month in which we began Jack's "Victory Lap" around the country, which finished 37 days and 10,000 miles later. We jumped in the old van and imposed on friends and family on our way to Baltimore, Fairfax, Charlottesville, Kingsport, Chattanooga, Vicksburg, New Orleans, Houston, Corpus Christi, San Antonio, Green Valley, Phoenix, San Diego, Los Angeles,

Las Vegas, the national parks in Utah and Arizona, and Kansas City. The three boys joined us in San Diego to celebrate Linda's mother's birthday (I won't say which, but it is some combination of zero and eight) along with other family members. Another great city. Also, if you haven't seen the canyon national parks in Utah and Arizona, they are spectacular...In November, Jack received a job offer to join the faculty at George Mason University, in Fairfax, VA., which he accepted. (God save the students!) He is now the most junior member of the faculty; however, he must have the longest title: Executive in Residence and Visiting Professor of Management at the Graduate Business Institute. He has an office big enough for himself and one guest chair, with a window view of a brick wall. He wanted a change, and he sure got it!...November and Thanksgiving took us back to Virginia, where Jack now works while imposing on friends for a room. Mike and Andy joined us at a friends' home (remember those folks from VA who live in VA and went to Music in the Mountains with us? Same folks.) for turkey and football. Too much of both! We also continued our annual tradition of joining Jack's Aunt and Uncle and their family for a Thanksgiving drink. Who would have thought that all these Miami folks would end up in Virginia?...In December, we will return to Blacksburg (which the Va. Tech students affectionately call "Bleaksburg") for Linda's niece's (Megan's) graduation. Then it's home to Connecticut for the holidays, hopefully, for the last time. If we don't sell this house soon, Jack is going to run out of friends in VA (which, knowing Jack, won't take long!)....Linda went from being a frequent homebody, to a frequent traveler, and back to frequent homebody all in one year. She still does tennis and teaches some, but her main job is to sell the damn house... Mike finishes his four-year hitch in the Army in May (he spent November in the Mojave Desert playing a very expensive version of laser-tag) and is preparing applications to various MBA schools for September. 26 years old and still writing essays...Steve moved to Phoenix where he heard there really were jobs for mechanical engineers. Sure enough, he found one at a company called AmSafe. The next time you are on an airplane, turn over the seat belt buckle and it will probably say AmSafe. Steve is in charge of the seatbelt webbing, making him the "Web Master". Sounds cool...Andy worked at the Univ. of Virginia over the summer, helping the business school install new computers and networks. Then he entered the business school in the fall, so he had a head start on their systems. In October, we went to Parents' Weekend to see Andy receive Intermediate Honors for having a 3.5 average his first two years (Way to go, Andy!). While we were there, the business school had a reception for parents and we went, expecting to see Andy suck up to the faculty. What a surprise to us when, instead, the faculty sucked up to Andy, imploring him to help them build a web page on the Internet, or to fix their computer systems, etc. He graciously deigned to see what he could do for these poor beseeching souls!...This year the joke is on Jack (what, again?). Since he gained ten pounds in 37 days, Linda says, "Jack ate his way around the country" on his victory lap. Jack's answer is simple, he re-tired. (Get it? Spare tire? Around his waist? Oh, well!)

Whew, what a year! The best part of it all was the chance to spend time with many of the wonderful friends and relatives that we have around the world. I normally don't name folks in this letter, except for very special occasions; however, I want to thank many of you by name for the friendship, hospitality, and love you extended us this year. I hope I remember everyone, but, at my age, the memory is the second thing to go.

Jack's cousin, Pat Coleman for coming to Jack's Mom's services to represent his family, and to his wife, Dede for having us over. Tom and Ruth Ann Prevost for having us join them on the sailing trip. John and Judy Guido (the Virginia friends in England) for everything! Kim and Stephen (yes, there's another one in the world) Pendray, and all the other Pendrays in England that we met, for making us prouder to be Pendrays. Jan and Betsy Rumberger for the friendship, hospitality, and great South African wine. Nick Torelli (whom Jack finally found after thirty years of looking) and his wonderful wife, Nancy, for welcoming us to South San Francisco. John and Nettie Morse for being our permanent friends in the bay area. Jim and Ellen Mullen for joining us for the Music in the Mountains, inviting us to their Thanksgiving, and putting Jack up as an itinerant professor. John and Cindy de Santis for having us over, joining us in Switzerland, and being there when needed. Ken and Kathy Homa for being a halfway house in Baltimore, and good friends. Gordon and Susan Harvey for being great relatives. Art and Lucy Wittich for forty years of friendship. Inky Philips, Jack's "brother" since the '50s, and his terrific wife, Mary. Penny Pendray and her daughter, Betty, for being terrific step-relatives. Rex and Jackie Alfonso for having us in Houston, and as friends for forty years. Pat and Jan Miller for putting us up in Corpus (hope the wines were good!). Lemoyne and Delores Hall for showing us San Antonio. Bob and Gladys Lawrence for being Linda's wonderful parents, and gracious hosts and traveling companions. Pat and Lynne O'Malley, for picking up thirty years later as though it were yesterday. Jack, Babs, Jim, and Kathy Coleman for being wonderful Miami relatives in Virginia. The friends at CBIS who I hated to leave behind. The Fox Mill Dinner Group, for being the best thing that ever happened in our lives!

We love you all. You make our lives meaningful!

Merry Christmas and a Prosperous and Happy 1997!

The Pendrays

Hotel del Coronado in San Diego, CA

50 Years of Christmas Letters

My Mom

Julia Claire (Judy) Condon Pendray Hoeller (whew!) was born to Margaret Amelia (Meme) Johnson Condon (11/21/1887-6/12/1968) and Nicholas Jay (Daddy Nick) Condon (8/17/1887-10/28/1943) in Pensacola, FL, on May 12, 1913, and died in Miami on March 8, 1996, at the age of 82. She was the middle of five siblings: Margaret Muriel (Sister), Nicholas Meredith (Brother), Mom, John Amick (Jack), and Emily Amelia (Babie). From the locale and the nicknames, one might conclude that this was a very old-south, Irish family, and one would not win an award for figuring that out. As an example, even though my grandmother Meme had a son and a son-in-law who flew fighter planes in WW II, when she referred to "The War," she meant the Civil War, also known as the War of Northern Aggression in the Condon household. "Sherman" was a cussword in that house. One of my Condon ancestors is reputed to have fought on both sides of the Civil War, starting for the North and switching to the South in time for the defeat. Our family is known for its judgment and timing! My generation was, fortunately, the last American generation to be raised in a segregated South, as each of my secondary schools, including the University of Florida, integrated soon after I graduated. I always stood for the playing of *Dixie* in honor of my heritage, but now appreciate that the inhumane components of that heritage outweigh honoring the valor of the combatants. Civilization progresses slowly, in fits and starts, but in the right direction. Mom never progressed to this step.

Anyway, the Condon family moved to Miami in the early 1920s and settled in the new town of Coral Gables. Daddy Nick is reputed to have been one of the bookkeepers of the founder of the Gables, George Merrick, and to have invested his life's savings in the development of the Gables. George Merrick lost all of his fortune in the Florida bust of 1926, and Daddy Nick followed him into that same hole. (I believe I inherited my investment skills from Daddy Nick.) Merrick survived as a fishing guide in the Florida Keys, but the Condons stayed in Miami, living a couple of blocks from the border with Coral Gables. Mom attended Miami High School, but did not graduate. Brother was an early graduate of the fledgling University of Miami, having paid his way through school caddying for golfers at the Biltmore Hotel. In short, my mother was a third-generation old-south Floridian and a first-generation Coral Gabelite, and our Gables roots are deep.

Strangely, I only have two memories of my mother when I was a child, ages 6 and 7: The time she ran screaming into our Chattanooga bedroom in the middle of the night in order to put Tommy and me in the middle of a terrible fight that she had started with my dad, and her driving us back to Miami alone when she left my dad. I'm sure there were happy times, but they must have been blotted out by the scary memories. I have many other memories of her when I was a teenager and beyond, but they follow the same path so I will omit them, save the following example. Sorry for the bummer, but this is what I remember.

It seems that Mom, Dad, and Pop were at a Meter Convention, all being in the electric meter business. (Who knew that there were Meter Conventions? I can only envision members of the electrical engineering meter sub-cult gathering to discuss the creation and nurturing of their beloved meters. Guess you need to have been raised in an *Electrical World* magazine house to appreciate that.) Anyway, Mom somehow managed to get a fistfight started between Dad and Pop. While I can imagine a Meter Convention, I can't picture these two middle-aged, gentle souls, duking it out. Dad must have been the angrier of the two, as he bloodied Pop's nose, which brought an end to the fisticuffs. This would all be hilarious, except for the malevolent manipulator who instigated it, Mom.

Pop, Mom, and Dad at my wedding

Mom could be loving, fun, and personable, but those memories are simply eclipsed by the ones when "evil Mom" was present. No, Mom was not evil; she was mentally unstable and did evil things when off-kilter. Having read the book *Snakes in Suits* about psychopaths in the workplace, I think it is a reasonable hypothesis that Mom was a psychopath. Notice that psychopaths are considered to have a personality disorder, and not a mental illness. One of the dominant characteristics of a psychopath is the lack of remorse, which I observed over and over with Mom. Given her dramatic mood swings, I would also guess that she had some bipolar issues too.

50 Years of Christmas Letters

Hello Out There...

Fighting cholesterol, that's what I'm a doing. Scientific fact: drink red wine, take aspirin for the hangover, win the battle of cholesterol. Hell, I may live forever at this rate...This year's anti-cholesterol medication is from Booze-in-a-Box, Almaden cabernet sauvignon in fact. (Never met a wine I didn't like!) Jack loves the engineering of it. Airtight metallic bag of 5 liters of wine in a box with a spigot. Just open the icebox door and there it sits, with its little spigot all ready to pour. When it's running dry, he rips the bag out of the box and squeezes it dry, usually right in front of dinner guests. Jack is <u>not</u> in the running for sommelier of the year...Well, we bought a townhouse in Reston, VA, and sold the house in CT, in that order. Jack got tired of imposing on friends in VA (and were they ever tired of him!) so he went and bought a townhouse. Fortunately, Linda sold the house in CT within a month, so we didn't have to carry them both for long, thank the Lord. It was hard leaving 13 years of great friends in CT, but great returning to our friends of 20 to 30 years in VA. In March, we moved into the townhouse. It's on a small lake and the back faces west. In fact, Jack had stood in front of it several years ago when we first thought we were relocating to VA and said he wanted that house so he could watch sunsets from the deck. This time, it was for sale and we snapped it up. (Jack says he bought the site, and a townhouse happened to be on it.) We lost 800 square feet in the move, but still have two guest bedrooms and great sunsets. Y'all come see us...Jack spent the spring semester trying to figure out academia, while Linda spent it trying to get all our stuff into 800 fewer square feet. Neither succeeded...After school was out (with an empty nest, we thought we were finally finished with being bound by school schedules. Ha!), we jumped into the minivan for another little drive. First stop was Jack's 40th high school reunion in Coral Gables, FL, where Jack and all his friends pretended they were still 17 for several days. We also went out with Jack's stepfather who turned 93 this year. On the way back to VA, we stopped in Kansas City (a small detour according to Jack's map reading) for Linda's niece's (Megan) wedding. All the boys joined us for the event, which was held *al fresco* (no, everyone wore clothes, it means, "in the open air") at the groom's parents' house. A beautiful event and a great party...While in KC, we visited with some old friends from our previous life in VA, Don and Merrie Wehe. They live on a lake and have a pontoon party boat like ours, but with a real gas engine. (In Reston, only electric motors are allowed, so Jack bought the biggest one he could find and has the fastest pontoon boat on the lake. He can go 7 miles an hour and almost make a wake!) Anyway, Don is an experienced sailor and seaman, almost as good as Jack (can you see it coming?), and they motored out into the middle of the lake where the propeller promptly fell off the motor. If it hadn't been for some beer-guzzling teenagers passing by with a motor <u>with</u> <u>a</u> <u>propeller attached</u>, we might still be out there. It was a good time and great to see them again, even if we had to paddle...In KC we stayed with Pat and Lynne O'Malley, the same folks we imposed on last summer during Jack's retirement victory lap, but this time we brought our three boys with us to boot. They were wonderful hosts, but I won't be surprised if their copy of this letter is returned marked, "Moved, no forwarding address." We keep hoping they will come visit us and get even...On returning, we had a gathering of the founders of ASSIST, the company formed by nine Air Force types from the Pentagon in 1968. ASSIST didn't succeed, but everyone who was in it sure did...It's nice to be back in the Washington area again. (We refer to it as "moving back to America." In Connecticut it was a half-hour drive to the closest Pizza Hut.) We've done the Kennedy Center, Wolf Trap, and the George Mason Center for the Performing Arts...Jack and Linda spent two weeks in the UK (still burning those frequent flier miles) in July. Three days with friends from CT, John and Cindy de Santis, in their neat country house near Henley, and the rest with VA friends, John and Judy Guido, in their perfect London flat in Kensington. We took off for a wonderful week's drive to the Lake District and York. (Now that Jack has the title of "Professor," he had to stop at Oxford and Cambridge and see them. Not quite up to George Mason, but they'll do.) After dozens of trips to the UK, this was Jack's first tourist trip. What a great place to have great friends like the de Santises and the Guidos...In August we were visited by Jan and Betsy Rumberger, those wonderful friends who are the wonderful distributors of that wonderful South African wine that they always bring in those wonderful cases when they come. One wonderful evening, we went out on the float boat with some of that wonderful wine and watched a wonderful sunset followed by a wonderful moonrise. Wonderful wine! And wonderful friends!... The next weekend we went to Snowshoe, WV, for our annual Music in the Mountains weekend. Friends from Jack's days at Stanford (35 years ago!), Dick and Barbara Abbott, joined us. It was nice to have someone along who understood classical music. (Jack is still waiting for the bluegrass band.)...School started for Jack in late August. He's teaching two courses, an MBA course in international business and an MS in Technology Management course called, "Managing the Client Relationship." (One of his students wanted to know if it would be a problem to take the course without the required pre-requisite courses. Jack replied that he didn't think so, since he had never taken the pre-req's either.) Sharp students and a great faculty are keeping Jack on his toes... Thanksgiving saw all four boys, including Jack's nephew Sean, at the house. Gosh, can they put away the food! Linda's folks, Bob and Gladys Lawrence, were also in town, so we had a group of more than a dozen for dinner at Linda's sister's, Susan, new house. Good food, good family, unique American holiday...Linda has been more than occupied with the new house and old friends. (Even many of our friends from CT have come to visit, always a treat for us.) She has our quarter-acre looking like a public flower garden in the summer and the new house is as comfortable as if we had been here for years...Mike finished his four-year tour of the Army in May and set out on a U.S. victory lap that made his dad's look weak. He spent four months on the road, visiting friends, camping out, and enjoying the many national parks and sights of our big land. Now he's back home (they do come home again!), planning the next move in his life. Graduate school or job? A tough choice... Stephen is still in Phoenix making airplane seat belts. He got two raises within three months, so he must be doing OK. Steve's latest acquisition is a dirt-bike. As you in the North read this in the dark and cold of winter, just imagine ole Steve whizzing around the Arizona desert in the warm sun...Andy will finish the University of Virginia this year with a degree in business (they call it commerce at UVA). He will have a concentration in Management Information Systems (MIS) and also get a minor in Computer Science from the engineering school. He will probably stay another year and get an MS in MIS, at which point he should make enough money to support us all...Joke's on Jack again this year. He left the corporate world looking for something a little less demanding when he signed his contract with George Mason University agreeing to work four days a week for nine months a year with an 80% cut in compensation. Then he agreed to teach two new courses. His summer "off" was spent in preparing for the classes, and he's put in six-day weeks and sleepless nights all semester trying to keep ahead of the students. As Linda says, "Jack may not be very smart, but he's stubborn."

As we gather with our friends and family to celebrate the holiday season, we are particularly thankful for the good fortune that has allowed us to count you among those.

Have a Merry Christmas and a Happy and Prosperous 1998!

The Pendrays

CHRISTMAS 1998

G'day Mates:

Just practicing. Drinking Jacob's Creek cabernet sauvignon from Rowland Flat, South Australia. Just practicing. After drinking enough wine, jumping around like a kangaroo. Just practicing. After drinking more wine, curling up and sleeping like a koala. Just practicing. Guess what, we're off to Australia for most of 1999. If they'll give us a visa (funny how countries founded on immigrants, like the U.S. and Australia, don't want any more), Jack has been invited to consult and teach at the Graduate School of Management at the University of Western Australia in Perth. Perth is on the west coast of Australia and is a lot like San Diego was in the fifties, but without the sailors. Just over a million friendly folks and great weather. We leave on Jan 11th, come home for May and June, then return to Perth until early December. That way, we manage to have an endless summer in 1999. Why not? Most folks ask us what our plans are. Here they are: go there, find a place to live, find a car to drive, figure it out, don't worry, be happy....Back to 1998. January saw Jack still teaching in Virginia, so we were stuck in the school schedule. We did fly to Florida before the semester started and make a round robin of St. Pete, Naples, Miami, Cape Coral, and Sarasota (in that order, bad map reader. Jack?). Saw lots of old (guess we should start saying long-time) friends and relatives...The rest of the semester was pretty much trying to stay ahead of the students for Jack (he failed) and trying to stay ahead of Jack for Linda (a slam dunk)...We did get out to the Kennedy Center, Wolf Trap, and the George Mason Center for the Performing Arts quite a few times and Jack even fell awake on several occasions. Nice to be back in Washington where there are nice things to do in the several hours a day that the traffic is tolerable...Also nice to be so close to Charlottesville where Andy is in school. We keep showing up and surprising him. He's really thrilled by this...In May after the semester was over, we took off to Florida again, by car. Now that all the kids are gone, we finally got a Chrysler (now a German car!) minivan for the two of us and all of our junk to junket around in. Love the minivan, only one problem, it handles so well that we keep getting tickets for speeding...In June, Jack was asked by the MS in Technology Management students to teach their final class before graduating. He imparted all of his wisdom in about fifteen minutes and then took them all for beer. Maybe that's why they requested him...Oh yeah, in June we left for a month in Australia and two weeks in Europe. Jack discovered that most of those frequent flyer miles he had accumulated over the years were about to expire, so we blew them on a splurge. How about first class tickets to Perth, Sydney, London, and Paris? And how about first class tickets for Linda's parents to Melbourne, Perth, and Sydney? How about furnished apartments with spectacular views of the Indian Ocean in Perth and Sydney Harbour in Sydney? How about first class compartments on the trans-continental Indian Pacific train for three days across Australia? How about Linda's parents having the only private parlor room on the train with easy chairs, TV, and bar? How about trying to get Jack out of Linda's parents' parlor room? How about eating beans and bread for the next three years? ...What a great trip! Visited at least ten wineries, saw lots of sights (although some were blurry, humm), met scads of nice folks, ate tons of good food, and blah, blah, blah (what do you care? You had to be there.)...From Australia, we went to impose on our friends in London, the Guidos, and then took the TGV to Paris for several days, where we imposed on the family of the woman who used to be our baby sitter in France 25 years ago, Maryse Poullaouec. Since our youngest, Andy, spent the summer with them, we thought it only fitting that we impose also. Great folks, good times...In August, we came home and tried to figure out what was going on in the U.S. Something about the President and some intern? What's that all about?...Since Jack was, once again, retired after May, we were finally free of the school schedule, so we set out driving to Florida again in September (no speeding tickets this time, yeah!). Jack's stepdad (94 and going strong) is still in Miami, as well as his nephew, Sean, so we get to Florida a lot. Coming back, we stopped at Snowshoe, West Virginia, so Jack could ride an old steam logging railroad at the blinding speed of (maybe) ten miles per hour. We then went to Charlottesville to surprise Andy (thrilled, again)...In October, our friends who distribute that wonderful South African wine, Jan and Betsy Rumberger, joined us for a trip to West Virginia to ride yet another train to see the fall foliage. Great trip, crappy foliage. Too dry this year...Linda, her sister, Susan, and Susan's husband, Gordon, surprised Jack on his 59th with a kidnapping to Steamtown, PA, for a (guess what?) steam train ride and museum visit...In November, we had the usual Thanksgiving pig-out at Linda's sister's house. Jack's nephew came up from Miami, so the whole generation of nieces and nephews was there. What a great holiday Thanksgiving is. You eat and drink and watch football and don't even have to give presents or go to church...Linda had an exciting year, mostly riding trains with Jack. I forgot to mention the great Zig Zag train ride he found outside Sydney. This was such a popular train ride that Linda and Jack were the only passengers. Maybe that was because it was cold and rainy, but Jack thought it was cool because they let him ride with the engineer...She also is the charter member of an investment club (The ~~Beardstown~~ Reston Ladies), whose purpose is to make enough money to pay for Jack's train rides. She's also secretary of the neighborhood association, a job she will find difficult from Perth...Mike found gainful employment at Dominion Semiconductor, a 50/50 joint venture of IBM and Toshiba. He is an interface between the manufacturing floor and the information technology dept. Today, he passed his sixth exam and became a Microsoft Certified Systems Engineer (MCSE), which is a big deal. Using home study only, Mike passed all six exams in one try, and nobody does that...Steve has come home for the month before we leave for Perth. It's great to spend time with him since he's been in Arizona for three years. He quit Amsafe after several frustrating years, but he must have been indispensable there. They keep calling him to find out how to do things...Andy graduated, with honors, from the University of Virginia last May, with a degree in business and a minor in computer science. He spent the summer in Paris working for Network Computing Devices, and then returned to UVA to begin his work on an MS in Management Information Systems. We expect him to graduate in May...This year the joke is, again, on Jack. He got fired, again. Well, in fact, this is the first time he was ever fired, all his previous bosses just wish they had fired him. As reported two years ago, he retired, then accepted a teaching position at 20% of his previous compensation (he called it "community service"). Well, this year they fired him (in academia they have a euphemism for this called "not renewing your contract"). He found out when they distributed new business cards and he didn't get any, subtle. Only Jack could get fired from retirement! Oh well, he had fun and learned a lot.

As we sit around the fireplace (yeah, right, it was just 80 degrees here, a record breaker), our thoughts are of loving family and friends, good fortune, wonderful memories, and exciting prospects. May you all have a Merry Christmas and Happy and Prosperous 1999!

The Pendrays

273

50 Years of Christmas Letters

CHRISTMAS 1999

G'day Mates & Rellies: First, an apocryphal story, in Strine: It was tipped around the Uni that, since Jack was not a dinky di chalkie, the Uni was punting by letting him lead a stream of e-commerce. Naturally, Jack spat the dummy when accused of such a rort! Anyone get that? Translation: "Hello friends and relatives: First an apocryphal story, in Australian: It was predicted around the University that, since Jack was not a genuine teacher, the University was gambling by letting him lead a session of e-commerce. Naturally, Jack blew his top when accused of such a scam. As Churchill said, "Two countries separated by a common language"!...Welcome to the 29th perennial pernicious palaver per the perpetual peregrinations of the peripatetic Pendrays (off we all go to the dictionaries!)....We spent most of the year in Perth, where Jack was teaching in the Graduate School of Management (GSM) at the University of Western Australia (UWA), hence the basis for the apocryphal lead story...Australia is famous for its opals, in particular the black ones. The particular Black Opal that I'm observing is 88% cabernet sauvignon and 12% merlot, comes from the vineyards around Adelaide, and you can find it at your local wine shop for about twice what I buy it for in Perth...January 11th saw us off to Perth for their summer. Found an apartment on the Indian Ocean, rented a Toyota Camry with everything backwards for driving on the wrong side of the road, and settled in. Jack taught a course they must have made up for him called Contemporary Information Management Issues. He covered all the stuff he thought MBAs should know about how information technology is affecting business. He had a ball, and some of the students even said they enjoyed it too...In February, we partook of the Festival of Perth, sponsored by UWA, and attended many of the performances. We invited Jack's boss, the Director (Dean) of the GSM, and his wife to join us for the Three Penny Opera. It was awful and the air conditioning didn't work. First time we've ever apologized for inviting someone to a performance!...We found an Anglican Church (Episcopal to us) which reminds us of the one we loved so much in Connecticut. The rector and his wife are terrific, have become good friends, and have introduced us to many other new friends in the parish...March saw us off to Adelaide, Alice Springs, and Ayers Rock for a week. Adelaide is a beautiful city of about a million folks near the southern coast and is home to great winemaking areas, which we <u>had</u> to visit, so we did. Alice Springs is in the middle of the country, and is noted for that. It is also noted for having 20% of its population of 35,000 being Americans who support the "secret" CIA and NSA operations based there. The area "where the American spies live" is on the guided tour of the town! Ayers Rock is just that, a really big rock in the middle of nowhere. Folks like us, i.e., not too bright, pay good money to go see this rock...In April, Jack had a week off over Easter, so we went to Hong Kong, which is Chinese for "bring money." We stayed at the grand dame Peninsula Hotel, had a great time, and left lots of money...One of Jack's professor colleagues is a long-time member of the Royal Perth Yacht Club (those rascals who won the America's Cup from the U.S. for the first time!) and took Jack racing with him there. Due to having Jack as crew, they came in last, but they did better in the drinking-after-the-race activity...In May, we came home for several months, just in time for

Andy's graduation from UVA with his Master's degree in Management Information Systems. Well done, Andy. We're anticipating that he will soon be able to support us in the style to which we would like to become accustomed... We bought a condo in Sarasota and made that our permanent residence (since we aren't ever anywhere for long, might as well be from Florida). Didn't really have much time to spend on this process, so we bought our condo fully furnished, sight unseen. Luckily, we had a Realtor with good taste and we love our place in Siesta Key. Other friends from VA also own units there, so we had seen the condos before. We plan on spending most of our time there when we are in the States, but we're keeping the townhouse in VA as our second home. Jack says, "If we keep moving fast enough, 'they' will never catch us." Wonder who "they" are... We also went back to Connecticut for several days in June and visited friends there. Great to see them all again...Linda's folks, Bob and Gladys Lawrence, came to Virginia to celebrate their 60th wedding anniversary. Linda's sister and her husband, Susan and Gordon Harvey, threw a small party (dinner for about 60 folks!) for them. No one parties better than Bob & Gladdie and their friends...In August, we went to Seattle on our way back to Perth. Jack's brother and his wife, Keith & Renee, live there, and Jack's 95-year-old stepfather, Pop, made the move from Miami to Seattle this year. Pop made the flight in first class, and ate and drank everything they offered. Gets his money's worth, that fellow. It's really great having him three blocks from Keith and Renee, who see him all the time...Jack started teaching a course in electronic commerce in August. Since this was something exciting, about which he knew nothing, he volunteered to teach it. If his students learned half as much as he did, it was successful...September was kinda quiet, except for a steam train ride up the Avon Valley outside Perth. Shucks, even that was quiet, since the farm town we went to on a Sunday was closed...October was more exciting. Susan and Gordon came to celebrate our 33rd anniversary with us. We visited some of the restaurants around Perth and went down to the Margaret River region south of Perth to visit wineries (again)...Jack went to Shanghai for several days to teach e-commerce to a group of Chinese Chief Information Officers. Fascinating experience for Jack; not sure the Chinese got much out of it, as the business culture gap was significant...In November, Jack turned 60 for the first time. He promised himself that he would run six miles and weigh under 160 again before he turned 60, so he asked Linda to buy a scale that had both English and metric units on it. She did, it had stones and kilograms! Jack got down to 11 stones or 72 kgs., whatever that is, and declared victory. He did manage to run six miles on Oct 17th, declared another victory, and hasn't been close to that since...November saw the arrival of all the "kids" in Perth. Mike arrived on the 21st, and Steve, Sean (their cousin from Miami), and Andy and his girlfriend, Diana Cassell, arrived on the 26th. Since most of the group had lost Thanksgiving Day, literally, as they crossed the international dateline east of New Zealand, Linda prepared a Thanksgiving meal that was incredible. Considering that most of what we eat for Thanksgiving is not generally available in Australia, she did a Herculean job...Now that we had our merry group of 7, we set off for some adventures. Jack led the daytime excursions and Steve led the nightlife activities. Five days in Sydney included climbing the top of the Sydney Harbour Bridge. Six days in New Zealand included canyoning in jet boats and rafts, and a visit to the America's Cup Village in Auckland...Jack resigned his last Board seat in December. He was just not capable of doing the job for AppliedTheory from Australia (was he ever capable?). The week after he resigned, the stock went up 50%. The word really does get around fast...Linda still looks 39, making folks think that the old codger Jack is either a cradle-robber or has acquired a trophy wife. She has built up quite a group of friends and activities in Perth, but still relishes returning to her friends in the States...Mike has become a certified geek, having added a long list of computer-based certifications to his resume. Quite an accomplishment for someone who never took a class in these subjects. He has joined a new company, Compath, that specializes in supporting internet over cable-TV wires. On second thought, maybe Mike will be the one to support us in old age...After three years of laid-back living in Phoenix, Steve has moved back "home" to the faster East-Coast living of Stamford, CT. He's made the plunge into sales with a manufacturer's representative, Automation Associates, who sell high-tech manufacturing machines. Steve has Long Island and some of New York City as his territory, where we all know there is money to be made. On third thought, he may be our old-age pot of gold...Andy is at Price Waterhouse Coopers, helping them straighten out their networks. His job is in Maryland, but he lives in Virginia near the Pentagon... Obviously, we're just proud as hell of all of them and plan to retire (again) in luxury...The joke's on both Jack and Linda this year. They drive on the left in Australia, so all of the car controls are backwards. In particular, the windshield wiper control is where the turn indicator is on American cars. So, if you're ever in Perth and you see a car with the wipers on when it's a normal sunny day, wave, it's Jack and Linda...So here I sit with my empty bottle of wine and a fuzzy computer screen (it wasn't that way this morning!) thinking about all the years and all the family and friends and how lucky we have been to have all of these. May you all have a Merry Christmas and wonderful new century!

The Pendrays

The 1990s

50 Years of Christmas Letters

The 2000s

50 Years of Christmas Letters

CHRISTMAS 2000

Hello out there...Welcome to the 30th Pendray Christmas letter. To those of you who have read all 29 of the previous letters, I can only say: What's wrong with you?!...Bloody Mary is helping me write this year's missive, and quite a help she is. Not only does that show my flexibility in choice of beverages, but it seems appropriate since I started this process before noon...Since it's a Wednesday, I guess I'm taking the day off to write this, but how does one know that you're taking a day off in retirement? How does one go on vacation when retired? How do you know you're on vacation? Am I no longer entitled to vacation travel packages? Some of life's never-ending questions....A stupid year! One by one, we agreed to do things that, when put together, made for a stupid year. Started the year in Virginia, then went to Florida, then to Perth, then to Singapore, then back to Perth, then to Tasmania, back to Virginia, back to Florida, back to Virginia, back to Florida, back to Virginia, then to Connecticut, Vermont, and upstate New York, back to Virginia, back to Florida, back to Virginia, back to Connecticut, back to Virginia, then to London, Scotland, and Ireland, back to Virginia, back to Florida, and back to Virginia. See, really stupid! Fun, but stupid...On January 1st, we flew to our condo on Siesta Key, next to Sarasota, for a week. Jack went jogging one day and came home excited that he found a group of seven houses on a peninsula with water on both sides. So we bought one of them that week, without having ever been inside. That didn't matter since it was going to be dramatically renovated while we were in Australia, and we did get to see the plans before we left...So, we left for Perth, Jack stopping in Seattle to visit his brother, Keith, and 96-year-old stepfather, Pop, and Linda going via Tucson to visit with her mom and dad...We spent three months in Perth while Jack bamboozled some students at the University of Western Australia into thinking that he knew something about electronic commerce. While there, we got in a five-day trip to Singapore, which is sort of an elected dictatorship. Very safe and clean, but a little sterile. For example, there was an editorial in the newspaper advocating that they reconsider their outright ban on chewing gum. Racy stuff!...At the end of our stay in Perth, our friends of 37 years, Dick and Barbara Abbott, joined us. We toured south Western Australia, Tasmania (those devils!), and Melbourne together on our slow way home. Great friends, great trip...In May, we returned to Reston for a couple of weeks before heading off to Florida to see what this renovated house looked like. It looked like it wasn't finished! After several weeks of watching the workmen fiddle around (Jack said he finally understood the song "Send in the clowns"), we closed the sale so we could throw them out and get it finished ourselves. Little did we know that we had moved into a third-world country where almost all of the workmen are unreliable. (For example, they destroyed the lawn sprinkler system putting in some new palms. While repairing the sprinkler system, they cut the TV cable. While repairing the TV cable, they cut a phone line. While putting in a new phone line, they cut the new TV cable, so the cable guy came and fixed the old TV cable.) In short, Jack became the chief workman and handyman, and Linda became the furnisher/finisher. That pretty much took care of June and July (and October and November)...In August, we took a drive from Florida to Virginia, then continued driving on to Connecticut, Vermont, and Lake Placid, New York. We visited our son Steve and old friends in Connecticut, Jack's cousin and his wife, Jay and Anne, in Vermont, and spent a week helping our friends Lee and Nancy Keet celebrate their 40th wedding anniversary in Lake Placid. Nice to have such wonderful folks to mooch off of as we travel around...After driving back to Virginia, we flew back to Florida to see if we could make progress on the house. We didn't...Steve had some surgery in Connecticut, so we went back there for that. (It all seemed to go well, but the doc botched it and Steve almost bled to death the next week when we were in Ireland. He's fine now, but it was a scary thing.) ...In September, we toured Scotland and Ireland for the first time ever. It was a great trip in spite of the fact that the Irish roads make the Australian outback trails look like super highways (Jack's knuckles were white for weeks)...October put us back in Florida, where our long-time group of friends from Virginia joined us for a week of partying in our new, almost-finished-and-furnished house, all 17 of them. Fortunately, several of them have condos in the area, so there was room for all. Our unfurnished living room became the ballroom, and we're under orders that we can't furnish it now...After this gang left, we flew to New York to join our Australian minister and his wife, Ken and Fay Drayton, who were flying around the world. We did the New York

289

thing, plays, museums, etc., then the Washington thing, then we drove to Florida via Beaufort, SC, and Savannah, GA, to let them experience the Old South and our common British heritage. Another great trip with great friends...We stayed in Florida for Thanksgiving with 14 family members who came for the holiday weekend. Our dining room chairs arrived the day before Thanksgiving, so no one had to eat turkey standing up...We're in our townhouse in Reston, VA, for the month of December and are glad to settle in one place for almost a month... See, it was a stupid year! Fun, but stupid...Since we kept our townhouse in Reston, Linda has had to purchase all new furniture for the new house. What with all the packing and traveling, she hasn't been bored this year... Mike is still at Compath, where he took a stint as MIS manager this year. He continues to accumulate geek credentials at an amazing rate and has networked our computers in both Reston and Sarasota. Nice to know he's minding the house in Reston when we're not there...Steve is doing fine in Stamford, CT, now that his bout with the medical world is over. Still selling manufacturing devices and enjoying it. In his spare time, he's started a graduate class and also earned his PWC certificate. (For the uninitiated, that stands for Personal Water Craft. Steve gave us all lessons on the Jet Ski over Thanksgiving.)...Andy is still at Price Waterhouse Coopers as a technical consultant to its consultants. (When they get in deep doo-doo, they call Andy for help.) He moved, so that he is now about a mile from his office, which is a good thing in the Washington-area traffic...Joke's on Jack again this year. After working to get college degrees, have a professional career, build a nest egg, and then retire to a life of leisure, he finds that that life of leisure is actually as a full-time manual laborer/handyman working on his house. That's what he gets for jogging in nice neighborhoods!

Well, the second Bloody Mary is empty and it's about time for a nap, so I'll end this rambling by wishing you all a Merry Christmas and a Wonderful and Prosperous New Year!

The Pendrays

50 Years of Christmas Letters

CHRISTMAS 2001

Hello out there...Welcome to the 31st edition of the Pendray Christmas letter. Those of you receiving it for the first time will soon understand why those who have known us for a long time do not open mail from us this time of year...As tradition dictates, I have opened a beverage and have been re-reading some of the past Christmas letters for inspiration. There are so many past letters, I'm half through the bottle of 1990 Topolos Russian River Zinfandel and only ten percent through this letter. At that rate, I calculate it will take five bottles of wine to finish the letter, or is it six, or four, whatever it takes...Thanks to Lyn Hammers who gave us this wine; it's terrific. Did you know there are really only twelve bottles of wine in the world, but people keep passing them on as gifts? At the end of this letter, there will be only seven bottles left in the world, or is it four, or six, whatever...Things were quieter for us this year, so this letter may be less confusing than normal, or maybe not...We spent last Christmas and New Year's Eve in Virginia with family and friends, then flew to Florida on New Year's day for more partying with more friends...On Jan. 6 we flew back to VA to pack to leave on Jan. 14 for Australia, via Seattle. In Seattle, we spent a day with Jack's brother and his wife, Keith and Renee, and Jack's 97-year old stepfather, Pop, who is in a nursing home down the street from Keith and Renee. They're all having a great time together, which sure justifies our moving Pop from Miami to Seattle while he was still young, only 95...From Seattle we flew to Sydney, where we recovered from that horrendous jet-lag for several days before continuing on to Perth on the 18th (which is really the 17th here, but, being upside down, the Aussies have trouble with dates and stuff like that)....Jack taught his last semester in the MBA program at the University of Western Australia. He only had eight students sign up, so it's clear that word got out and he should have finished earlier. Nevertheless, he had a ball with such a light load, but drove those poor eight students nuts with too much attention...While Jack was harrying his small flock of eight unfortunate students, Linda was busy with her many Australian friends and activities, including a church group, a walking group (whose mission was to walk to the nearest coffee shop), a book club, and on and on...After Jack's class was over, we were joined by friends from Connecticut, Rich and Lin Jaffee, with whom we set off for another attempt to deplete the stocks of the southwestern Australian wineries. We were quite successful...Just before leaving Perth in April, we went to Broome, in northwestern Australia, with some Aussie friends, to find out how hot it really could get in Australia. Broome is famous for pearls, so Linda had to get two big ones...In April, we returned to the U.S., stopping for a week in Tucson to visit Linda's folks, always a pleasure...In May, Jack went to Miami for a reunion of his high school fraternity. About 200 old farts spent the weekend acting like 16-year olds. Naturally, Jack was very reserved and did not participate. Right!...We had two couples visit us from Australia, on separate occasions, and we showed them some of the eastern U.S. We're hoping that many more of them come to do the same...In June we settled in Florida for the summer to oversee projects on the money pit, otherwise known as our new home. (So far, we have spent the summers in FL and the winters in VA. I don't think that's how it's supposed to work.) We had a new boat dock built to hold all of Jack's toys, the new 23 foot runabout boat and the two jet skis. The lift for the boat even has a remote control, bringing the number of remote controllers in the house to about twenty. (Linda hasn't a clue how most of them work, so Jack is finally master of his domain, or so he thinks.) In July, all of the boys visited to play with the toys, which they did...Also in July, Linda's folks moved from Arizona to a retirement community between our house in Sarasota and Tampa. It's really terrific having them close again after so many years apart. Their retirement complex is great. Even the food is good, and it's all-you-can-eat for about $4 a meal. Jack wants to get on the entrance waitlist, but Linda thinks he'd put on too much weight...Skipping ahead, (hallelujah!) in October, our long-time eating and drinking group (guess which of those dominates) from VA came to FL for ten days. These 17 folks played with all the toys, drank all the booze, ate all the food, then left...After we had an entire new roof put on the house (don't ask!), we had the family, fourteen of them, to FL for Thanksgiving. Same thing with the toys, booze, food, and leaving...After they left, the fifteen new doors to replace the fifteen new doors on our house finally arrived (don't ask!). We hope to have them installed when we return in Jan. ...Jack has had a pretty rewarding year, both as an MBA professor and as a free manual laborer. For one of these, he was worth every cent he received...Linda has started to build a new social life in Florida to add to her social life in Virginia and replace the one in Australia. Fortunately, we're in a great neighborhood with terrific neighbors... Has anyone noticed that the economy is somewhat weak?...Mike missed the family gathering at Thanksgiving because he had to stay in Virginia and work on a proposal for his company. The next Tuesday, they laid him off! With all his geek credentials he shouldn't have trouble finding a new job, and it should be a no-brainer to find a better company. Mike finally made us grandparents. He adopted Linda's sister's husband's daughter's (whew!) dog, Riley, giving us our first granddog... Steve is still in Stamford, CT. He also was laid off, in June, as a result of the economy. In Sept., he had a new job offer, which evaporated on Sep 11th. While he's looking for work, he's making good use of his time applying for MBA programs for next year, taking classes in bartending and French (could he become a French bartender?), and helping Jack repair and maintain his water toys... Andy is still at a large consulting company, who shall remain unnamed to protect the guilty. This year, he was given a promotion, a 10 out of 10 on his performance evaluation, and a simultaneous cut in pay. Like Mike and Steve, his education, experience, and abilities provide confidence and security, but this sure isn't how I recall companies treated folks... Has anyone noticed that the economy is somewhat weak?...This year's joke is on both Jack and Linda. In the spring, they signed up for a series of summer shows at the Wolf Trap Theatre. Since they spent the entire summer supervising work on the money pit (don't ask!), they missed them all. They sent all the tickets to Linda's sister's (here we go again) husband, Gordon, who had a great time. Gordon hopes that we repeat the experience next year. Dream on, Gordon.

For a serious thought this year, let's make sure that Bin Laden and the events of Sep 11th don't destroy the free, open, and trusting society that is America. If we let that happen, he wins. Love, cherish, and protect one another at this time of year, and throughout the year. Merry Christmas and a Prosperous and Safe New Year to all of you, our dear friends and relatives.

The Pendrays

Festive Riley

50 Years of Christmas Letters

CHRISTMAS 2002

Hello out there...Bubble, bubble, toil, and trouble, i.e., champagne, more champagne, toil over the Christmas letter, which will trouble all of our friends when they read this 32nd edition of the Pendray pageant. By tradition, I sip something, re-read past editions of this, and write until the computer screen image is blurry. It's only 10 a.m., but tradition will be honored! I should be in bed early today, about 2 p.m. I figure. This year's mind lubricant is a bottle of Chandon California champagne. We have a case of this stuff left over from Linda's niece's wedding, so Christmas promises to be very merry around here, albeit a little blurry...Now that we are really fully retired, life is a little slower, so maybe this letter will be shorter (dream on!)... We did start the year with a quiet New Year's in Florida; we slept right through it...Since our three sons were all in various states of economic uncertainty, two unemployed, one uncertain with his job, they came down at the end of January to spend a week with us. Steve flew from CT, and Mike and Andy drove from VA. Having a choice between Andy's commodious Ford Explorer and our minuscule VW bug, they chose the bug for the trip. When they arrived, we were surprised to see them in the bug, especially when our 95-pound granddog also emerged from the car. Looked like a circus act! Unfortunately, it's true, intelligence is an inherited trait...While the boys were in Florida, Jack decided to fall off his dock while attempting to get on the boat, alone. He hit his side on the side of the boat and broke two ribs (he heard them go crack, crack). Lying suspended in the ropes between the dock and boat, he decided not to drop into the water, since he couldn't breathe, but rather climbed back up onto the dock, hobbled into the house and asked Steve and Linda to take him to the hospital. If you've never broken a rib, don't, it smarts...In February, we went to VA for two weeks to be sure we didn't forget what true winter was like, but rushed back in time for a visit from Jack's old (long-time?) buddy from high school, Inky Philips, and his wife, Mary. No friends like old (long-time?) friends...March saw us in Naples (the Florida one) with the Abbotts and Mertens, more of those old (yeah, yeah) friends...Jack went to visit his brother, Keith, Keith's wife, Renee, and his stepdad, Pop, in Seattle, as Pop was in failing health...Two chapters in the Book of Life were closed in April. Pop left us for greener pastures on the 18th. He had 97 years of unbending faith, love, and caring for others. Fortunately, he had the last several years in Seattle, where Keith and Renee surrounded him with love and attention. Funny, how the loss of someone who loved, sheltered, and nurtured you leaves such a big, empty hole. In Chattanooga, Jack's stepmom, Penny, 96, went to her reward within ten days of Pop's doing so. We are proud that Penny bore the Pendray name. She was enveloped by the love of her daughter, Betty, until the end...April also had its joys. We finally installed the new doors which replaced the new doors on our house (don't ask)! After the new doors were replaced, we had a skilled carpenter spend several weeks fixing the new doors. Now, when it rains the doors don't leak; however, the new roof does (don't ask!)...We went sailing from St. Vincent to Grenada with our old (actually quite a bit younger than us) friends, the Guidos, at the end of the month. You know how that goes: sail several hours a day, eat and (mostly) drink the rest. A great time...In May, we spent two weeks in VA, when we sold the Reston townhouse to Mike and Andy. That'll teach 'em to move home! Now, when we go to VA, we're guests, but they keep asking us to fix this, and replace that. That'll teach us!...In June, we finally got it right and drove to VA for the summer. Unfortunately, this year the summer in VA was hotter than the summer in Florida. Go figure. So, we drove on to CT for one of Steve's old (still young) friend's weddings and a chance to visit our many wonderful friends in CT. Since we gave them short notice of our coming, they were all still there and we had some terrific reunions...July saw us off to Pearisburg, VA, (you know, right next to Ripplemead) for the housewarming of Megan (Linda's niece) and Curtis. Even took the granddog, who almost drowned trying to keep up swimming with our canoes in the New River. Granddog now has a life vest, with a handle, for easy lifting of this 95-pound dog!...Went back to FL for several weeks to see if the house was still there...In Aug., we went to Boston for the retirement party of Jack's friend, Bill Harper. Lesson learned: don't invite

Jack to a party, he'll come. It was great, and we had a chance to visit Linda's college sorority sister, Karen Back, and her husband, Don Bachman, at their place on Cape Cod. No friends like old (yeah, yeah) friends...We also slipped down to Norfolk for Jay and Charlene Foley's retirement from the Navy (another lesson learned by the unwary, invite them and they <u>will</u> come). The Navy really knows how to put on a ceremony, but it might have had something to do with Jay's two stars and Char's receiving the highest civilian medal given by the Navy...Sept. saw us off to Australia, this time as just tourists. We hooked up with friends in Brisbane, Dennis and Kay Neil, who had driven across the Australian desert from Perth, and rode with them down the east coast to Canberra. From there, we flew to Perth, where we stayed with the Plowmans and the Draytons (got it yet?, invite them and they <u>will</u> come). We saw most of our relatively new, old (ha, ha) friends in Perth and had a great visit...Our neighbor in Perth, Ruth Cocks, came back with us. We spent three days in LA on the way back and did all the tourist things, city tour, Hollywood, Disneyland, and Universal Studios. All those roller coasters and not one upchuck! We set out with Ruth from VA to drive to FL, going through Williamsburg to the outer banks of NC. We stayed at beautiful downtown Ocracoke, NC, Myrtle Beach, and Charleston, SC, and Jekyll Island, GA. After a few days in Sarasota, we drove to Flamingo, in the Everglades, and Key West for two nights. Saw lots of strange animals, both in the Everglades and Key West...In Nov., we flew to College Station to visit the Guidos and see a Texas A&M football game. Those Aggies take football very seriously!...We also had Thanksgiving in Nov., because that's when it is. We were in FL and had an intimate gathering of 22 of our closest relatives, and near-relatives, for dinner. The crowd stayed over for the wedding of Linda's niece, Kelly, to Kenny Clark on the beach at Siesta Key on Saturday. It was a great event, good folks, food, beverages, and perfect weather...We're driving to VA with Linda's folks for Christmas. Gonna be houseguests of Mike and Andy, again. You gotta love it!... Linda had one of those decadal birthdays this year. Yes, she's 40...Mike got tired of traveling six days a week and found a job in what he calls "a real company," BearingPoint, ex KPMG Consulting. He's happier, and so is his dog, Riley, now that Mike's home more...Steve started his two-year MBA program at Vanderbilt, in Nashville, in September. Not only is Vandy a great school and MBA program, they gave Steve a scholarship to come there. He likes Vandy and Nashville, but there's no sign yet of the really big money, from country music...Andy hung on and watched Price Waterhouse Coopers Consulting struggle until IBM finally picked them up for a song. Next week, he starts a new job in Reston at Predictive Technologies, with a nice increase in pay. IBM's loss. You may see Andy zipping around Reston these days in his new black Subaru WRX, a hot car...The annual joke this year is on Jack. Having broken two ribs trying to step on the boat, he tried it again six months later, after his ribs had healed. This time, he only tore his groin. In three days, he was black and blue from knee to knee, if you can imagine what that entails. He's healed again, but Linda has forbidden him to go near the dock alone.

50 Years of Christmas Letters

In these troubled times, we rely and depend on our family and friends, more than ever, for love, comfort, and cheer. May you all have a Merry Christmas and Happy, and Peaceful, New Year.

The Pendrays

"Pop"

Within a year from when my mom took us back to Miami after her divorce, she had pursued and married Richard (Dick) Hoeller, who had been a roommate of my dad's in Miami when they were both bachelors. Somehow, Mom had finagled another man into loving her. To spite my dad, Mom started calling Tommy and me by the last name of Hoeller, and had us call Dick, "Pop." To this day, there are ex-students of the Sts. Peter & Paul school in Miami who think of us as Hoellers. Dad forced her to go back to Pendray in one of many legal confrontations he had with Mom.

Luckily, Pop was another great and gentle guy, and, because of circumstances, he raised Tommy and me in place of our dad, who was cut out of our lives by our Mom. While Mom favored corporal punishment, Pop would just lecture us when we needed correction. And lecture he did, on and on and on. At one point, Tommy and I begged him to please just spank us, which I don't recall him ever doing. He was quiet, soft spoken, and incredibly hard working. During his 50 years at Florida Power & Light in Miami, I can't remember a time when he didn't have a second job that he worked to provide for his family of Mom, Tommy, me, and his son, my younger brother, Keith, a genuine Hoeller. Even after he retired, Pop worked as long as he was physically able as a parking lot attendant for an over-busy 7-11 strip mall in South Miami. Now, one could understand that he would do anything to get out of that house, which is surely true, but he also really loved people and interacting with them. He got his fair share of obnoxious Miami drivers in his parking lot, but everyone appreciated the calm and considerate manner in which he did his job. I bet he would handle the toughest cases by quietly lecturing them, on and on and on, until they moved their cars, begging for mercy.

Pop had a droll sense of humor. He loved puns and *double entendres.* Being a very quiet person, he mostly told his jokes to himself. If you happened to be nearby and listened intently, you might hear one. My favorite one had to do with my high school, Coral Gables High. Every time he would drive by Gables High School, if you listened closely, you would hear him say, "Hi, school." It never failed. I always chuckled; it never failed.

Pop was quite an American success story. Born on September 6, 1904, in Bad Salzungen, Germany, his parents died during WW I while he was a teenager. Since none of his large family could take him in, he was partially raised by a kind neighbor. Circa 1923, he immigrated to the U.S., where he stayed with his aunt in Washington, D.C., while learning English. Circa 1924, he worked his way to Miami doing odd jobs, including working on the railroad to Key West. He taught himself electrical engineering and worked as a meter expert in the distribution division of Florida Power & Light, alongside my dad, who spent his life doing the same thing for FP&L and the TVA. Pop ended his 50-year career at FP&L as the director of all outside landscaping and line clearance for south Florida, a huge responsibility.

When Linda and I were married, my mother, father, and stepfather were all in attendance, and my older brother, Tom, was my best man. At the reception following the wedding, I noticed that all my family's men had flower *boutonnieres*, except for Pop, who seemed naked without one. Until the end of my time, I will deeply regret that I didn't think to order one for the one person who deserved it the most, Pop.

When we were living outside Paris in the early '70s, Mom and Pop flew over and visited us. While there, they flew to Germany where his surviving family members, a sister and others, I believe, came through the Iron Curtain from East Germany and visited them. After over 50 years of sparse contact, this reunion happily closed his family loop.

Three brothers: me, Tom, and Keith at Tom's wedding

Tom, my older brother and fellow traveler through youth, contracted cancer and died less than a month past his fortieth birthday. He spent his last months at the home of Mom and Pop, under the attentive love and care of Pop. While I was flying to Miami, Tom died in the hospital with Pop at his side. Tom left a six-year-old son, Sean, whose only immediate Miami relatives from his father's side were Mom and Pop. Sean was fortunate to have a Grandma and "Grandpop" to give him some continuity and contact with his father's family. Grandpop doted on Sean whenever he got the chance.

When Mom developed Alzheimer's, they moved into Fair Havens retirement home in Miami Springs. There, Pop cared for her until that dreadful disease took her life. Now, Pop had a strong faith in a benevolent God and a glorious hereafter. After Mom's memorial service, I tried to console Pop by saying, "Mom is up there waiting for you." Pop replied, "Well, she's going to have to wait a while." Pop loved life and enjoyed another six years after Mom's death. We flew him to Seattle under the care of the Director of Nursing at Fair Havens, Karen Kennedy, who cherished Pop. Keith and his wife, Renee, had found a retirement home a few blocks from their house in north Seattle, and Pop spent the last years of his life under their watchful care with many hours of loving family experiences. The Grand Old Man died there on April 18, 2002, at the age of 97.

I loved and respected Pop dearly, and I'm ever thankful that Mom had made us call him "Pop." The most puzzling thing about Pop that I will never understand is why he loved and stayed with Mom right up until her end, but I thank God that he did!

Pop, the parking lot attendant

CHRISTMAS 2003

Hello out there...Here comes the 33rd version of this infamous letter, so 3 must not be a lucky number for any of y'all...Devil's Lair (no, that's not the name of Jack's home office). It's the wine that is serving as encouragement to me to continue writing this letter. No sober person would ever do this. Anyway, Devil's Lair is my favorite Australian Chardonnay and is almost impossible to find in the U.S. It's made in a small winery in the Margaret River region south of Perth, and they probably only let five cases out of the country every year. Two weeks ago, a friend sent me to a local wine shop, and there were all five cases for 2001! So I bought a case and only have two bottles left now. Gotta go back and buy those other four cases. There goes the food budget for the month... Last December we drove to Virginia for the holidays, picking up Linda's parents, in Tampa, and Steve, in Nashville. We had our first white Christmas since forever, gentle snow on both Christmas Eve and day, really beautiful. Then it turned to frozen slush and ice, and we jumped in the car and drove back to Florida. It was tough reading about the horrible winter in VA, but we called now and then with words of encouragement. Hey, it was tough here, too. It reached 50 one night and we actually burned the dust off the gas logs. Terrible smell!...We stayed in Sarasota for most of the winter (we're not as dumb as we look). During one cold snap (it was below 70 for days on end!), we went to Miami for the weekend to visit our nephew, Sean. It was pretty cold there, too. I had to wear long-sleeved shirts—in the evening...In March, we took a quick trip to VA to see if winter was still there. It was, so we came home...At the end of March, our notorious Gourmet Group from VA came here for a week of eating, drinking, and general carousing. We did...The highlight of April was Jack's jury duty. They call him every year, but he never gets selected to a jury. Guess our judicial system still works after all...In May, we repeated last year's sailing adventure, but with the four Pendray boys as crew, Mike, Sean, Steve, and Andy. Since no one knew how to sail (Jack fakes it), we rented the biggest boat we could afford and got a 46-foot catamaran to take, one-way, from St. Vincent to Grenada, with two-day stopovers at each end. It's impossible to tip over a catamaran that big, so we didn't. It was a wonderful boat, with four staterooms and four heads, two engines, generator, air conditioning, etc. We'll never rent a monohull again. We ate ashore a lot, as each of the four guys had to pay for a dinner ashore. It was a contest to see who could order the most outrageously expensive item...When we returned, we had the leak in our new roof repaired, again. Finally, when it rains here, all of the water stays outside. Ah, the little victories of life...In June we drove from Sarasota to Virginia, via Ft. Lauderdale (map reading is not Jack's forte). Actually, Steve was in Lauderdale on a summer internship with American Express...We "summered" in VA with Mike and Andy, and got to use all of our tickets to Wolf Trap...We returned to FL for a week in July to check on the house and enjoy a weekend visit from Steve, Sean, and four of the Amex interns from Ft. Lauderdale. It did give Jack a start to see the boat being pulled home by one of the jet skis, but the problem was just a loose dead-man's lanyard on the boat...Oh yeah, we also went to Alaska in July. We flew to Anchorage, took a train to Fairbanks (Jack likes trains), met two couples from the notorious Gourmet Group, the Gios and the Mannings, in Fairbanks, joined a Princess tour which took the train back to Anchorage (Jack really likes trains), took a Princess cruise down the inland passage to Vancouver, met some Pendrays in Victoria, took a train to Seattle (really, Jack!), visited Jack's brother and his wife, Keith and Renee, in Seattle, then flew back to VA. Alaska is everything they say it is, and so are the cruises. The ship was riding at least a foot higher in the water after Jack, Jim, and John ate tons of food and drank gallons of beer and wine...Before leaving VA in September, we went to the funeral of Jack's uncle, Jack Coleman. He was a really nice guy, and we'll miss him greatly...We drove home via

Nashville to spend the night with Steve at Vanderbilt. Nice school, nice city...We got home in time to go to the memorial service for Kerry Byrd, Linda's ex brother-in-law and father of our nieces, Kelly and Megan. Another really nice guy who we'll miss... November saw us off to Lampasas, TX. (Jack always wanted to go there, but never thought he'd really make it.) The big event was the wedding of one of the notorious Gourmet Group's kids (the group is notorious, not the kid), Mike Guido. It was another excuse for the notorious Gourmet Group to party, so we did...On returning to Sarasota, we prepared for the Thanksgiving dinner for 15 of us. Not as big a crowd as last year, but just as much fun...The first weekend in Dec., we welcomed three of Jack's old friends from the Ching Tang fraternity at Coral Gables High School: Paul Huck, Tom Prebianca, and Bob Victor. Paul and Tom were with their wives, Donna and Aleta, but Mitzi Victor had the good fortune to have a cold and miss the event. The gruesome foursome spent half the night pretending they were 15 again, and the rest trying to figure out what happened during the last fifty years. It was a blast...Jack started studying Spanish this year. Growing up in Miami, he knows a few Spanish words, but he's now learning some he can actually use in mixed society...Linda is settling in to FL. She has a new morning walking partner, has joined the church book club, and sees her parents and aunt in Tampa frequently. She got her Christmas present in November this year, a new driveway. Ain't Jack romantic...Mike now sports around Virginia in a new Infiniti G35 coupe. Sometimes, you also see his best friend, Riley, hanging his head and tongue out the window. Mike is still at BearingPoint. They keep trying to send him to Iraq where they have a consulting contract, but, so far, he's stayed at local clients. Mike and Andy attended motorcycle school and got their licenses endorsed to drive bikes. We can hardly wait for the Harley hogs to appear...Steve finishes his MBA in May and has accepted a job at American Express in Ft. Lauderdale. Well done, Steve! We look forward to having him closer...Andy now works for Sygate Technologies. The company is in California, Andy's territory is Europe, and he lives in Virginia. Andy travels a bit. His schedule is a lot like Jack's was and they often compare travel horror stories...The joke this year is on Sean, our nephew. On the sailing trip, each person was given a specific job to learn. Since Sean was the only non-engineer, he was assigned the job of tending the automatic anchor windlass. Well, the windlass had two parts missing, so it was not automatic at all, but was an engineering nightmare. The anchor rode was all chain, and it would slip off the windlass and all 250 feet of it would run out, making a big pile of chain on the ocean floor and a lot of noise doing it, until it hit the end (which was, fortunately, well fastened to the boat). This provided great amusement to the other boaters at anchor in the harbor, and, naturally, we all pointed at Sean to be sure they knew who was responsible for the windlass. To his credit, Sean soon figured out the problem and stopped it from happening, but it was good for a laugh until then.

A prayer: There are those who seek to destroy our country, our freedoms, and our culture. As our country struggles to fight them, God give us the wisdom and courage to do so without destroying our freedoms and culture in the struggle.

May you all have a Merry Christmas and a Happy, and Peaceful, 2004.

The Pendrays

CHRISTMAS 2004

Hola Fuera Allí (Hello Out There): In honor of Jack's third year of embarrassing himself in Spanish classes at the local community education center, parts of this letter will be bilingual. This year's locution lubricant is a Jose Cuervo Especial Margarita (Special Joe Crow Margaret). About the only Spanish phrase that Jack has mastered is "Más margaritas, por favor" (More Margarets, please). His teacher says that he has a wonderful French accent and could pass himself off anywhere in the world as a Frenchman speaking Spanish horribly. He may try this next time he's in France and see what they do with that...We ended last year in Virginia, where we had a wonderful white Christmas, but will spend this Christmas in Florida, where it will probably be 80 degrees and sunny. Imagine snuggling around the Yule log in that!...Jan., Feb., Mar., & early Apr. were quiet in Sarasota, enjoying guests from Virginia, Germany, Virginia (different folks), and Pennsylvania...April 9th, Jack and a long-time friend from high school, college, and beyond, Inky Philips, set out on a two-week geezers' road trip around the South in Jack's antique car (it's a 2001 Oldsmobile, but they don't make Oldsmobiles anymore). They went to Cedar Key (llave de cedro), Mexico Beach (la playa de México), Pensacola (OK, I quit!), Biloxi, New Orleans, Natchez, Memphis (to visit Graceland, for sure), Corinth/Shilo, Chattanooga/Chickamauga, Savannah, and back to Cedar Key. They had a great time of drinking, eating, drinking, singing, drinking, driving (not while drinking, which seriously limited the amount of driving time in any one day). It did take them a while to figure out that most folks thought they were a gay couple, but, when one of the bellmen considerately laid out the two hotel robes on the same bed with chocolates on both pillows (in a two-bedroom suite), that was a tip-off...May was a fun month. Steve received his MBA, with honors, from Vanderbilt, so we all went to Nashville to share in his glory. Then we all went to France to celebrate. Steve's girlfriend, Stephanie, and his cousin, Sean, joined us. We spent two days in Paris, then took a TGV (Tren a Grande Velocidad, said with a good French accent) to a barge near Bordeaux. We got on the barge, floated down to Bordeaux, and tied up for five days to visit wineries. The barge had seven guests (us) and a crew of three. We were coddled, fed, cared for, and otherwise spoiled. The barge had a fully stocked, self-serve bar that was open 24/7. After the second day, the chef asked if we were likely to continue consuming a whole bottle of Bailey's every night. We said yes, and he stocked up (so we did!). TGV back to Paris for one night, then home. Great trip!...In June, we celebrated 65 years of marriage and love between Linda's folks,

The 2000s

Bob and Gladdie. Even though Bob was in the hospital at the time, he was present in spirit and reminiscences...Also in June, we attended a reunion at the Glass House in Virginia. This was a bachelor pad for junior officers where Jack lived, and is where Jack & Linda had their wedding reception. It was great to see all the knights errant again, gray hair and all... July was a tragic month for us, as Linda's dad, Bob, died on July 8th. We miss his steadfast love, constant support, unquestioning friendship, and, mostly, his quick smile and laughing eyes. Linda lost a loving, and loved, father; Jack lost his role model in life. In Sept., on what would have been Bob's 90th birthday, Gladdie had a memorial service for him, where Jack's old friend, Inky Philips, a retired Army Colonel and Chaplain, helped us through the remembrances...The summer got crazy. Andy accepted a new job, as a Product Manager, with his California company, which required a move to California. Mike was recalled by the U.S. Army, which required that he report to Ft. Jackson, SC, on his way to Iraq...In Sept., we decided to take Linda's mom, Gladdie, to Montross, Virginia, to visit her old house, where we all have many great memories. We asked the other family members if they might want to come along, and most said yes! So, we rented a 5-bedroom house at Stratford Hall, Robert E. Lee's birthplace, and had a great time visiting old friends and remembering good times...In Oct. we closed the sale on the guys' townhouse (they were both gone by then), and rushed off to Linda's reunion at William & Mary (I won't say which, but it's some combination of 0 and 4). It was a great time and W&M even won the football game...In late Oct., our infamous Gourmet Group from Virginia came to FL for a week. Jack took the opportunity to throw himself a surprise birthday party in honor of his becoming a ward of the State (eligible for Medicare at age 65). The surprise was Jack dancing the geezer YMCA with his walker...In early Nov., we went to Orlando for a Sigma Nu reunion, where we watched UF beat FSU. Go Gators!...Thanksgiving (Gracias Dando) was in Sarasota. Mike and Steve made it (the Army let Mike loose for two days), but Andy was in Connecticut for his 10th high school reunion...Mike was doing well as a Senior Consultant at Bearing Point, getting a promotion and raise, until the Army decided that he was crucial to winning the war in Iraq. We all thought Mike would be the oldest Captain in the Army, until he told us about the average age of the other reservists that have been recalled. (We used to fight wars with our young, but I guess that's not the case anymore.) After spending several weeks at Ft. Benning in a big tent with 250 soldiers from his unit (a really big tent!), he is now in a small tent with only 25 soldiers. They have been promised that the showers will be installed any day now. Being one of the leaders of his unit, Mike was selected to go to Kuwait as one of the advance party preparing for their deployment in Iraq, leaving Dec 22nd, so it looks like he will miss this and next Christmas. His dog, Riley, and car are in the tender care of Steve and Stephanie until he returns...Steve had so much fun at Vanderbilt that he didn't want to leave, but they made him graduate anyway. He took a job with American Express in Ft. Lauderdale as a Project Manager. His job is to help AmEx do their processes more effectively. He's only four hours away, which he can make in three hours now that he has Mike's car... Andy decided to live in Palo Alto and commute across the bay to Sygate in Fremont, CA. He now lives several miles from where Jack lived when he went to school there 40 years ago. Hope he has as much fun as Jack did there. Now that he's close to Napa Valley, we've made our plans to go visit him next spring, and frequently thereafter...This year, the joke is on us. Remember that townhouse that we sold Mike and Andy in Reston several years ago, including most of the junk we had accumulated over thirty years? We thought we had found an effortless way to get rid of our junk! Well, they asked us to sell the house, get rid of the junk, and otherwise take care of things while they were busy moving. They left, we did. Whew!.... Well, Joe Crow and Margaret (Jose Cuervo y Margarita) have run out on me, so I'll sign off until next year.

To plagiarize, 2004 was the best of times, it was the worst of times. We are blessed with our family and friends, and would have it no other way. Feliz Navidad!

The PENDRAYS

Early Lawrence family photo: Bob, Susan, Gladys, and Linda

My 65th Birthday Party

The only birthday that I remember clearly was my 65th in Sarasota. I rented the Ca' d'Zan, the home of John Ringling, for the evening. The house was open, privately, to the party guests, and it was fully staffed by docents, who joined the party for dinner. We had dinner and dancing to a live band on the terrace. The back of the house faces west, and we had a spectacular sunset that evening. It was all in honor of my "becoming a ward of the state," as I joined the ranks of Medicare health care. A birthday to remember!

50 Years of Christmas Letters

John Ringling's Ca' d'Zan in Sarasota

CHRISTMAS 2005

Hello out there...Some of you are receiving this annual letter for the 35th time, but we haven't heard anything from any of you folks for about ten years. Could it be a cause-effect relationship?...This year I'm horsing around with a bottle of The Footbolt Shiraz. Footbolt was the name of the race horse whose winnings funded the startup of the d'Arenberg winery in the McLaren Vale near Adelaide, Australia. It's excellent wine, so there will be no neigh-saying...Jan. was a quiet month in which we had the house painted, and so was Feb., and so was March, at least as far as the painting goes. Don't ask...In March, we had the first reunion of folks who lived in the same apt. complex as Jack when he was in grad school at Stanford in '62-'64. Couples came from California and Istanbul, Turkey. Another couple was supposed to come from Germany, but Klaus had a bicycle accident, so they came a little late, in Sept.! Since all the guys were single back then, we didn't talk too much about past exploits, but the only noticeable difference in the guys was the much higher price they were willing to pay for wine...At the end of Mar., we had the second annual reunion of our Connecticut neighborhood gang. Good wine, good food, funny stories, funny people. (In Aug. we had the third annual reunion of this same

327

group at the Homas' in Annapolis. At this rate, we'll all celebrate the reunion of 2050, whether we make it there or not.)...In Apr. and May we set out on our son-to-son trip. We had Steve take us to the cruise ship in Ft. Lauderdale so we could cruise through the Panama Canal to go stay with Andy in Palo Alto. Jack called this the OFA cruise. When you take a 14-day cruise during the school year, where there is lots of sea time and not much to do but eat, drink, and vegetate, it's an OFA cruise, mostly Old Fat Americans. Jack is slowly joining this group. We spent a week in CA with Andy, including 3 days in Napa Valley where Andy showed us some of the better wineries, through cloudy eyes after a while...Back home in late May, we had a bunch of Chinks over for a weekend. These Chinks were all Floridians. You see, Jack's high school fraternity was called Ching Tang, nicknamed Chinks, since Greek letter high-school fraternities were illegal way back then. Some of these Chinks were also grade school and junior high school friends of Jack's. Jack and Bobby Victor had even had matching Hopalong Cassidy cowboy outfits in 5th grade, which they stopped wearing after high school...Jack's stepsister, Betty, drove down from Chattanooga to soak up a little Florida sun, hot tub, and gin & tonic...In June we had guests from Australia, Chris & Chris, yep, Christine and Christopher, both docs to boot. We did a mini-tour of FL, ending with a visit to Cape Canaveral where Discovery was ready to launch. Very impressive use of taxpayers' dollars...During the heat of July, we escaped to Steamboat Springs to visit Florida neighbors, Dee and Jim Gutfreund. It was great, even though it was almost as hot as FL. We made one road trip together to Aspen, where Jack had booked a non-airconditioned hotel. Oops...In Aug. more Aussies came to visit. Roger is a prof at UWA, where Jack taught briefly, and is a member of the Royal Perth Yacht Club. When we were living in Perth, Roger invited Jack to crew for him in a sailing race. They came in dead last, a

The 2000s

first for Roger, but Roger still invited Jack to the RPYC, but only to drink...Sept. started on a sad note. We went to VA to attend the funerals of two dear friends, Anita Nilsen and Dee Lobley, who died within 24 hours of each other. The world will miss the joy that these two folks brought to their friends and relations...The Pfitzners finally arrived in Sept. for the March reunion, better late than never. We left them in charge of the house and dog, actually Mike's dog, Riley, and went to Australia for six weeks. While we were gone, Karin & Klaus got the opportunity to track the various hurricanes, which, fortunately, missed Sarasota... In Oct., as we were returning from Oz, as it's referred to by the Aussies, Wilma blew our way. It missed us, but hit Steve in Ft. Lauderdale. So, we got home, unpacked, and drove to Lauderdale to help Steve cut up the fallen trees in his girlfriend's (Stephanie's) yard. Two weeks without power was a test of their mettle. (We left after one night, taking Riley, the dog, with us.)...In Nov. we drove back to South Florida to deliver Riley and visit Jack's nephew, Sean, in his new apt. in Coral Gables. Jack spends all his time in Coral Gables, where he grew up, saying what used to be where, but ain't no more. We stayed with one of those Chinks while there, the Hucks, and saw other old (better say long-time) friends...We had lots of family here for Thanksgiving. There were 16 of us ranging from 2 months to 89 years, but Andy stayed in CA and Mike stayed in Iraq (against his will; the Army's not very understanding). I counted; we drank two cases of wine that week. That's a lot of thanks. Now that the wine is restocked, we'll hang around here for Christmas. Sure hope the snow isn't too deep in FL. There's even a very small chance that Mike will be back by then, but more likely he'll return in Jan....Jack was recruited onto the vestry at our local Episcopal church, so you know how desperate they must be. He's still taking Spanish classes, but not advancing very well. Since he misses every other semester and forgets everything, he keeps re-taking the same class.

329

In Jan., he'll take Spanish IV for the third time, if the teacher doesn't put him back into Spanish III...Linda spends a lot of time in various church activities, which has folks asking why Jack, and not Linda, is on the vestry. She can often be seen scooting around town in her minivan, doing good deeds and getting things to keep the household functioning. In fact, it's now a new Toyota minivan, leather, moonroof, subwoofer, and all...Mike spent this year in Iraq fighting the bad guys. It's a thankless job, but let's hope the long-term outcome will justify the sacrifices. Someone sure needs to do something about that mess over there, and, if not us, who? Mike did get two weeks' leave in Virginia in October, while we were in Australia, naturally. The Army is certainly not very understanding. He's looking forward to returning to his job at Bearing Point in VA when the Army finally lets him go... Steve learned about FL hurricanes first hand this year. He is now a qualified expert in generator connection and maintenance, yard cleanup, and shutter placement and removal, having practiced the latter several times this year alone. Steve and Stephanie are in the process of relocating to New York City, where Steph is already working at the headquarters of American Express. Steve is posting for Amex jobs there, which is good since they are buying a coop apt there...Andy is enjoying Palo Alto, even though he is working ungodly hours. His company was sold to Symantec and lots of folks have left. Andy has been asked to add the duties of some of these departing folks to his duties. That probably won't encourage him to stay either... Lastly, Riley, our peripatetic granddog, has got to be one of the best traveled dogs in Florida. Being often swapped between Steve & Steph in Ft. Lauderdale and us here is Sarasota, he knows all the rest stops on I-75 intimately. Surely, Riley will be the happiest one to see Mike come back home...The enclosed photo this year is a fraud, being from 2004 rather than 2005. Since Mike spent the year in Iraq and wasn't available for the family photo (the Army is still not very understanding), we used this one taken last year. It shows Steve, Steph, Jack, Linda, Andy, Sean, and Mike outside a winery (big surprise) in Bordeaux, France...The joke this year is on Andy. He suggested that we visit d'Arenberg winery during our tour of Adelaide, which we did. The tasting room was excellent, and they use Riedel glasses for their free tastings of all of their wines (unlike Napa Valley where you pay to taste in cheap glasses). We were given a long list of wines that were available for tasting, and didn't know which to select. So, we called Andy and asked him which we should try. He was not pleased to be stuck in California traffic talking to us as we tasted some of his favorite wines in Adelaide. Guess he won't give us any more recommendations!

We wish you all a Merry Christmas and a 2006 in which we have peace.

The Pendrays

50 Years of Christmas Letters

My Elementary School Days

Normal Park (Chattanooga) 1945-46

Since I did first and half of second grades at Normal Park about 75 years ago, my memory is very cloudy. Other than remembering the walk to school up a steep hill on cold days, I only have two clear memories.

The first one is of a Boy Scout or PTA meeting where a hypnotist performed. My dad was called up on stage to be hypnotized. The guy had my dad leaping around the stage trying to catch butterflies with an imaginary hat. Not like my dad, at all, but he was a team player and a good sport. I'll never know how much was real.

In the second grade, the teacher gave me a stapler to staple some papers onto a bulletin board. I drove a staple right through my little thumb, thereby fastening it securely to the bulletin board. Never will forget that one.

About ten years ago, I found out one of our best friends in Sarasota, Shari Sadler, had been a teacher at Normal Park while her husband, Jack, worked for DuPont in Chattanooga. It was long after my time there, but, still, a small world story.

Toothless cowboy on fake bronco

Sts. Peter & Paul (Miami) 1947-1950

I went to this Catholic school for grades last-half of 2 through 6, and I have a few memories still.

I was on the school safety patrol back before schools had crossing guards. We little kids would just step into the middle of one of the busiest roads in Miami, SW 12th Ave., hold up our hands and stop traffic. Sometimes, one kid would signal to stop while another was signaling to go, and the drivers would just stop and laugh until we sorted it out. Do not try this in Miami today!

In the 5th grade, I had Sister Sebastian, who believed I couldn't be as bad as I acted. When she found out that I was an avid reader, she would have me sit in front of the class and read stories to the class for hours (or so it seemed).

Bobby Peterson used to beat me up. I'm still afraid of Bobby Peterson, wherever he is.

I still can't get the 7's times-table right. Why is 7 so hard?

My best friend in 1949 and '50 was Peter Desjardins, pronounced diss-jar-dens. Remember that.

One day in the mid '70s, I was having lunch in Paris with an old Sigma Nu frat brother of mine from UF, Dennis Germaske. He said he knew a guy that I should meet, a French/American named Pierre Dayjhardan, with whom Dennis had gone to Miami Edison High School. He set up the meet, and, sure enough, it was the same guy, gone French, including the pronunciation of his name. Seems that Peter's folks were French, and he had been raised bi-cultural, which I never knew. Small world.

CHRISTMAS 2006

Hello out there...This is the 36th edition of the never-popular Pendray Christmas letter. Any of you that have actually read all 35 previous editions please check yourself into a psych ward immediately...As usual, I am imbibing a judiciously selected alcoholic beverage to provide me the courage to write this. It goes like this: drink, think, type; drink, drink, think, type; drank, thank, tip; drunk, thunk, thud...This year's courage is coming from a Turley red Zinfandel from Napa Valley. Specifically, this is a 2004 from their Rattlesnake Ridge vineyard, which somehow seems appropriate for me. For the three of you who are not wine experts, Turley is the king of red zins. I know this because one of our Connecticut friends, Lyn Hammers, is a wine expert (and sometime radiologist) and is one of the few folks who is actually allowed to buy Turley wine (their waiting list is huge). So, by "judiciously selected," above, I meant that Lyn selected the wine and let me have some of it. He warned me that it needed to be opened and allowed to breathe a while before drinking. Three and a half minutes seems about right to me...This year really started with a great Christmas present last year. The Army let Mike come home from Iraq in time for

Christmas. We went to get him at the Sarasota airport, and here came Capt. Pendray strolling down the empty corridor in his desert camos with no other passengers in sight. The crew on his Delta flight had asked all the other passengers to stay in their seats while Mike got off the plane, to a hearty round of applause from the passengers and crew. Mike spent a couple of months with us before returning to his job in northern Virginia, which almost made up for the time we missed him while he was in Iraq...Jan. through April were quiet months for us in Sarasota. This is the season of the "snow birds" here, when the population doubles and the traffic increases by a factor of ten. Jack calls these his shut-in months, as he doesn't like to go out. Nevertheless, we did manage to get out to the occasional restaurant and performance, and even partied some with friends and visitors...In May, we took a two-week trip to South Africa, stopping in London to visit with Jack's relative, Kim Pendray, and his wife, Marion. The trip to Africa was a tour set up by the Stanford Alumni Ass'n. Talk about roughing it! We had our own private luxury train in South Africa, and private aircraft to fly to Victoria Falls and Botswana. Every time we did something dirty, like ride in a Land Rover to see animals (I think it's called safari, but it had nothing to do with tents, campfires, or crawly things), they would welcome us back with hot towels and champagne. It was tough, but we held up. We went from Cape Town to Kimberly to Johannesburg/Pretoria to Kruger Nat'l Park to Victoria Falls, Zambia, to the Chobe Nat'l Park in Botswana. I could fill the page with this trip, but will settle for saying that it was exceptional...A week after returning from Africa, we jumped in the minivan and drove to Saratoga Springs, NY, stopping on our way in Virginia, Pennsylvania, and Vermont to visit friends and relatives. After the Saratoga Springs wedding of Kevin

Jaffe, the son of ex-neighbors from CT, our old neighborhood gang from Trumbull, CT, returned to Trumbull where we continued drinking, eating, and otherwise making fools of ourselves for several more days...On our way back home, we stopped in Virginia again to help Mike move into his new apartment in Dunn Loring. He now has nothing in storage, hooray!...In July, we celebrated the 90th birthday of Linda's mom, Gladys. Friends and relatives, including all of her grandkids and great grandkids, came to Tampa from all over the country for the bash. She stills throws quite a party!...In August we stayed home to enjoy the heat and humidity. How did folks live here before air conditioning? Must have really affected their brains. Wait a minute, isn't Jack a Florida native who was raised in Miami before air conditioning? A case in point...Sept. saw us on the road again, starting with a four-day trip to Coral Gables for Jack's high school fraternity reunion. Over 100 old "Chinks" (the nickname for the Ching Tang fraternity, composed entirely of American white guys) gathered to see if they could remember what it was like to be 17. It turns out they could all remember what high school was like, but what happened yesterday was often a mystery...A day after returning from Miami, we set out for Rome to pick up a Princess cruise around Italy and Greece. Mind you, this was no ordinary cruise, as the infamous Gourmet Group from Northern Virginia was aboard. Yep, 16 of us ex-neighbors from Fox Mill estates settled in to see if we could drink all the booze on the ship. In the dining room, we had two tables, and two kinds of reactions from the neighboring tables: they either found other tables or asked to join us. A great trip, and we're all still friends, which shows how big a ship it must have been. The cruise ended in Venice. Ever been there? There are no vehicles, just canals, which means that you get to schlep (ETYMOLOGY: Yiddish *shlepn*, to drag, pull, from Middle Low German) everything around crowded medieval alleys. (Schlep is a great word, and I think it's onomatopoetic. It's exactly the sound one makes when carrying large baggage around the alleys of Venice. In fact, it's hard to carry on a conversation in Venice because of the noise of all the schlepping around you.)...Ten days after returning from Europe, we flew off to Hawaii for the wedding of the other Jaffe son, Chad, whom we call "4" because he spent so much time at our house in CT we made him our fourth son. Those Jaffes managed to marry off both of their sons in one year. We asked them what the formula was, but they wouldn't share...We had a quiet Thanksgiving in FL with Linda's mom and long-time friends Dick and Barbara Abbott...Christmas will be less quiet, as all of the "boys," Stephanie, and Jack's nephew, Sean, will be here. Gotta remember to protect my Turley from them...Other than playing travel agent, studying Spanish (notice that I didn't say "learning" Spanish), and cheering for the Florida Gators, Jack lives a quiet life... Linda still keeps everything running, in spite of Jack's efforts, and has the chance to spend quite a bit of quality time with her mom, who is only 45 minutes away...Mike is back at his job at BearingPoint, and gone from home 12 hours a day to do that. We tried returning Riley to Mike when we went to VA, but he didn't take to doggy day-care, so he's back with his grandfolks in Sarasota. Mike manages to get vacations to FL, when Riley has the best of both worlds: Mike and the swimming pool in the same place...Stephen got a job with American Express in New York, so he moved there. Oh yeah, HE GOT ENGAGED! Stephanie Warren agreed to be his wife and they're planning on a wedding in the spring. They met in the MBA program at Vanderbilt. Stephanie is terrific, and we are beside ourselves with joy. (What does that mean anyway? How can you be beside yourself? A little bit more of this Turley and I might just figure it out.)...Andrew is still in Palo Alto and still with Symantec, the company that acquired his old company. So goes corporate America. They gave him a new job where he only has to work eleven-hour days, so he decided to give it a try...Gotta include Riley, the Labrador. He is pretty well recovered from the pinched nerve in his neck. His vet, his neurosurgeon, and his chiropractor all contributed to his recovery. We're glad to be supporters of the dog care infrastructure of Sarasota...The joke this year is on us, again. On our trip to Hawaii, Jack, the travel planner, planned a three-day stop in San Francisco on the way back to spend time with Andy. Naturally, Andy's company sent him to Florida for the exact same three days! We probably passed in the air coming home. We enjoyed staying in Andy's apartment and visited many old friends in the San Francisco area, including Jack's cousin Jens Hansen and family...Well, the Turley's gone, and I'm gone, thud.

We wish you all a Merry Christmas and a Happy and Prosperous 2007.

50 Years of Christmas Letters

CHRISTMAS 2007

Hello out there...What you have in your hand is America's final answer to the telemarketing and Christmas catalogs problem, the 37th annual Pendray Christmas letter. We have started sending copies of this letter to all of those folks who call or send us unsolicited mail, and they promptly send us a "Do not reply" letter with a promise to remove us from their lists. There is even a rumor that the Democrats are proposing to establish a "Do not write" list to send us for anyone wishing to get off our mailing list. This should sew up the election for them, and force us to outsource this mailing to India, where the do-not-call list does not seem to apply...My liquid courage this year is a bottle of Trapiche Malbec wine from the Mendoza region of Argentina. We discovered Mendoza Malbec during our trip to Buenos Aires last year, or was that this year?; whenever. It's 13.5 % alcohol and costs about $8 at the supermarket. How could that be bad?...Checking over my diary for this year, I see that the most exciting thing we did in Jan. was to have colonoscopies. Mind you, in Sarasota, aka the land of the driverless Cadillac (little old folks driving big cars; get it?), medical procedures are one of the most popular subjects of conversation, along with ailment oneupsmanship (my illness is bigger than yours!). Having passed everything to pass our colonoscopies (an <u>inside</u> joke), we headed for Buenos Aires in February (it was <u>this</u> year, whaddaya know!). Actually, we went to Virginia first and spent several days with long-time friends (I don't say <u>old</u> friends anymore), the Giaquintos. I should probably say long-suffering friends, as we go to Virginia often and usually stay with them. In fact, I think they can declare us as dependents this year. Anyway, we went to Buenos Aires (loved it) and joined a small-ship cruise that floated around the mouth of the Rio Platte for seven days, mostly eating and drinking (included, so just imagine). We must have covered all of 200 miles, but did get to Punta del Este and Montevideo. At the end, we flew to Iguazu Falls, on the border with Brazil, so we have now seen all of the big three: Niagara, Victoria, and Iguazu Falls, all impressive...In March, some of the infamous Gourmet Group from Virginia spent a few days in FL, and many beverages were consumed. Also, we went to Key West for a few days to scout out the site for the rehearsal dinner in May. Oh, yeah, Steve and Stephanie got married! How about that! Steve Pendray and Stephanie Warren were married in Key West on May 26th. Not only did a Pendray boy finally get married, he married a great girl. Stephanie and her family are all terrific, and we are fortunate to have them in our lives. We had told Steve & Steph that the end of May would be very hot and humid in Key West, but, as usual, the "kids" were right, the weather was perfect, as were the parties, wedding, and reception. It was a class act all the way and really fun...Jack went to his 50th high school reunion in Coral Gables right after the wedding. His life-long friend, Inky Philips, rented a two-bedroom suite overlooking Biscayne Bay and invited Jack to join him, so they became the center of the snack and beverage activity of the reunion...After Jack's reunion, we went back to Virginia (staying with the Giaquintos, again!) for the funeral of the husband of Linda's "second mother," Jean Hipps. Bill Hipps was an Air Force general, and the service at Arlington Cemetery was as impressive as the life of the man it honored...After having traveled <u>away</u> from Florida during the beautiful winter months, we decided to spend the summer <u>in</u> Florida. Stupid! It sure is hot and humid here in the summer! Jack got bad cabin fever, so, in Sept., we gave up and rented a small house in Cashiers, NC, for a week to check out the area. The weather was cool and Jack had an old friend (actually younger than Jack), Tom Prebianca, and his wife, Aleta, there to show us around. We've rented a house there for the month of July next year, but haven't yet figured out what to do about June and August...Also in Sept., Linda slipped off for a weekend in New York with a group of the gals from the Virginia Gourmet Group. If spending money is any measure, they had a fantastic time...Linda then slipped off again with her mom for a weekend with relatives in So. California in Oct. Since her mom paid for this trip, Jack has no idea how much fun they had, but the hearsay is rampant... Mike came to visit us in Oct., or so we say. We know he really came to schmooze with his dog, Riley, who stays with us due to Mike's demanding work schedule. He came for three days, but stayed for five, due to canceled flights (ain't flying fun nowadays!). We (especially Riley) were delighted to have him a couple of extra days and he was able to join us for our anniversary steak dinner. Yep, we celebrated 41 years of happy marriage, attributed mainly to Saint Linda's (that's what our Virginia friends call her) patience with Jack (I won't say what he's called by our friends)...In Nov., we went back to Virginia (yep, stayed with the Giaquintos again. See?)

for the wedding of Scott Homa, son of Ken and Kathy Homa, our neighbors in CT. Another great wedding and it was good to see our old CT gang there...After coming home, we took off to spend Thanksgiving with Andy in San Francisco. Naturally, we went via Chicago. Really. In his summer cabin fever, Jack booked us on what he calls a 1920s trip. We stayed at the Palmer House in Chicago, took a deluxe Pullman train to San Francisco, and stayed at the Stanford Court Hotel on Knob Hill for four days. Andy came in from Palo Alto and spent three days in the hotel with us. We did all the touristy things and had a ball. We had Thanksgiving dinner at Julius' Castle restaurant on Telegraph Hill overlooking the bay. Jack and Linda had the traditional turkey dinner and Andy had the very traditional osso buco (from the Italian Thanksgiving tradition, I guess)...Steve arrived on Sat., Dec. 8, for a long weekend with us. We suspect he also really wanted to schmooze with Riley, and we sure enjoyed his visit. He probably will need the R&R, as the whole family is going to New York for Christmas, and Christmas dinner is at Steve and Stephanie's apt. Should make for a close family...Linda is still busy keeping the house running and keeping up with the trips that Jack planned during his summer cabin fever. She also gets to spend time with her mom, Gladys, who lives less than an hour away and who celebrated her 91st this year. Gladys is still sharper than all of us put together!...Jack spends his time planning trips, and then taking them...Mike is still in Virginia working for Bearing Point. So far, the Army has not called him again, for which we are all thankful...Steve and Stephanie are still in New York working for American Express. We are looking forward to sharing a bit of their lifestyle over Christmas...Andy is still working at Symantec and living in Palo Alto. After the acquisition of his prior company by Symantec, he seems happy with the new environment, and they seem to recognize what a valuable resource he is...This year the joke is on Jack. After five years of studying Spanish, he tried to use some of it in Punta del Este to order three scoops of ice cream and wanted to pay in U.S. dollars. It seems that the server understood that he wanted three different flavors and to pay in Brazilian reals. The ice cream melted by the time they got that straightened out!...Well the Malbec bottle is as empty as my brain, so I'll close before the computer monitor becomes too fuzzy.

We wish you all a Merry Christmas and a Happy and Prosperous 2008.

The Pendrays

Mike, Andy, Stephanie, Steve, Gladys Lawrence, Linda, Jack

CHRISTMAS 2008

Hello out there...I've been asked to keep this letter to one page (or much less); however, my tests indicate that most folks my age would have trouble reading it compressed to one page, so two pages it is. This is the 38th edition of the Pendray Christmas Letter, and those of you who have received it before are probably already on your way to the trash bin with it, thereby demonstrating good taste and wisdom...The liquid language loquacity lubricant this year is a bottle of Drylands Sauvignon Blanc from the Marlborough region of New Zealand. It's exorbitant price of darn nearly $10 is justified by the high-tech screw top which will allow me to efficaciously re-cap the bottle when this letter is completed, if there is any wine left (fat chance!). Since it's a white wine, I have to keep the bottle in the frig and walk there for refills. (I'm on my first trip there now.)...We finished last year with a flourish by spending Christmas in New York City (spending being the operative word). In fact, all of us went, Jack, Linda, Mike, Sean (Jack's nephew), and Andy. Since Steve and Stephanie's one bedroom apt seemed a little tight for all of us, we stayed at

349

a Holiday Inn across the street from them, where we could actually see into their apt from our rooms. After the second day, their blinds never opened again. We saw the Rockettes' Christmas show and *Jersey Boys* and ate at Café Un Deux Trois, several great neighborhood restaurants close to S & S's apt, and had our last lunch at Tavern on the Green. On Christmas Day, two friends of S & S's joined all of us for a spectacular dinner that Steph and Steve somehow prepared and served in their one-bedroom apt. Balanchine could not have choreographed a better ballet than the one of Steph and Steve preparing this huge meal in their one-butt-at-a-time apt kitchen...(walk to frig for refill)....Jan. and early Feb. were quietly spent in Sarasota, and Andy squeezed in a visit of several days. Toward the end of Feb., our long-time friends, Karin and Klaus Pfitzner, arrived from Germany to care for Riley, the Labrador, while we went off to South America for three weeks. The good part for K&K is that a house and pool came with Riley, along with Florida weather...We headed off on a tour/cruise/expedition of Chile, Easter Island, Peru, and Ecuador. Saw lots of fascinating things, like really big stone statues, archaeological sites, cities, and wildlife, including blue-footed boobies (not what you think, buster, it's a bird!). Mike came and relieved the Pfitzners of dog care, so he was here for a few days after we returned...In April, we picked up Linda's mom, Gladys, in Tampa, and drove over to spend a weekend in Melbourne with Jean Hipps, Linda's "second mom." We spent a lot of that weekend remembering how many parties we had shared together, and we continued the tradition...(Dance to frig for refill)...In May, we threw Riley in the minivan and drove to Virginia to visit friends and Mike

350

and to go to the Baltimore wedding of Jay Homa, who used to live next to us in CT. Great wedding and great friends...Steve & Steph came to visit Riley for a few days in June. We were also here, so we got to spend some quality time together. (We often say that we wouldn't see any of the kids if Riley wasn't here. He's quite well loved by all.)...July gets really hot and humid in Florida, so we have joined the migration to the mountains of NC for July. (It was Riley's first use of his custom-made minivan cushions. Between liking the cool weather in NC and traveling ensconced in his cushions, he wouldn't get out of the minivan for several hours after we returned home.) We rented a house for the month and hosted family, friends, and some of Jack's old high-school fraternity brothers and their wives...August was still hot in FL, so we got together with some of Jack's college fraternity brothers, and wives, and went "tubing" in the Ichetucknee River, north of Gainesville, FL. This is an old tradition at the University of Florida were you get in an inner tube with drinks and drift down a crystal clear, cold river until you can't feel anything anymore...(Ramble to frig for refill)...Sept. was the month when we checked off one of the items on Jack's bucket list: we walked into, and rafted out of, the Grand Canyon. There were nine of us: Linda, Jack, Steve, Steph, Carl Warren (Steph's dad), Sean, Andy, Kim Truong (Andy's girlfriend), and Susan Harvey (Linda's sister). Six wonderful days of strenuous activity and thrills. The tour leaders even baked Linda a birthday cake in the canyon. The trip was just too fantastic to describe. We combined it with stays, coming and going, at Rich and Linda Jaffe's terrific house in Scottsdale. More great old friends...October was quiet again, mostly because Jack's knees were still recovering from the canyon. He's glad he didn't wait any longer to do the canyon, and a little earlier would have been better...Nov. is the month of that uniquely American holiday, Thanksgiving. This year, everyone came! There were 30 folks here, spread over two houses as Linda's sister rented a house close to us for the week. It was quite a feast and gabfest. Mike stayed here for two weeks after Thanksgiving, which gave his dog, Riley, a chance to follow him around...(Wobble to frig for refill)... Jack is still studying Spanish; not learning, just studying. He rides his bike around Sarasota, dodging the old folks driving their cars while napping...Linda is now famous on Siesta Key. As training for the Grand Canyon hike, she spent every August morning walking around the Key in full hiking gear: boots, backpack, water bottles, etc. Just ask anyone about the "crazy hiker lady." She spends lots of time on church activities and sees her mom fairly often. Gladdie is 92 years young this year, and still sharper than the rest of us...Mike is still working at Bearing Point, which has started sending him to interesting places like Japan and Guam (Guam?). He's the only member of the family that was smart enough to go to cash, so he missed the market crash. I think he's in the wrong business! Mike chose not to do the Grand Canyon trip. He said he had done enough hiking and camping in Iraq...Steve and Stephanie are still employed at American Express, no small feat given the current state of the financial industry. Between family trips and friends' weddings, they traveled a lot this year...Andy is also still employed by the same company, Symantec. His girlfriend, Kim, took Mike's place on the Grand Canyon trip, and she definitely had more fun than anyone, except maybe Linda's sister, Susan. OK, it's a tie, they were both outlandish…Riley is 11 ½ and going strong. He is the star of his own webcam, which was set up by Steve and Steph so they all could watch him sleep in my office… The joke this year is on Steve. While we were in Cashiers, NC, this July, he came to visit us (Riley, really) for a few days when Steph had a business trip to Phoenix. His flight home was an afternoon non-stop from Charlotte to NYC, so we stopped at Chimney Rock to do a little hiking on his way to Charlotte. It was really hot and humid, so the hike turned into a sweaty affair. No problem for Steve: quick flight to NY, shower, and to bed. Delta had other ideas. They canceled his non-stop, put him on a flight to Atlanta, canceled his flight from Atlanta, lost his luggage, and told him he was on his own til the next day. Ain't flying getting better and better!…May your investments be all in cash and your job be indispensable!…(Crawl to bed for a nap)…

We wish you all a Merry Christmas and a secure and sane 2009!

The Pendrays

The Crystal Room of The Tavern on the Green in Central Park,
New York City

My Eleven Jobs

(I clearly had a problem holding a job!)

Headquarters, USAF, The Pentagon

June 1964 – June 1968

Please Take this Job

Towards the end of my studies at Stanford, I was sleeping off a good party the night before when the phone next to my bed rang in the early morning, say 7 a.m. I groggily picked up the phone and growled "Hello" into it. A man's firm voice on the other end said, "Lieutenant Pendray, please." Well, that got my attention because few people knew I was in the Air Force, much less a lieutenant, but rather just knew me as a Stanford student who partied a lot. Anyway, I cleared my voice a bit and responded, "That is I." He announced that he was Col. Gregg calling from HQ USAF in the Pentagon. Shocked, I actually sat up at attention in bed and said, "Yes, sir." Col. Gregg said that he was the commander of the USAF Data Services Center (DSC), which supplied the computer and software support to HQ USAF and to the Office of the Secretary of Defense (OSD), Bob McNamara being in that job at the time. Gregg went on at some length extolling the virtues and excitement of working in the Data Services Center at the Pentagon, and then asked, in a supplicating manner, if I might be interested in coming there as my assignment after Stanford. I replied that it sounded very interesting, but that I was a bit confused. I told him that, while being new to the ways of the Air Force, I didn't think it worked this way and I thought that orders just arrived and you went. He laughed, and explained that junior officers—lieutenants and captains—were very rare in the Pentagon, and they could not be assigned there without agreeing to it. So, I agreed, "Yes, Sir!" and got orders for my first real job, a lulu.

Systems Programming at HQ USAF

I was assigned to the systems programming department in the DSC as a systems programmer. Systems programming was responsible for the software that was fundamental to the operation of the computer: the operating system and its ancillary systems. I was given the job of helping improve the performance of the systems and procedures. We didn't actually write the code for the operating system, IBM did that, but we did control and teach how it was used, and diagnose problems. Additionally, when they found out that I knew COBOL, I became the systems programmer for COBOL. This was 1964, and COBOL was still new to DSC, but it was a DOD-dictated programming language of preference. Most of DOD's programs were in Fortran, assembler, or a special in-house developed system called TRIM. My job was to help them convert all of the non-scientific applications to COBOL, which was most of the applications for both USAF and OSD. I was responsible for the COBOL compiler maintenance and use, setting up training in COBOL for the applications programmers, and leading one of the first big COBOL-based projects, the automation of the budgeting and review process for the Command, Control, and Communications (CC&C) budget of the Air Force.

I could go on for hours about my experiences at the Pentagon, but, instead, I'll just tell some amusing things that happened there, in their context.

Pentagon Stories

Al Merten, my roommate and friend, burned through his Stanford MS in a year (a very bright guy), so he was still a 2nd Lt. when he got to the Pentagon. One day, Al and I were walking down one of the corridors of the Pentagon and passed a 4-star admiral and his entourage. In the Pentagon, there was no saluting nor wall-hugging, so we just breezed on by, until we heard someone loudly say, "Lieutenants!" Since we were the only lieutenants within hearing and seeing range, we thought maybe he meant us, so we turned around and the 4-star commanded, "Come here," which we sure did. We were wondering what the hell we had done wrong now, so we marched up and said, "Sir?" The 4-star reached out and rubbed Alan's 2nd Lt.'s gold bar and said, "I haven't seen one of those in many years; I just had to touch it." Everyone laughed and we went our merry way, whew.

There was a full colonel, Bud Laedtke, in charge of the physical facilities of DSC: the computer hardware, the magnetic tape vault (huge!), and just about everything but software. This was a big job, almost as big as Col. Gregg's, to whom Laedtke reported. There was a huge room of computers, with two 7094 II's, two 7080's, a dozen 1401's, and scads of punched card handling and printing hardware. Col. Laedtke had an executive officer,

Major John, and the two of them shared a large office with their admin assistant, Evie Gemmel, with a glass wall looking into the computer room. Col. Laedtke asked Col. Gregg if he could borrow me for a few months to help him increase the efficiency of his computer operations and tape vault storage. A desk and a big high-backed executive swivel chair just like theirs was squeezed in for me in their shared office, and Laedtke asked me to just observe and listen to what went on and give him my feedback and ideas, which I did. I was not used to the fancy executive chair, and one day in the middle of one of the Col.'s staff meetings, I leaned back too far and went crashing down behind my desk. On my knees, this very red-faced lieutenant peeked over the top of his desk to see a stunned group all trying not to laugh. One day, Maj. John told me that I had on a non-regulation name tag and that someone would say something to me about it, at which Col. Laedtke and Mrs. Gemmel lifted their heads to see my response. My name tag was from my ROTC days, and was slightly different. I was still a 1st Lt. and John was a senior Major, but, me being obnoxious me, I responded, "Who would say something?" Obviously, John was saying something about it, but he stammered around a bit and blurted out, "Col. Cloninger might say something." Well, I had just taken a field trip with Frank Cloninger, so I

359

marched down to his office, showed him my name tag and asked him if he saw any problem with it. He said it was fine, so I marched back into Col. Laedtke's office and told Maj. John that Col. Cloninger thought my name tag was fine. Laedtke and Gemmel almost fell out of their chairs. John was a nice, but frustrated guy who resented my being in the office with them and let me know it. I now regret embarrassing him like that, but it makes a funny Pentagon story.

One day I was sitting at my desk in the programmers' bullpen and the head of DSC, Col. Sam Cravens, who had replaced Col. Gregg, came in and stood by my desk. I was deeply involved in programming and didn't notice him until some of the other officers called my attention to his presence. I should have stood up, but was so flustered that I forgot to, so Sam just sat down in my guest chair. Col. Cravens was a good guy, and we had become somewhat friendly, even though I was a Cpt. and he a full-bull, but I should have stood, dumb me. Anyway, he asked me if I remembered that he was giving me an Air Force Commendation Medal the next day? (The senior civil servant who headed the CC&C budget process had recommended Alan Shapiro and me for the medal because the COBOL budget automation process had worked quite well.) Everyone in the bullpen could hear our conversation, and I saw all the programming pencils stop moving. I replied that I sure did remember and said that Linda was coming in for the ceremony. He then asked if I was aware that I would need to wear a uniform at the ceremony, to which I said yes. He then said that it had to be a class A blue dress uniform, and he paused. A bit perplexed as to where this was all going, I just kinda nodded and stared. Then he asked rather loudly, "Do you have one?" The whole bullpen broke out in laughter. You see, at Stanford and at the Pentagon, uniforms were not required, so I seldom wore one, except in the summer when the open-collared uniform was allowed; otherwise, it was coat and tie or class A uniform, and I chose coat and tie. I always said that the class A blue uniform was designed to be used everywhere, so it was comfortable nowhere. Anyway, this ends my story of the only day in six years of service that I had to wear my uniform, to get a medal.

B/Gen. Bill Pratt was in charge of all USAF computer activities and I have several stories with him.

One time I had to brief Gen. Pratt on a subject that I now forget, and I had prepared a set of flip charts with lots of details and content, which pretty much represented everything I was going to say. I started the presentation by reading the contents of the first flip chart, and turned the page to the second one. Gen. Pratt stopped me and asked if all the pages contained what I was going to say, and I said "Yes, sir." He said, "I can read faster than you can talk, so be quiet and turn the pages when I say. If I have any questions, I'll stop and ask them." He had no questions, but, at the end, he referred me to Lt. Col. Dick Bassler to teach me how to make a presentation. Dick taught me a lot and became a good friend.

Being a lowly Brigadier General, a one star, in the Pentagon, Gen. Pratt was not entitled to an officer aide, which generals usually have. Whenever a social event happened that required an aide, Gen. Pratt would call on one of us junior officers in the DSC to serve in that function. He called on me twice. On one instance, I was standing next to Gen. Pratt while he was talking to the Comptroller of the Air Force, a 3-star named Gen. Milton. Now, the Asst. Secy. of the Air Force had asked the DSC to prepare a short course on computer concepts and systems analysis to be given to the general staff, who were being driven crazy by Sec. Def. Bob McNamara with all his talk of computers and systems analysis. I was one of the 3-man team who was chosen to prepare and give this short course, and Lt. Gen. Milton was one of the folks who took the course, over his lunches. He ate, we talked.

Anyway, Pratt notices that Milton's drink is empty, takes it from Milton and hands it to me to go get it refilled. That's what aides do, so I start off to the bar, but Milton grabs his glass away from me, hands it back to Pratt, and says, "You get it for me, Bill. Jack is my professor and I have some questions for him." I'm thinking, "Sh—, I'm a dead duck!" Pratt, being the cool dude that he was, reaches out to the first junior officer going by, hands him the glass with instructions, and continues in our conversation with Milton. All ended well, thanks to B/Gen. Bill Pratt.

Having survived four years in the Pentagon, I looked at my probable career path in the Air Force and realized that I would probably bounce from AF Command headquarters to Pentagon and back all of my career. This seemed to me to be a high-stress, low-reward path to oblivion, so I reluctantly decided to resign. I was a regular officer, not a reserve officer, so the Air Force did not have to accept my resignation. It being the middle of the war in Vietnam, I was worried, but my resignation was accepted, and I've always thought that Bill Pratt may have had to approve it, and did. My last social event as an Air Force officer was a boat cruise on the Potomac with the Data Services Center staff. Gen. Pratt was the guest brass aboard and he gave a speech. At the end of the speech, he said something to the effect that the Air Force does not usually recognize resigning officers, but he wanted to make an exception for me. He thanked me for my service and wished me good luck. Then he made some crack about something in my apparel, to which I responded that at least I didn't wear goofy golfing hats on boat trips. Pratt was a big golfer and had one of his hats on. He kinda scowled and called me up front and center. I was thinking, crap, I've done it again. When I got up front, he took his hat off and put it on my head and said, "Now you do!" I wore it the rest of the cruise. The hat was way too big for me, but I kept it for years with great pride and fond memories.

My last duty in the Pentagon was as a computer selection officer on loan to the Air Force computer acquisition department. When I reported to the full colonel (whose name I forget) who ran the department, he welcomed me and briefed me on their operation. At the end of the briefing, he said that I had to come in early every Thursday and make the coffee for the department. I protested that I was a Captain and thought that my coffee-making days were behind me. He said, "Shut up. My day to make the coffee is Monday." That's the Pentagon, where rank is everywhere and often means little. When the Colonel returned me to

DSC, he did write a good review of my work for him, so I guess my coffee was pretty good.

In summary, my days at the Pentagon were stressful and frustrating, but it was a great experience and school. As one of our Air Force officers, Marty Binkin, said one day, "The Pentagon experience can only be appreciated over your shoulder, looking back." Once again, I was protected from myself and mentored by many fine senior officers, including General Pratt, Colonels Gregg, Craven, Laedtke, Burrell (my boss, mentor, and role model), and many others. Belated thanks, guys.

ASSIST

June 1968–January 1970

When I was released from the USAF in June of 1968, ASSIST had already been founded by nine of us Air Force officers who all planned to resign or retire within the year. It was the heyday of computer services and software development companies, and 20 years before the Internet dotcom boom (and bust). Several of us worked full time, others moonlighted, and two did other things while they waited to see if the company survived. I was the Chief Technical Officer and VP. We also hired some of our active-duty Pentagon USAF friends as moonlighters, and, eventually, full-time employees. None of us had any business experience, but we had a great deal of brains and computer expertise at our beck and call. That wasn't enough.

We managed to win two major contracts. One was with the Brookings Institution for whom we developed a system to give easy access to the data of the 1970 census. We were paid by the hour, billed lots of hours, and made a reasonable profit. The second was a contract to automate the union contract at the DuPont plant in Waynesboro, VA, (exactly 10 miles from where I sit today as I write this 50 years later!). This was a fixed-price contract and the cost estimate was made by the ASSIST CTO, me. I grossly under-estimated the size and difficulty of the job, and we lost a ton of money trying to deliver as promised. (This was the first of many lousy development estimates in my life.) When the Brookings job finished, and all we had left was the money pit at DuPont, we defaulted on the contract and liquidated the ASSIST company.

When we realized that we were in deep doo-doo, we had set out to find some venture investors in the D.C. area. While it was late in the game and we were deep in the hole, we did have a chance. If we could finish the DuPont job in Waynesboro, there were several other DuPont plants waiting to buy the system, which would have been very profitable. So, we put together a slick presentation explaining this opportunity, and showing how hard we had worked for little compensation for two years. At one of the presentations, after we had given our pitch, the wizened potential investor looked at us and said, "What else have you put into your company other than stupidity?" We got the message and closed the company.

While at high cost and personal sacrifice, we all learned a lot about doing business, which most of us put to good use later. Nevertheless, there were two lessons that I did not learn at ASSIST, nor ever: How to interview and hire a good salesperson (who may only be very good at selling him/herself), and how to estimate a systems development project (a black art never fully conquered by me, nor by the industry).

CDSIL

February 1970–October 1970

A successful Washington-based professional services company (a rent-a-programmer body shop) named Computer Data Systems Inc. (CDS) formed a joint venture with the UK's mini-version of IBM, named International Computers Limited (ICL). The

JV was called Computer Data Systems International Limited (CDSIL) and the objective was to open a chain of computer services companies across continental Europe using ICL mainframe computers. The CEO, Joe, was one of the founders of CDS and was one of those salesmen who was very good at selling himself, and hot air. (I learned later that he was being forced out of CDS when he formed the joint venture CDSIL, and the JV was structured so that CDS had no liability from it.)

Being out of work, despondent from the failure of ASSIST, and having always wanted to live in Europe, specifically Germany, I was easy prey for Joe and accepted the CTO job at CDSIL, based in Paris, which was not exactly Germany, but close. Off I went to Paris to see it for myself, and there was, indeed, an office, a nice computer room with a big ICL 1904 in it, several employees, and an office for me. Based upon this in-depth analysis, I called Linda back in Falls Church, informed her that I was pleased with the new job and facilities, and asked her to sell the house and get ready to move to Paris, and, oh, don't forget to include bringing our 3-month-old son, Mike. She did all that, so that when I returned to the U.S. we were able to close the house sale, pack up, and schedule the flights for her and Mike before I had to fly back to Paris.

CDSIL had offices and computers in Paris and Geneva, a complete staff at the "C" level (e.g., CEO, CFO, etc.), some employees, and, apparently no customers. I spent my time learning the ICL operating system and French, the operating system being elementary and incomplete, while French was very difficult and complicated. I had taken one quarter of German at Stanford to see what a foreign language was like, having never had a language in school, but my twelve words of German only got me into trouble in France. One of the things that Joe told me was that he wanted me to help manage the Geneva shop, and that it was crucial that I go to Geneva at least every three months, and to be sure to get my passport stamped each time. We spent several months looking for customers, installing computers, hiring employees, and spending ICL's investment money, when ICL started to get itchy and threatened to cut off the funds, or so I heard.

One day near the end of the summer, Joe announced that he needed to return to Washington to solidify additional funding for CDSIL and would return soon. Well, when he got back to Washington, he called his administrative assistant back in Paris and told her to tell everyone that he wasn't coming back, the company was closed, our recent paychecks would bounce, and the company credit cards that we all carried were canceled. That was all true. He had returned with his wife and family, and shipped their household back. Moreover, it seemed that CDSIL was operating illegally in France, we were all illegal immigrants working illegally, and we were on tourist visas, which we had to renew by leaving the country every three months. Golly! There we were, stranded and illegal. Fortunately, we had sold our house in Falls Church and had that profit in the Bank of America branch in Paris, so I decided to stay and try to find work, as we were fascinated by France and the friends we had made there.

TECSI-GSI

January 1971–August 1979

TECSI

After CDSIL collapsed, ICL offered me a job as the head of its operating system team. The OS was called George III, so maybe they felt it appropriate that an American lead it since we had conquered George III once already. It was based in London, which was tempting; however, the salary of 5,000 pounds a year was not.

From our attempts to acquire customers in Paris for CDSIL, I had met a few folks in the computer services business, and one of them contacted me after it became known that CDSIL had folded. He knew a guy who was helping a French company staff a new startup, and they wanted to meet me. I met first with two of the young founders of the startup, TECSI, both of whom had just returned from the U.S. where they each earned PhDs, one from Berkeley and one from Stanford. Since I had an early Computer Science degree from Stanford and also knew how to spell COBOL, they offered me a deal. They would pay for me to go to the Berlitz total immersion French school for the month of December if I would agree to accept a job offer from them in January, contingent on their winning either of the two major contracts they were in the process of bidding on. Having nothing better to do, and liking the guys I had met, I accepted.

December at Berlitz was the hardest month of my life! I discovered that I am far from gifted in languages, and the 12-hour days of Berlitz were excruciating. At the end of December, I was absolutely exhausted, but I could ask for the bathroom and some other things in French. On the other side of the deal, TECSI had won both of the large contracts, so I was hired. One of the contracts was from the government and involved helping the French customs evaluate and select a general contractor to automate the air freight customs operations at the new airport under construction at Roissy en France, now called CDG. The second was from Air France and also involved automating its air freight customs processing. I was assigned to the government customs contract.

There were two serious bids that had to be evaluated for the CDG air freight customs job, one from Computer Sciences and one from SESA. (Little did I know that I would eventually work for both of these companies.) The project was a major effort and the proposals were quite different. CSC had just completed a similar project for the UK, and its proposal, based on IBM computers, was short and clear. SESA had never done such a project, and its proposal was large, wordy, confusing, and more expensive, but it was from a French company and based on the French national computers from CII. No one involved, neither the government client nor the consultants engaged, had a clue as to how to evaluate the bids and decide, except for me. Having spent about half my time in the Pentagon doing exactly this, I was an expert! So, I really did take charge of the process, in English, with translation and presentation help from the other TECSI guys, and we developed the appropriate cost/performance formulas and applied them to the proposals. Needless to say, the CSC bid was twice as good at half the price, because the company had just successfully done it in the UK. Enter French politics, exit Jack Pendray. The French awarded the job to CSC, with SESA in an overseeing role, and using the French

CII computers. As part of the job, CSC had to largely expand and improve the operating system for the CII computers, as well as install their application. It actually worked out well, except for the French taxpayer, as CSC was paid properly for its work, SESA learned a lot about project management from CSC, CII got its operating system brought up to snuff by CSC, and the customs got a system that worked. A rare success story of large computer systems integration projects.

From there, I went onto a project assisting one of France's largest banks in increasing the performance of its systems. After analyses, we had the company add a high-speed swapping drum to its configuration, by which the company avoided acquiring another complete system from IBM. They saved lots of francs and were quite pleased.

My last major project was for a sister company of TECSI within the CGE group (which had acquired a controlling interest in TECSI), a telephone switch manufacturer called Alcatel. Alcatel was one of two or three telephone equipment companies charged with leaping a generation of telephone network switches to bring France out of the telephonic dark ages into the future. TECSI had a major role in the development of France's first computer-based telephone switches, both the small regional and

373

large nodal switches. During the start-up phase of the project, I headed TECSI's software team for the big switch. Both switches were quite successful and vaulted France from third-world to state-of-the-art telephone networks.

I was made a "Senior," the TECSI name for a VP, after my second year, and Directeur General Adjoint, the EVP and COO, after my third year. The founding CEO Jacques Bentz continued as CEO but was promoted to a larger job within our direct parent company, GSI, so I effectively ran the company except for intra-company political matters, where Jacques led and protected me. My promotion to general manager, as an American in a very French large company, was unusual, but that is a different story told elsewhere in my written ramblings.

One of the initiatives I am most proud of was TECSI-Week. As I had found out at ASSIST and CDSIL, technology-trained folks are usually poor business people, but are quick learners. My first year as GM of TECSI, I decided to take all 30 TECSI employees, with their families, to Istanbul for a week of training in sales methodology and client management. They were all skeptical of this, as sales is seen as a low-life activity by professional people in France, and elsewhere. I hired a professional large-account sales organization that taught the Xerox method of selling value. After the week, there were 30 folks who had caught the fever and became experts in selling, and then delivering, value to clients. In fact, one of the most aggressively opposed consultants, a near founder, was so persuaded that he spent the rest of his fruitful career teaching sales methodology in France. The second year, we all went to Athens, Greece, for a week to learn how to organize and give presentations, both written and spoken. It was given by a consultant who taught it to McKinsey consultants. Another watershed event for the technical folks, including me. TECSI-Week was so successful that the parent company, GSI, which had thought it a giant boondoggle when I first proposed TECSI-Week, later adopted the idea as GSI-Week.

My last year in France, TECSI was consolidated with some other GSI software and consulting activities throughout Europe into the Consulting and Software Services (CSS) division, about 100 skilled professionals, which I led. Thanks to the political, financial, and management strength of the Compagnie Generale d'Electricite (CGE) group (now called Alcatel), of which GSI was a subsidiary, all went very well and work was a rewarding pleasure. TECSI was my best job ever!

One recent story of which I am proud. In May of 2019, Linda and I rented an apartment in Paris for two weeks with the purpose of finding and visiting with some of the founders and near-founder employees of TECSI. We had ten of them join us for small lunches, dinners, and house parties, many of them coming from distant parts of France for the occasion. Each had his own "Jack Story" to tell, some of them even positive. The person who opposed the sales training, and then spent the rest of his career doing just that, Raymond Maugey, was one of them. He told Linda that I had changed his life for the better, high praise. He also told Linda that when they hired me at TECSI, he had made the comment to the founders, "Jack has been instrumental in two failed companies. What could go wrong?"

General de Service Informatique (GSI)

On my return to the U.S. in July of 1975, I was still head of CSS in Europe, and I founded GSI-USA with the idea of using it to do acquisitions for GSI in the U.S. Since I was in Europe over half the time, my efforts in the U.S. got off to a slow start. On top of it all, I was given the responsibility for chairing the annual GSI-Week in Venice, Italy, during my first year back.

The age of the mini-computer was in its early phase, so I thought it would be good to find an acquisition and application that got GSI involved in this growing technology. I settled on the application of business management for small and medium distributors of discrete products. It was an application that had many thousands of possible clients worldwide, and for which mini-computers were a very cost-efficient solution.

Transcomm Data Systems was a small 20-person company outside Pittsburgh that was founded by some young computer whizzes recently graduated from Carnegie Mellon. They had exactly the type of system that I was looking for, running on PDP 11 mini-computers. They agreed to be acquired by GSI-USA and joined the GSI group. I also had found a sole operator with some complementary software in Denver, and he became the distributor of the Transcomm software in the west. I left GSI the next year, but I was pleased to see on a much later visit to GSI in Paris that the Transcomm system had become one of GSI's successful international products.

One final story of my GSI days. At the first GSI-Week after Transcomm joined GSI, the president of Transcomm and his wife joined with all the other GSI managers in Corsica. The Chairman of the Board of GSI, a bigwig from the parent company

CGE, was the guest of honor, and the Transcomm president's wife was seated next to him at the evening gala. She would have been in her 20s, and he in his 50s, I think. When the dancing started, not many people hit the dance floor, and she asked the chairman why folks didn't dance much in France. He promptly asked her to dance, whisked her away, and whirled around the dance floor with her in high style. She had the pleasure of dancing with a great gentleman, Edouard Balladur, who was to be the Prime Minister of France from 1993 to 1995, and unsuccessful presidential candidate in 1995!

Datagram vs. Virtual Circuit

Circa 1974

First, some background. The Internet is based on packet switched (PS) data networks that are all interconnected. The first significant PS network was the ARPANET, funded by the Defense Advanced Research Projects Agency (DARPA) and directed by Dr. Larry Roberts, an MIT genius. The Internet infrastructure was based on ARPANET and its technology, to which were later added the interface of browsers to give us the World Wide Web. Prior to the PS data networks, data networks were based on switches that connected transmission wires to form point-to-point physical circuits, similar to long-distance telephone technology. In PS technology, data messages were broken into small packets and the packets were sent over the network to their destination end point, where they were re-assembled into the message. ARPANET used a method of packet switching, called datagram, where each packet was sent into the network and made its way through the network nodes independently of other packets from the same message. When, and if, all the packets arrived at the end point, they were re-assembled into the message. A competing technique was developed in which the network assigned resources in nodes to a message, and the packets were all then sent in order through the network using the same path, called a virtual circuit.

In 1974, the French telephone company PTT was seeking suppliers that could build the Transpac PS network for public use. I thought TECSI/GSI/CGE was well positioned to seek this business because we were a preferred supplier for the PTT's telephone network. At that time, the clear leader in PS technology was ARPANET, so I contacted the prime contractor, Bolt Beranek and Newman (BBN), with the idea of using its technology to form a bid for the PTT's Transpac. BBN informed me that it was forming a subsidiary company, Telenet, for the purpose of selling PS networks, and data transmission services over Telenet's proprietary PS network, to be built, and that I should contact Telenet's president, Dr. Larry Roberts of ARPANET fame. Larry and his sidekick, Dr. Barry Wessler, also of ARPANET fame, received me well and we agreed to jointly bid the Transpac project with TECSI/GSI/CGE as prime contractor, and using the Telenet, i.e., modified ARPANET, technology. With lots of help from TECSI/GSI/CGE people of power and connections, we set up a day-long meeting in Paris with the PTT to make an informal presentation to gauge their reaction. I arranged for four of the key ARPANET founders to make presentations, and, hopefully, wow and convince the PTT. Doctors Larry Roberts, Barry Wessler, Leonard Kleinrock, and Howard Frank were all participants, and all were impressive folks.

On the PTT side, there was an internal technical struggle over datagram versus virtual circuit. The PTT had a research datagram PS network up and running, with strong supporters, but the head of the Transpac project, Dr. Remi Despres, was a strong supporter of the virtual circuit approach. So, the main goal of our team was to convince Remi that datagram was preferable (because that is what we had to sell, using ARPANET technology). At the end of the presentations, there was a free-flow conversation between Larry and Remi about the merits of the two methods. After about a half hour, as I recall, Larry conceded to Remi that he, Remi, was correct and the virtual circuit was better than the datagram, mainly because of its better control of network congestion. While I was privileged to have been a front-row witness to this watershed moment in the emergence of the Internet infrastructure, it shot my marketing effort in the head. Our chief salesman, Larry Roberts, was also an honest scientist, and I respected him for that, but we did not bother to make a bid for Transpac using the datagram technology.

Epilogue: Telenet soon developed and announced a virtual circuit front end for its datagram network, and converted to 100% virtual circuit technology in 1980. Roberts and Wessler, as Telenet representatives, worked closely with Despres in the development of the X.25 standard PS protocol, based on virtual circuits. The PTT awarded the contract to SESA for the development of Transpac. This work resulted in SESA's PS network products that I sold for SESA-Honeywell in the 1980s. When I joined SESA in 1979, Remi Despres was its in-house chief scientist, or something like that, and a nice guy to work with.

I'll never forget the presentation Larry Roberts gave me in his office in 1974 in which he accurately predicted and described a networked world-to-be coming in several years. His vision was prescient, but it took a lot more than several years. In 1986, he gave a paper in which he said, "If we look forward to the year 2000, based on historical trends, computers will be about 500 times cheaper per computation than today. Almost all devices in the home, office or plant will have complex computers incorporated into them." Again, his vision was perfect, but he was off by 10 years or so. Larry died on Dec 26, 2018, a great loss. To many, including me, he was the Father of the Internet, and I'm proud to have known him.

SESA Honeywell

August 1979–March 1983

SESA was another French software development company in which CGE had an investment. SESA did the major software for France's backbone packet switching network, Transpac, which was the precursor of the Internet in France, similar to the ARPANET in the U.S. SESA had also developed some hardware for packet switches, which were also part of the French backbone network.

Prior to the Internet, large companies maintained their own telecommunications networks using point-to-point transmission lines leased from the various telephone companies. The opportunity to sell packet-switching technology to these large companies was large, as the intelligent networking of the leased lines provided great improvements in service and much lower cost through efficient utilization of the leased lines. In essence, many companies built their own private Internet before the one we know today existed. The biggest market for such private packet-switching networks was in the U.S., and SESA had the knowledge, the hardware, and the software, but not the U.S. infrastructure and financial credibility needed to be a viable contender. The company recruited me to build that, and I was eager to do so. I knew something about this technology, as I had tried, unsuccessfully, to get TECSI/GSI into this business in France by proposing the ARPANET technology to the French government in competition with SESA's offering. In this effort, I worked with the founders of the ARPANET backbone, which became the Internet backbone in the U.S. after the crucial software interfaces were added, but that is another story that I have told elsewhere.

It was decided that SESA needed an American partner in order to respond to the concerns of U.S. infrastructure and financial strength. I contacted many companies and found that Honeywell was entering the telecommunications business by offering private voice networks and equipment. I contacted Honeywell and it agreed to become a

49% partner in a joint venture founded as SESA-Honeywell Communications (SHC). I was the President and I had two VPs, one from SESA and one from Honeywell. We opened our office in Herndon, Virginia, hired staff and started marketing private networks based on the hardware and software of SESA. We sold, installed, and maintained three networks: a 3-node network for Honeywell, a 3-node network for Chase Manhattan Bank, and a 1-node network for Lincoln (Nebraska) Telephone. We were doing well.

Well, not as well as I thought. It became apparent that the SESA packet switch node hardware failed often and needed frequent manual intervention. Our maintenance folks figured out what the main problem was, a sensitive connector, but there was no work around. This was not a big problem for telephone companies, as the nodes were installed in central offices that were staffed around the clock with maintenance personnel, but it was not feasible for commercial organizations to staff maintenance like this. The three clients were unhappy and no easy fix was on the horizon. SESA and Honeywell, mostly the latter, reimbursed the clients and removed the networks, and SHC gracefully ceased operations. I was unemployed, again.

CSC

March 1983–December 1983

I don't recall how it happened, but after SHC folded I was put in contact with Computer Sciences Corporation's Federal Systems Group in VA. CSC had just finished doing the software and systems work on the CIA's large data network, again using packet switching technology, and they saw the opportunity for selling private networks such as we had done at SHC. I was recruited as the VP for Private Data Networks with the idea of selling the CIA-proven technology to government and commercial clients.

When I got to CSC I started looking at the ownership issue of the CIA-developed system I was to sell. Usually, work done for the government entered public domain and was available for re-use by anyone, but I wondered about the CIA. It turned out that CSC had developed the software as a sub-contractor to MA-Comm, the prime contractor, and only MA-Comm had the right to re-use it. Since CSC had developed the software, it was unclear if it could re-use that, but it only ran on MA-Comm's hardware. So, the boss of CSC Federal set up a meeting with the president of MA-Comm to propose that we combine to sell private networks using MA-Comm hardware and CSC software. Well, it became clear in a hurry that MA-Comm had big eyes for the market too, and didn't want to combine, nor let CSC use the software, nor let CSC buy MA-Comm hardware. I was a VP without anything to sell!

CSC was a little embarrassed over not having done its homework before hiring me, and they talked to me about becoming their VP for their internal networks. That turned out to be a political football within CSC, as the East Coast, federal systems, and the West Coast, commercial systems, both wanted to control the internal network. Since each had about half of the revenues of the company, it was an internal stand-off. I passed on the opportunity and resigned. In less than six months, I was unemployed, again.

Bunker Ramo Information Systems

December 1983–December 1984

Near the end of my brief tenure at CSC, I was contacted by a head-hunter who represented a Connecticut company, Bunker Ramo. I met with the president, visited the facility in Trumbull, CT, and took the job. Bunker did two things: platform systems for banks and information for stockbrokers. I was the VP of Brokerage Systems. We provided real-time stock quote terminals and database information to stockbrokers. Bunker was number two or three in this business, which was dominated by Quotron. The third player was ADP, which also offered back-office processing services to brokers. Bunker had 30,000 Bunker-manufactured terminals connected to brokers' desks by a network of point-to-point leased lines. The host computers were also unique to, and assembled by, Bunker. I started the conversion to commercial off-the-shelf hardware.

At the end of 1984, it became widely known that Bunker was for sale, and that the likely acquirer was ADP. It made sense for ADP, as it would expand its customer base and move the Bunker clients to its network. None of this made sense for me, as ADP already had a good network and management. I was looking for opportunities, again.

Vanguard Atlantic

January 1985–December 1992

Lee Keet founded one of the early software development and products companies, Turnkey Systems Inc., in the '60s, and I had negotiated with Lee for TECSI to distribute his products in France. It had been a good relationship for both, and we were good business associates. TSI was in Norwalk, CT, and I made contact with Lee when we

387

moved to Trumbull for Bunker Ramo. By then, Lee had sold TSI to Dun & Bradstreet and was running D&B's software products division in Wilton, CT. At dinner one night at our house in Trumbull, Lee said that he was leaving D&B and starting his own boutique investment and merchant banking company to specialize in computer services and software companies. Having done quite a bit of merger and acquisition (M&A) work for GSI and SESA, I was very interested in what he was doing and asked Lee if he could use a partner. He said yes, and I took a 15% ownership in the company, Vanguard Atlantic, Ltd. (VAL). Lee rented an old Victorian house in Wilton, CT, two blocks from his home, hired an administrative assistant, and we set up offices.

VAL did two things: investment banking (IB), where we helped companies with their M&A endeavors, and merchant banking (MB), where we acquired companies using our own, i.e., Lee's, financial resources. We each had our own IB clients; for example, Lee had Coopers & Lybrand and I had NYNEX, the old NY and New England Telephone Company. In marketing our IB activity, we self-published a weekly newsletter and co-authored a book on strategic corporate development through acquisitions. We were moderately successful in this very crowded market space of well-known, established competitors.

While the IB business provided good market exposure and paid our bills, it was merchant banking that was the high reward, high risk opportunity area for VAL. Our first acquisition was to purchase Lee's old companies from D&B, which was struggling in the software products market after Lee's departure. These included TSI as the crown jewel and several other smaller companies. We changed management of the different units and disposed of the smaller ones in one way or another, concentrating our efforts on TSI.

TSI had made its success in data entry and telecommunications interface products, both of which were obsolescent, and a new product was needed. We led TSI through a strategic re-think which steered it into the emerging market of electronic data interchange, where its skills and experience were immediately applicable. TSI produced a data mapping product called Mercator, which was very well received by the market. Somewhere along the line, VAL had brought in a large NY venture investor, Warburg Pincus, with an eye on taking TSI public. TSI did an IPO in 1997, I think, and was caught up in the stock craziness of the dotcom boom, which produced a small paper fortune for many of the shareholders, including me. It crashed along with the dotcom crash, which was exacerbated by a financial reporting scandal concerning TSI's books. The company was eventually acquired by another at a negligible price. Nevertheless, the merchant banking effort of VAL was a success which, exaggerated by the dotcom market madness, produced a paper fortune for many. I did diversify some of my investment gains in TSI, but I rode most of it to the ground, thereby turning my small fortune into a tiny fortune. Dumb me!

The second major MB activity of VAL was called ECsoft. Based on the success of TSI, Warburg supported our effort to build a chain of companies to distribute software products throughout the common market countries, focused on development and performance tools for software creation. ECsoft acquired several small companies in Europe and negotiated distribution relationships for some software products, but there were problems with this. One problem was strategic, in that we concentrated on software products for the large computer mainframes right at the time when the migration to client/server architecture was taking off. The second huge problem was tactical in that two of the company acquisitions, both made by me, were disastrous. I totally misjudged the companies that I recommended ECsoft acquire in Spain and France. In Spain, the situation degenerated into a union brawl and the COO of ECsoft, Leo Apotheker, had to spend many months personally managing and closing the operation.

Needless to say, my usefulness at ECsoft was over and I withdrew from participation. This was a major setback for VAL, and soul-wrenching for me, so we negotiated my graceful departure from full-time employment at VAL with an ongoing consulting relationship for a while. I stayed on the board of TSI until 1999, but in 1992 I was unemployed, again.

The story did have a happy ending for VAL, ECsoft, and its investors. Lee, Leo, and the ECsoft management team converted ECsoft into a successful software development company which resulted in an IPO a few years later. I tip my hat with thanks to Lee, Leo, and the team. As for me, my time at Vanguard provided a lifetime of financial security. Again, thanks to Lee and the Vanguard team.

CBIS

January 1993–July 1996

As I was gracefully, and somewhat shamefacedly, leaving Vanguard, one of the younger TSI board members from Warburg Pincus approached me. His father, Dr. Shelly Horing, was the president of Cincinnati Bell Information Systems (CBIS), a subsidiary of Cincinnati Bell, and he was looking for a new president of the international division of

391

CBIS. Introductions were made and I joined CBIS as president of the international group. Shelly Horing had retired from Bell Labs and was recruited by Cincinnati Bell to run CBIS. He was an old-school gentleman from the Bell Labs culture and was a pleasure to work for.

Cincinnati Bell was a small Bell operating company and one of only two Bell companies that were allowed to diversify into computer services after the breakup of the Bell system. It had done a good job of building CBIS, and CBIS was the dominant supplier of billing services for the cell phone industry. If you received a cell phone bill in 1994, there was a 70% chance that it was produced by CBIS. Market dominance like that is always very profitable. However, in my opinion and using hindsight, three strategic mistakes were made in the growth of CBIS:

1. It purchased a large government body-shop contractor, a very low-margin business in which it had no experience nor competitive advantage. This business was a misfit in the CBIS culture, and a drag on profits for years.

2. The international group was involved in many different kinds of non-billing software projects, with the only common denominator being that all the customers were telephone companies. Again, CBIS brought little competitive advantage to this

business, other than telephone company credibility. I would also add that international business was a poor cultural fit in CBIS, a provincial regional company having few folks with international experience.

3. CBIS had made no efforts to enter the international cell phone billing business, which it dominated in the U.S., because the rest of the world used GSM cell technology, with which CBIS had no experience.

In my first six months at CBIS, I concentrated on issue #2 above, because international was losing money on most of the projects in which it was involved. We canceled some projects, closed some offices, notably Germany, and re-negotiated the three surviving contracts, the Dutch PTT, the Swiss PTT, and Telstra in Australia, all of which had large cost overruns.

That done, I started to look for a European GSM billing company that CBIS could buy, which would get us in the international business that we knew so well in the U.S. And then my boss and protector, Shelly Horing, was replaced, oops!

Cincinnati Bell hired two guys from Procter & Gamble to turn around CBIS. They came in like Batman and Robin, but I soon decided they were Joker and Robin. The new boss, Joker, was a paradox to me. He didn't seem very bright, was crude, treated his employees like dirt, had no knowledge of the information services industry, but he had amazingly good business instincts. I couldn't figure out how Robin got along with him, because Robin was smart, a nice guy, and a motivational leader. Perhaps Robin was calling all the shots behind the scene all along. Needless to say, Joker and I didn't get along, but I had negotiated a good contract with CBIS when I joined, they had no one to replace me, and they, correctly, had little interest in the international software projects business, so I stayed on. It did not go well. Eventually, Joker retired and Robin became CEO, but, unfortunately, my bridges with both had long ago been burned. On my first annual performance review with Robin, we negotiated my exit where he honored my contract and gave me a profitable and positive public sendoff. Financially secure, I was unemployed, again.

GMU

November 1996–December 1998

During my final year at CBIS I had had enough experience at being unemployed that I knew it was going to happen again soon. I noticed an ad in the Wall Street Journal. George Mason University in Fairfax, VA, where we had lived for so many years, was looking for an Executive in Residence and Visiting Professor of Management for its graduate business school. The school offered the usual MBA and a new degree, the Master's in Technology Management (MTM). I applied and, after a years-long process, was offered the job. The job represented an 80% cut in compensation, but we were financially comfortable by then, so I took it.

On my first day, I showed up with my business suit and tie on, and was shown to my office, which had a desk, a chair for me, one chair for a visitor, and a hat rack in a maybe 12' by 8' office. Coming from CBIS where I had three offices around the world that were each at least four times this size, it was a change. So, I settled in and looked over university and course materials until lunch time. When I left for lunch, I stopped by the business school's secretary to report that I was leaving for lunch, when I would be back, and how I could be reached, as I had done for the last ten years of my working life. She looked up and said, "So what?" I knew I had found a home in a different kind of environment! Universities do not operate in teams, but rather as individual performers. It didn't take me long to ditch the suit and tie, keep sporadic office hours, and always avoid the Northern Virginia traffic.

One of the professors at the school was Bob Buzzell, who had recently retired from the Harvard Business School, where he was a chaired marketing professor and chairman of the marketing department. Bob enjoyed teaching and had joined GMU when he retired back home to Alexandria, VA. Bob took pity on me and became a mentor and friend. One time I asked him what was the most important thing I could do for the students, and he said, "Make them write." So, I gave many written assignments. What Bob did not tell me was that I would have to assess, i.e., grade, all these writings! Boy, did I burn some midnight oil. Since we taught mainly using the case method, I soon found that I could ask any relevant question about a case, read all the written answers that came in, and deduce what the right answer was when my reading was over. Then I would go back and grade the papers. The nice thing about teaching in MBA programs is that the students, who mostly have work experience and are highly motivated, collectively know more than the professor, and they will teach one another if properly stimulated. It is called "Being the guide on the side" as opposed to "Being the sage on the stage." I loved being on the side. All I had to do was stir up the students and step back and learn.

One of my *leitmotifs* in business is "Everyone is in sales, most folks just don't know it." In business, as in life, one is always trying to explain, convince, persuade, justify, defend, etc....These are all forms of selling. So, I asked permission to develop and give a course in sales for the Master's in Technology Management program. Now, I really identified with the MTM program, since I had mismanaged so much technology in my life. The MTM was an executive degree that was given to a cohort of working professionals mainly on weekends and evenings. Almost all of the students were middle-level managers in technology companies and were sponsored by their employers who paid their tuition. Anyway, back to my sales course proposal. I was rapidly informed that sales is a skill, not a knowledge, and that universities don't teach skills, but rather they create and impart knowledge. Management obviously being an acceptable knowledge, I developed a course called, "Managing the Client Relationship." Since client relationships start with sales, I snuck it into the course. Similarly to my experience long ago at TECSI, the reluctant and resistant technical students were taken by the course and became believers in selling and delivering value to clients.

Each year the graduating MTM student cohort selected a professor to give the students their last class before graduation, a high honor. My last year, they selected me. I gave a lecture entitled "What Now, or So What?" My premise was that they had acquired lots of new knowledge (and some skills, shh!), but it remained up to them to demonstrate it in their workplace or the degree would just be "so what?" We met for 15 minutes and adjourned for beers at a local bar.

My contract at GMU was for two years. At the end, the entire structure of the graduate school, and its management, had changed. I can only imagine the new dean questioning what this lowly Master's degree guy was doing in the faculty. It had been a fun and positive experience for me, but I was unemployed, again.

UWA

January 1999–June 2001

In June of 1998, we took an around-the-world trip with Linda's parents. Perth, Australia, was one of our stops, and I had contacted the director of The Graduate School of Management (GSM) at The University of Western Australia, one of Australia's premier universities. David Plowman received me and was interested in my joining his staff at the GSM, where he wanted to strengthen the technology aspect of the MBA program. He said he couldn't offer me much money (about enough to cover our expenses and travel), and I replied that was fine with me as I didn't intend to work too hard. He laughed and we had a deal. It turned out that I had lied, as I worked my tail off and loved every minute of it. In the beginning, I taught two consecutive quarters followed by a quarter off back in the U.S., and then I went to alternating quarters teaching in Perth and being home in the U.S. We did this for almost three years, which gave us plenty of travel. Perth is almost the antipode of Washington D.C., so it was about a 12,000 mile trip no matter which way we went.

In January of 1999, we flew to Perth to begin the winter quarter at UWA. I developed and taught courses in computer applications in business and the management of technology. The students were excellent, with a high percentage of students from nearby Asia, especially Indonesia, Hong Kong, and Singapore. My teaching method was case-based, and class participation was an important part of the process and the final grades. I soon learned that I had to reduce the class participation component, as it was foreign to most of the Asians. Apparently in Asia, the student listened, without saying much.

As I had done in my previous teaching at GMU, I gave a lot of writing assignments. I limited the written assignment responses to only one page. This was for two reasons. First, I knew that in the real world of business it was rare that decision makers had the time or inclination to read more than one page of a report before deciding to toss it or to continue to the second page. Secondly, I wanted to avoid students taking many pages to tell me everything about a subject rather being concise and to the point. This one-page edict produced a funny effect. I received papers with zero margins, tiny fonts, and very sparse punctuation. Against my normal no-rules teaching approach, I had to specify minimum margins and font size and re-emphasize that conciseness was the goal.

One day towards the end my first year at GSM, David Plowman wandered casually into my office and asked me if I knew anything about the Internet and e-commerce. I puffed up and proudly said that I knew some of the founders of the Internet and understood the disruptive opportunity of e-commerce on the World Wide Web. He said something like, fine, develop and give an e-commerce course for GSM. Back to burning midnight oil! I became the first person at UWA to teach an e-commerce course, which was a lot of fun. I had great students sign up for that course: a computer science professor at UWA, the head of the cardiology unit at Perth's largest hospital, engineers, lawyers, optometrists, and Indian chiefs (not really, that's an American thing). After an introduction to the Internet and the concepts of Internet-based e-commerce, I broke the class into teams of five people and asked each team to pick an application suitable for e-commerce and bring up a prototype website for it. As proof to my class that anyone could build a website, I built a simple website for my family to follow our experiences in Perth. We had demonstrable websites for a winery, a medical prescription transmission system, an ice cream factory, and others. What fun!

On my office door there was a slide-in name tag that said, "Jack Pendray." During my second year at GSM, David came by and replaced it with a new one that said, "Professor Jack Pendray." I thanked him, but was wondering why it had taken a year to get my name tag right. Remember this name tag story for later.

At the end of my second year at GSM, I decided to march in the graduation processional and attend the ceremony, as many of the students I had taught were receiving their MBAs. I donned my Master's robe with my Stanford hood and reported to the area where the "learned academy" queued up for the march. There was a list posted of all the faculty members who were marching, and their position in the queue, ranked by academic stature and seniority. My name was not on the list. In a small panic, I found the executive admin person for GSM and asked her why I wasn't on the list. She responded that I was on the "other" list and I had to report to the other area reserved for full professors, deans, and the university big wigs. I said, "Nope, not me." She replied, "Yep, you," and took me over to the bigwig area and pointed out my name on the list, with queue position #1. I almost fainted—what a huge screw-up someone had made. She took me in and explained that the marching order is in reverse order, with the lowest person going first, which made some sense. So, there I was in my dowdy Master's robe surrounded by academic royalty from all over the world in all their finery, plumes, puffed hats, brilliant colors, and all with the three sleeve stripes of a doctorate. I was led to my place as first in line and given a seal of the university to carry, symbolizing the beginning of the bigwigs group. I was perplexed and terrified that the screw-up would be discovered and I would be ejected in a mini-scandal, but then I noticed that the guy next to me, position #2, only had a Master's robe and hood too, so I smiled at him as a fellow victim of some giant mistake. He asked if my hood was from Stanford, which surprised me that he recognized the colors, and I replied it was. He then introduced himself as the dean of the law school and I almost fell over. You see, in Australia, the LLB degree is considered to be what it is called, a Bachelor's degree, and not a doctorate. The dean only had an LLB and an LLM! I later found out that he was also a QC, Queen's Counsel, the highest legal recognition granted in the British Commonwealth. And the poor guy had to follow me! In we marched, after all of the rest of the lower "learned academy" had been seated. I was in a daze and really confused.

The next day, I was seated in my office and the GSM executive administrator wandered in and sat down. She said something like, "You don't know, do you?" I said that I guessed not, since I had no idea what she was talking about. "You're an adjunct professor now," she said. Offended, I replied that I thought I was full-time and not part-time, which is what adjunct professor means in the U.S. She then said something like, "No, you are an Adjunct Professor, which is an honorary title given by the university and is equivalent to Full Professor." I almost fell out of my chair, but that explained a lot. She explained that David had nominated me to the Faculty Senate, or their version of that, and the Vice Chancellor (President) of UWA had then written the president of GMU asking about me and what title I should receive. By fantastic luck, the President of GMU was Alan Merten, my old Stanford buddy, roommate, and lifelong friend, who had, by coincidence, become President of GMU around the same time I had joined GMU. Apparently, Alan said I was OK and suggested they use the same title I had had at GMU, so my title got longer when I became Adjunct Professor, Executive in Residence, and Visiting Professor of Management.

403

Still in disbelief, I walked the halls of GSM, and, sure enough, the only door name tags that said Professor were the real Full Professors, and me. Get that! Australians are very low key, and David did all this without any fuss. Thanks, David.

When I left GSM, I was no longer unemployed. I was retired!

CHRISTMAS 2009

Hello out there...If you have ever received this letter before and you voluntarily opened this one, you need professional help! This is the 39th time that Pendrays' parental periodic publication in perfect prose is posted to people for purely Platonic purposes...I thought about consuming a bottle of Far Niente Chardonnay while composing this letter, but then realized that a $45 bottle of wine whose name translates to "no worries" was not very representative of 2009. Instead, I'm working on a box of Target's Wine Cube Sauvignon Blanc, which, at about $4.50 per equivalent bottle, is quite representative of this past year. Each of these boxes holds four bottles of wine in a plastic bladder with a spigot that doesn't allow air in as you consume it; therefore, the box can be opened for some time without the wine going bad. Why, we have had some boxes last as long as two days before we finished them off...January through April were stay-at-home months while we welcomed, and partied with, our many snow-bird friends who were in Florida awaiting the ground thawing up north. The ground thawed, they left, and we became bored...Normally, we would have scheduled an annual family trip around this time of year, but Jack had sent an email to all the family saying that, due to the economy and resulting diminished personal prosperity, there would be no vacations this year. Well, the younger generation protested vehemently by waving around handfuls of depreciating dollars, which we hope is a new family tradition! So, Jack served as travel agent and arranged for Mike to rent a 9-bedroom villa in Tuscany for two weeks at the end of May, and for the others to rent a 9-passenger Mercedes Benz air-conditioned (not easy to find in Europe) minibus for the same two weeks. Mike, the host, was kind enough to invite the rest of us to stay at his villa, and Jack became the main chauffeur of the minibus. Steve and Stephanie couldn't make it due to last-minute conflicts, but Jack, Linda, Mike, Andy, Kim (Andy's girlfriend, then), Sean (Jack's nephew), Meg (Linda's niece), Barbara and Charles Grimsley (Jack's cousin and her husband), and Bill and Kelly Schoonmaker (Mike's friends) did all manage to join in the fun. The Villa Catola was in the town of Bucine, population 6,000, which was perfect. The train station to Florence (1 hour) and Rome (3 hours) was a two-minute walk from the villa, and the town had a grocery store, two cafes, and three restaurants. Everyone came and went as they pleased, except when we all piled in the minibus to go visit wineries, medieval towns, or sights like Pisa. The day that Barbara and Charles Grimsley arrived, Bucine started its annual town fair, so we told Barbara that it was in her honor and she was the Queen of Bucine. Charles was feeling a little left out, so we also declared him to be the other Queen of Bucine. Barbara seemed to enjoy being the queen more than Charles...June was a quiet month as the Florida heat and humidity settled in and the sound of cicadas yielded to that of air conditioners...Having paid for a house in Cashiers, NC, before the economic collapse, we honored our reservations and spent July there. We shared the house (and costs) on Lake Glenville with our long-time friends, Judy and John Guido. It was a large house with a separate garage apartment, so we had visits from friends and family members from both families. We drove up with 12 Target Wine Cubes (equivalent to 48 bottles of wine), and the Guidos showed up with an equal amount of wine plus other spirits. We both went home empty. I think we had a good time, but no one remembers...During the last week in Cashiers, we took the family Labrador, Riley, to the local vet to check out a cough he had developed. The vet found a mass on Riley's throat. On returning to Sarasota, a biopsy confirmed that Riley had an untreatable thyroid cancer with a prognosis of 2 to 6 months. We set out to make those good months, with determination that he would enjoy the rest of his life and not suffer...In August, we were invited to spend time in Colorado with Sarasota neighbors, Natalie and Ray Gibson, and then travel to Montana to visit with our daughter-in-law's parents, Sharon and Carl Warren. Thanks to the capable and loving care of our dog-sitter, Darlene McGuigan, we were able to seize this opportunity to mooch off these generous folks. No better hosts can be found than the Gibsons and Stephanie's parents. We had a blast!...Mike and Andy both came to Sarasota over the Labor Day weekend to spend quality time with Riley (and their parents), which Steve and Steph had had the opportunity to do at the end of our stay in Cashiers. It was very sad to watch them say goodbye to the old boy for the last time...Trying to imagine what Riley would have on his "bucket list," we spent a lot of time driving him to places we thought he would enjoy, including a week back in Cashiers in September to escape the continuing heat of Florida. We rented the same place that we had rented in 2008, a house with a huge yard, screened-in porch, and a creek on three sides. Did you read about the floods in Atlanta in September? They were really centered in Cashiers. We had two hours of sunshine in the week, but Riley thought that lying on the couch of the porch in the cool weather was divine, and so did we. The last night, we were evacuated to a motel as the creek rose and rose and rose...At the end of October, and thanks again to Darlene's loving care of Riley, we were able to slip away to join Australian friends who were visiting the U.S. We joined Chris and Chris (not a typo) Lawson-Smith in Charleston for two days, then went to Savannah for another couple of days, and then took them home for several days before they returned to Oz. This was a great respite for us, what better way to get away than with great friends?...On Friday the 13th of November, our family lost its "best friend," Mike's dog, Riley. He spent twelve years loving his way into the hearts of all the members of our family, who had had many dogs before, but none were as special as Riley. It's been a month now, and I can sense that the sharp pain of absence is beginning to morph into fond memories, filled with fun and laughter, that will remain with us the rest of our days...Thanksgiving saw the whole family reunited in Sarasota with 15 folks around the table. We gave our thanks for the life of Riley, who had, indeed, led a "life of Riley," while missing his presence...Jack continues to study Spanish, never learning much...Linda stays busy keeping Jack out of trouble, being a mainstay of our church, and running the household... Mike's company was acquired by Deloitte & Touche, so he now works for a huge enterprise. They must recognize his worth, because they put him on an assignment that is close to where he lives. In Washington, that is really recognition!...Steve and Stephanie continue to love Manhattan (in spite of both of them having been called for grand juries) and American Express continues to employ them, which is a really good thing in Manhattan...Andy stays in Palo Alto working for Symantec, which is also a good thing in California. We owe him special thanks for spending most of his Thanksgiving holiday fixing our computers...

The 2000s

This year, the joke is again on Jack. When he turned 60 in Perth, he strove to run 6 miles and get his weight under 160 pounds, goals he achieved. Turning 70 this year, he strove to run .7 miles (notice the decimal point) and be under 170 pounds, goals he also achieved!... We're off to Virginia to spend Christmas with Mike, Jack's relatives, and dear friends. Mooching is becoming our lifestyle, as we are staying in the Reston apartment of Linda's sister and brother-in-law, Susan and Gordon Harvey. We're even having Christmas Eve dinner with the two Queens of Bucine. It doesn't get any better!!!

We wish you all a Merry Christmas and economic recovery in 2010!

The Pendrays

50 Years of Christmas Letters

The 2010s

50 Years of Christmas Letters

CHRISTMAS 2010

Hello out there...The cartoonist Bruce Tinsley, who draws the comic *Mallard Fillmore,* has recently been railing about what a scourge Christmas letters are. (Definition. Scourge: any means of inflicting severe punishment, suffering, or vengeance. Upon reflection, this 40th edition of this letter meets all three criteria.) I was not aware that we had any cartoonists on our mailing list, but, obviously, one of you must be using Bruce Tinsley as a pseudonym...Bloody Marys, made with Mr. & Mrs. T's mix and really cheap vodka (I found a vodka from Lake Alfred, FL, presumably made by moonlighting Univ. of FL graduate students) are serving as fodder to facilitate the flying fingers fleetingly fleeing the unfeeling facetious failure forecast for this forum. I started this letter at 0900 (that's 9 a.m. for draft-dodgers), so give me a break; after all, there are some rules to the consumption of alcoholic beverages. (Jack's favorite such rule is

413

"It's five o'clock somewhere.") Second Bloody Mary coming up right now...As forecast in last year's letter, we did, indeed, spend last Christmas in northern Virginia, in the super apartment of Linda's sister and brother-in-law, Susan and Gordon Harvey, who, wisely, left town for the holidays. They left us with their cat (Jack's highly allergic), four feet of compressed ice and snow surrounding their building, and a little popcorn dog that needed to turn some of that snow yellow every couple of hours. We visited many friends and family, had a great time, and appreciate Florida winters more than ever...January was quiet, excepting a visit from our old, er...long-time, friends, Dick and Barbara Abbott and Al and Sally Merten. A visit from these folks is not quiet, but sure is fun...In Feb., our old, er...long-time, friends from Virginia arrived in town for periods which varied between one and six weeks. The twenty members of the infamous Gourmet Group crescendoed their partying skills into a grand finale road-trip to visit Ken and Marie Hannum in Sebring, FL, where we inducted Ken into the Gourmet Group, a dubious honor which he graciously accepted... We spent a lot of March stuck in traffic in Sarasota. The population here doubles in the winter. We politely smile and wave, as we know they are all driving somewhere to leave money. Old, er...long-time, friends from Conn., Gus and

Nancy Serra, joined the traffic with us for a few days. Great to see them again...April was mostly spent doing things locally with local friends, excepting when we went to Egypt. Jack has a bucket list of things he wants to see that are older than he is (so Egypt barely made the cut). We went on a tour with Overseas Adventure Travel (OAT), who, somehow, manages to provide great tours for half the price of others. Mike came along with us and instructed us on the various types of automatic weapons that our Egyptian-government-provided guards were carrying. We had a fabulous time and never felt insecure or unwelcome. What incredible accomplishments the Egyptians achieved four thousand years ago. Egypt should be on everyone's bucket list...In early June, we sneaked off to The Big Apple for three days to visit Steve and Stephanie. Saw *Wicked.* We paid wicked prices for wicked entertainment and sustenance, guess that's one of the definitions of New York... At the end of June, Jack had rotator cuff repair surgery, which caused us to cancel our annual peregrination to North Carolina. He sported a very fancy sling, with a special bolster, for six weeks, causing some other sling-wearing friends of his to have "sling envy." Truly, one can compete in anything...(Time to go get Bloody Mary number 3. Better hurry and finish this before the nap arrives.)...July and early Aug.

were very quiet, as Jack laid around watching Netflix movies, showing off his fancy sling, and seeking sympathy from anyone dumb enough to ask, "How are you?"...At the end of Aug., we celebrated Jack's sling-freedom by traveling to Elk Rapids, MI, where Susan and Gordon have a "secret" condo. Well, it's not a secret anymore and they can just put our name on the guestroom door! Really, they've been trying to get us to come there and visit, but we kept thinking, "Michigan?!" Turns out it isn't covered with snow and ice all year, instead, it's a super place (in certain months!). Steve and Stephanie joined us there, and we had a great time. To paraphrase Arnie, "We'll be back!!"...Since we hadn't seen Andy for a while, we went to CA in Sep. Mike heard about the trip, so he joined us too. Three days in Yosemite were followed by some days in Palo Alto, then we continued on to Linda's 50th high school reunion in Carmel. (For those of you making the calculation, you should know that Linda is very bright and went to high school at the age of 4.) Her high school was in Munich, but, considering that the dollar is almost worthless in Europe, they had the reunion in CA. It was a terrific time and very satisfying to see that all those "military brats" turned out so well...Oct. was taken up by watching football and going to Peru. While Machu Picchu is 3,000 years younger than Egypt, it is still slightly older than

Jack, so it was on his list. Once again, we went with OAT, and had a great experience. OAT has a group maximum of 16, so we provided half a group with Mike, Mike's friends, Bill and Kelly Schoonmaker, Sean, Sean's friend Joe Carey, Andy, and us. Great group, great trip...Nov. is the month that America owns, because of Thanksgiving. Among the many great things our forefathers left us, Thanksgiving is one of the best. We had all the "kids" here for the week, with eleven family members at the table to share the turkey, ham, five pies, and too much other food. While everyone was in town, we had a visit from "Bob" and his humans. Bob is a guide dog-in-training from Southeast Guide Dogs, and we partially sponsor him. Bob is named after Linda's dad, and is in the Paws for Patriots program, which provides guide dogs to veterans. He is in the care of puppy-raisers for 18 months, who brought him to visit. We all loved having a yellow Labrador in the house again...Dec. will have the usual Christmas festivities, which we will share with some of Linda's family and our old, er...yeah, yeah, friends, the Abbotts, including their daughter, Tori, who is Jack's goddaughter, and her family. However, prior to Christmas, we have an event of almost equal importance. Linda's grandniece, Cheyenne Roché, will celebrate her Sweet Sixteen party and family members are coming from all corners for the event. We're expecting a real blast...Linda is more active than ever in church, looks after her mother, Jack, her kids, her nieces and nephew, and anyone needing looking after (some of our friends call her "Saint Linda," which has to do mostly with that part about looking after Jack), and still finds time to travel and enjoy life...Mike now works for Knowledge Consulting Group, a small consulting firm in Reston, VA, and will probably move to Reston so he can walk to the office. His current assignment is to review IT practices at the different federal district courts, which takes him to many interesting U.S. cities... Steve & Stephanie still live in Manhattan and both work for American Express. They live an exciting and hectic urban life, which we share with them occasionally, which rapidly exhausts us...Andy is still at Symantec, living in Palo Alto amongst the other computer wizards. He is right at home there, and doing very well...The joke is on Jack, again, this year (he's so easy!). For fifteen years, his right arm hurt and he was convinced that it was due to neurological problems emanating from herniated cervical disks. Recently, a friend was describing his symptoms of a torn rotator cuff, which sounded just like Jack's "disk-caused" problems. Consulting a specialist, Jack explained his symptoms and his self-diagnosis, but the specialist disagreed. Long story (15 years) cut

418

short: after rotator cuff repair, Jack's arm is fine and no longer hurts. Moral of this story: don't seek medical advice from Jack!...Well, the Bloody Marys are finished, and so am I.

We wish you all a Merry Christmas and an economic recovery in 2011! (All I had to do was change the year from last year's ending, as the recovery is still "just around the corner." Since they say that the Great Recession ended in 2009, this must be the economic equivalent of "Mission Accomplished"!)

The PENDRAYS

50 Years of Christmas Letters

CHRISTMAS 2011

Hello out there...Hard to believe that "they" have let me live long enough to write 41 of these. No better justification for capital punishment exists...As a consequence of the astoundingly rapid economic recovery resulting from the inspirational, courageous, and intelligent leadership provided by our elected officials in Washington (and I include all of them), I have been able to upscale my letter-launching lubricant from Target box wine to Yellowtail Shiraz, at five bucks a bottle. I'm getting a late start this year, as it is already 10:30 a.m., and I'm only on my third glass...All of our extended family were here for Thanksgiving, and I decided to try some of their work methods to produce this letter. I closely observed our prostrate progeny poised in precarious positions pounding on peculiar personal productivity products, and then tried to imitate them. I sprawled out awkwardly on the couch with my ear-buds deeply ensconced in my ear canals, put some cacophonic vibes on my iPod, placed my laptop on my ample "lap," took a glass of wine in my left hand, used my right hand to dial on my cellphone, and proceeded to type on my keyboard with my nose. How <u>do</u> they ever get anything done!... In Feb., our infamous Gourmet Group from Virginia (whose specialty is pizza) descended on Sarasota in what has become an annual tradition. Word has gotten out that they come in February; consequently, Feb. is now known as "very low season" in Sarasota...In March, we visited our oldest, Mike, in his new digs in Reston, Va. While he ended up with a landlord of questionable merit (Linda's sister, Susan, and her husband, Gordon), his new apt is in the vibrant Reston Town Center, which is terrific...In April we took the following trip, expressed in airline-speak: TPA-SFO-SYD-BNE-PER-SYD-SFO-TPA. (Anyone understanding this travels way too much.) In summary, we went to Perth for 3 weeks, stopping both ways to visit our youngest, Andy, in San Francisco, and spending a week with Nick and Nettie Gibson in Brisbane on our way to Perth. We had heard that our Anglican church in Perth was having a party for its 100th anniversary, so we went. They had a grand celebration, including the publishing of a book on the history of the church. We were called up on stage to receive the first copy of the book, a grand honor. I guess they figured that anyone traveling 25,000 miles to get a book deserved the first copy. I apologize for the list of names, but I can't not thank the wonderful Australian friends who welcomed us to Australia way back then, and, again, in April and May: John and Rosemary Pearman, Ken and Fay Drayton, Chris and Chris Lawson-Smith, Dennis and Kay Neil, David and Cathie Plowman, Ruth Cocks, Clive and Barbara Brans, Bruce and Wendy McCallum, Roger and Kay Smith, Anna Oehler, Charlie Gunnigham, Nick and Dianne Streuli, and others. What great folks! What a great country!...In Sydney, we caught up with a bunch of Pendrays from all over whose paths happened to cross in Sydney. Chris Pendray, from Utah, and his wife, Paula, an Aussie, and their daughters Ella and Tiana live in Sydney. Simon Pendray, from England, and his girlfriend, Camilla Lawson, also from England, met in Sydney where they both were working. Another fun gathering of Pendrays...We spent most of May recovering from jet lag. That's a looooong trip...In June, Jack and his life-long friend, Frank Molinari, went to the 55th reunion of their high school class in Coral Gables. Jack was informed that an informal survey was taken among the "girls" and that he and another guy were voted "best preserved." Must have something to do with being pickled in alcohol...Mike came down to help us celebrate the 4th of July. We ran Linda's dad's funeral flag up the pole, as is our custom on important holidays...July 28th we celebrated the 95th birthday of Linda's mom, Gladys Lawrence. Although in declining health, Gladdie was in full form and provided a great party for her two daughters, five grandchildren, five great-grandchildren, and other extended family...We spent August in FL doing what one does in FL in Aug., sweating...Escaping the heat of FL, we spent Sept. just south of Asheville, NC. We had several visitors join us, including our middle son, Steve, and his wife, Stephanie. Steve spent most of his week there replacing the steering rack of their BMW, and loved it. Engineers are different. Steph spent most of her vacation knitting in the garage keeping Steve company while he worked under their car...On Sep 25th, Linda's mom left us. Linda and Susan were both with her during her last days and final moments, and she went peacefully, surrounded by love and wonderful memories. Gladdie was one of the greatest of the aptly named "Greatest Generation," and she lives on in the spirit and memories of those she touched...In Oct., we went from NC to visit Ray and Natalie Gibson in Big Canoe, GA. No, they don't live in a big canoe, but rather in a really cool log cabin. "Big Canoe" is a place. Only in Georgia!...Jack's home town of Coral Gables opened a museum in the old jail, which seems strangely appropriate. We went down for the occasion and mooched a room off Paul and Donna Huck. Great to have some quality time with these dear long-time friends. While there, we had a chance to spend time with Jack's cousin, Pat, and his wife, Dede, as well as with Jack's nephew, Sean. Although old and infamous enough to be historical, Jack is not in the museum...November is famous in our family for two reasons, Thanksgiving and candy day. Now, you may not know about candy day, but it's big. On Nov. 1, Target puts its Halloween candy on sale. At 8 o'clock, Jack was there and ready for the race to the candy stalls, accompanied by an embarrassed Linda. By 8:30, he was at the check-out with over $100 worth of Reese's cups and other various chocolate goodies...Nov. also has a lesser event, Thanksgiving, a holiday with no gift-giving guilt, but rather just an obligation to eat yourself silly. Upholding our end, we did. Almost everyone came: Mike, Steve, Andy, Sean, Steph, Susan, and Kelly and her kids. Gladdie's absence was palpable...Dec. promises to be another family celebration. We're all going to Reston to celebrate Christmas with Mike. Susan and Gordon are wisely leaving town, so we are going to occupy their place as our participation in the "Occupy..." movement. Look for us on TV with our tents pitched in their living room...Linda has had her usual quiet year being useful in Sarasota when she's not traveling around the world. She organizes several different groups at our church as well as keeping the family in line...Jack continues his Spanish classes, learning less each week than he forgets...As mentioned, Mike has a new apartment in Reston. He can walk the mile to work when the weather is good, or if it's lousy when he sure can't drive. He still travels to federal courthouses about one week in four to audit their computer security. He's going to see every major U.S. city before it's over...Steve and Steph are still in NYC, and both still working for American Express (which is a good thing in this economy). They do a lot of traveling, as they seem to have a destination wedding, bachelor party, etc., in some exotic place every weekend...Andy was evicted from his apt in Palo Alto, as it was sold and being renovated. He took this as an opportunity to buy a neat townhouse in Sunnyvale. Now, instead of being five miles from work, he is two miles from work. Speaking of work, he got a promotion to Director at Symantec. Given that this happened during a layoff at Symantec, that's a real accomplishment...This year the joke is on Jack (too easy!). Jack got new eye lenses in Jan. as part of his cataract surgery. The new rule is "Put glasses on at 40, throw them away at 70," but Jack managed to break this rule. He got Restor lenses, which provide 9 different focal points (ask an engineer near you). Naturally, none of the 9 corresponds to his ideal reading, computing, or driving distances, so he ordered a bunch of glasses on the web for $9 a pair. For Jack the rule is "Put glasses on at 40, buy three different kinds at 72"…The bottle of Yellowtail is finished, and so am I.

We wish you all a very Merry Christmas and Happy New Year. May 2012 bring peace and prosperity to you, your family, and our country.

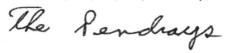

1st row, l to r: Hailey Carter, Georgi Clark, Gladys, Jake Carter, Cheyenne Roche, Sammy Clark

2nd row: Jack & Linda, Steve & Stephanie, Gordon & Susan Harvey, Kelly Clark, Mike, Lynne Harvey, Meg & Curtis Carter, Sean, Andy

Bob, Linda, and Gladdie—guess when!

Interesting Happenings in Australia

From Linda

Wining around Adelaide

With Fay and Ken Drayton we visited the wineries surrounding Adelaide in South Australia, spending lots of time at d'Arenberg in McLaren Vale sipping Dead Arm on Andrew's recommendation. As we stood at the empty tasting bar at 10 a.m., we called Andrew in California to get his help....he was amazed and jealous to learn there was no tasting fee and no limit to the caliber and number of wines we could try! Lunch on the patio was delightful and necessary to absorb all the wine imbibed. After lunch, we drove to Hahndorf, a quaint tourist town where Jack bought a genuine didgeridoo, an Aboriginal wind musical instrument. From Wikipedia: "The didgeridoo is played with continuously vibrating lips to produce the drone while using a special breathing technique called circular breathing. This requires breathing in through the nose whilst simultaneously expelling stored air out of the mouth using the tongue and cheeks." Since Jack has barely mastered breathing through his nose, he has not learned to play his didgeridoo.

Drinking to Michael Crawford at Leeuwin Estate

In 1999 I was reading the local paper (which we picked up each morning from Mick and Linda at the local convenience store at the corner of Marine Parade). An article announcing the 2000 Leeuwin Estate Concert Series in Margaret River caught my eye. Michael Crawford would be performing there on Feb 5th and 6th, 2000! We had become big Michael Crawford fans after listening to his Andrew Lloyd Webber recordings. And we would become even bigger fans as we rented the British comedy series *Some Mothers Do 'Ave 'Em* from the 1970s and learned what an amazing slapstick comedian he was as well. I called the phone number in the paper but was told no phone orders and no credit card orders. I could drive to Margaret River or to Fremantle to fill out a request and pay for tickets...but there was no assurance I would get tickets, as it was close to selling out already. I called Jack to tell him what I was up to. His answer was, "Buy 4 tickets!" I checked a map and, nervously, got in our rental car and cautiously drove on the left-hand side of the road to

Fremantle. (Less than 10 miles but seemed much further!) I finally found a parking spot and their funny little office, filled out an application, and wrote them a check. Eventually, we returned to the U.S. for a few months and then back to Australia. The tickets were waiting for us on our return! Now to find a place to stay....We hadn't realized what a big deal this was and that all of Perth would be going. We did find accommodations and the Draytons accompanied us on this great weekend.

Leeuwin Estate is a privately owned winery whose owners, the Horgan family, started the Leeuwin Concert Series in 1985. It is an outdoor venue on their beautiful property three hours south of Perth and has put Western Australia on the map. It was a favorite place for us to take our visitors long before we had heard of their concerts.

The Leeuwin Bandshell and Crowd

The Michael Crawford Program

From Jack

Training with the Crocodile Hunter

For 150 years the Australians tried to build a north-south railway across Australia from Darwin to Adelaide, and they finally opened it in January of 2004. The passenger train is called the Ghan, after the Afghans who would lead the camel caravans along the route before there were good highways or railroads. (Australian factoid: When the Afghans departed, they left the camels in the outback to fend for themselves. The camels did a remarkable job, as Australia is now home to the largest herd of feral camels in the world, there being over a million of them today. Their numbers are expected to double every 8 to 9 years, which will mean more camels than Aussies in 70 years!) Anyway, having already done the 4-day west-to-east Indian Pacific train in 1998 and being a train nut, I had to ride the new train as soon as I got back to Australia, which was September of 2005.

Fay and Ken Drayton came from Perth to join us, and on the 28th of September, 2005, we boarded the Ghan in Darwin for the three-day, two-night journey to Adelaide. There was one cabin on the Ghan that was actually two first-class cabins combined, and I had reserved that for Linda and me (I said I was a train nut!). We boarded and away we went, for a couple of hours. The train stopped at the town of Katherine so we could make an excursion into Katherine Gorge on the Katherine River. This involved some hiking, a boat ride, and sightseeing. As we were leaving to return to the train, there were some stone steps to climb, and I noticed a toddler struggling to climb up the steps on his own, but under his mother's close supervision. In spite of her appearance as an attractive, young, healthy woman, I thought that maybe she was too fatigued to carry the tot, so I asked if she needed any help. She replied in a surprising (for Australia) American accent that no help was possible, as the boy was very independent and determined to climb the stairs on his own. I made some crack that at least he would probably sleep well that night, and she laughed and said she sure hoped so. I wished her luck and moved on.

The next day as the train trundled across the outback, the train's conductor knocked on our cabin door and asked if we were Americans. We admitted being guilty, and he asked if we would like to walk back to the end of the train to the Chairman's Coach and meet Terri Irwin, as she had invited us to join her for drinks and snacks. We went! As we wobbled our way back to the rear of the train, the conductor explained that Steve and Terri Irwin had their family and film crew aboard in two private cars and were filming their trip for a TV special. We were warmly greeted by Terri, and, sure enough Terri was the young mother with the independent toddler from the day before. We were offered drinks and snacks, chatted a while and discussed her roots of Eugene, Oregon, and she then asked if we would be willing to be interviewed for the show as Americans visiting Australia on the Ghan. The film crew turned on the lights and cameras, and we were on our way to becoming stars on worldwide television! After the interview and more adult beverages and sandwiches, Terri offered to show us the private cars. In one of the rooms of the last car, we found Steve playing with his two kids, Bindi and Robert (the independent stair climber). Terri introduced us and we talked with the family for a while. It rapidly became apparent that Steve was a soft-spoken, shy, and gentle person, the exact opposite of his TV persona. Later, Terri affirmed that this was true and that it was one of the reasons why she did the interviews instead of Steve. At the end of the trip, we took a photo of the Irwins waving good-bye to us at the Adelaide train station.

The Irwin Family Filming

Steve and Terri Irwin Wave Good-Bye to Us

I recently found the TV show that resulted from this Ghan trip, and, alas, our blooming TV stardom was nipped in the bud by the editors, who did not include our interview. It is a series of five 10-minute segments, and it brought back some great memories for us.
See:
   https://www.youtube.com/watch?v=aX3FrEmNgME

Like much of the world, we were devastated by Steve Irwin's freak accident and death on

September 4th of 2006, less than a year after our shared train trip. A tragic loss to his young family, and to us all.

Meeting the Original Crocodile Hunter

In April of 2001 after the end of my last term at the University of Western Australia in Perth, we traveled to Broome, north of Perth, with two good friends we had made in our town of Cottesloe, Bill and Pauline Worcester. As we entered Broome by car, a large tourist attraction was on the right, The Malcolm Douglas Crocodile Park, which is well known in WA, and all of Australia. Pauline suggested we stop in as she had a question for them. We observed Pauline at the ticket counter having a conversation with the agent, who ended up shaking her head no in answer to the question. Pauline returned to us while the agent got on the phone. Pauline explained that she and Bill had been raised with Malcolm Douglas on the island of Nauru, but she was told that Malcolm was out of town. Pauline had explained to the agent their childhood link with Malcolm and left a quick message of hello. As we were leaving, the agent frantically chased after us and announced that Mr. Douglas was, after all, in town, and that we should pass through a private gate and proceed to his residence at the end of the road. We did. Malcolm was waiting and warmly greeted the Worcesters like the childhood friends they were. We were

435

invited into his living room and his wife, Valerie, served a nice high tea for all. After an hour or so of reminiscences and updates on his latest projects, we were invited for a private tour of the crocodile park, led by Douglas. At one point of the tour, he jumped into one of the crocodile pens, hung a dead chicken on a pole, and handed the pole to Linda with instructions to hang the chicken over the pond. Seconds later, a huge croc shot straight up out of the water, grabbed the chicken, and returned to the pond, leaving a startled and somewhat terrified Linda holding an empty pole. That was the last time any of us ever got near a crocodile!

Malcolm Douglas was a TV star within Australia, but not so much outside. In fact, he was called the Crocodile Hunter before Steve Irwin became famous under that name. Like Irwin, he died from a freak accident, but his death involved a vehicle, not a stingray.

So, in our time in Australia, we were fortunate to have met both of the famous Crocodile Hunters. We are still looking for Crocodile Dundee!

Sailing with the Governor of Western Australia

Probably in 2000, we were invited by our same friends, Bill and Pauline Worcester, to join a sail on the tall ship *Leeuwin* sailing out of Perth's port town of Fremantle.

STS *Leeuwin II*

Bill and Pauline worked on the ship as volunteers, Bill in the kitchen and Pauline as Purser. It turned out that the Governor of Western Australia, Major General Michael Jeffery AC CVO MC, was on board, and they introduced us to him. We spent some time chatting about my teaching job at UWA, American politics, and the daring exploits of the sailors in the rigging handling the sails. Governor Jeffery was a nice, down-to-earth person, as are most Aussies. Later that year, I had another event where I crossed paths with him, the graduation ceremony at UWA, but we didn't say more than hello to each other there. Since the processional line marching in was ordered by rank and academic status, least important first, I was first in the long line, and he was last!

General Jeffery went on to become the Governor-General of Australia from 2003 to 2008. The Governor-General of Australia is the Queen's representative, and, as such, has to approve all Australian legislation, appoint judges and ambassadors, and is also commander-in-chief of the Australian Defence Force. Nowadays, the Governor-General usually just rubber-stamps the recommendations of the Australian Prime Minister, but he has the veto right to say *no*.

On Top of Down Under

At the end of November of 1999, the four guys, Mike, Sean, Steve, and Andy flew to Perth to celebrate Thanksgiving. Andy also brought his then-girlfriend, Diana Cassell, so we had a merry group of seven. They left the U.S. the day before Thanksgiving and landed in Australia the day after Thanksgiving, having lost Thanksgiving Day crossing the international dateline. I've never figured out how that happens. Anyway, Linda prepared a traditional American turkey dinner, which was consumed by them in the fog of 12 hours of jet lag. After a quick visit around Perth, we all flew to Sydney, where we spent five days before flying on to New Zealand for a six-day visit on our way back to the U.S. In Sydney, they had recently started walking tours to the top of the Sydney Harbour Bridge, so we did that. Actually, Linda did not join us because she thought we were all crazy. So, the six crazy people paid their money, got suited up in special jump suits (they did not call them that!), and were attached to an ingenious tether line hooked to a bar which smoothly accompanied us throughout the whole walk to the top and back. It was a marvel of Aussie engineering. What a thrill it was!

Sydney Harbour and Opera House in Background

Downtown Sydney in Background

The picture of the bridge that follows is perfect for us. If you can magnify enough, you will see a small group of very tiny people standing at the rail to the left of the two flagpoles and middle post at the top of the bridge. While that probably isn't us, it is exactly where we were on our climb. Of further note, if you look under the bridge to the land beyond, you will see three tall buildings. We stayed in furnished apartments on the 9th and 10th floors of the middle building, overlooking the bridge and opera house. Spectacular!

Sydney Harbour Bridge

Dining with Australia's Famous Seat Designer

On a trip to Brisbane in April of 2011, we reconnected with Riegels Landing neighbors Nick Gibson and his wife Nettie McQueen, who had returned from Sarasota to their home in Brisbane. We loved visiting them in their home, which was designed by Nick's dad, architect Robin Gibson. Nick loves to tell this story of his dad, one of Australia's most famous architects, having designed the Queensland Art Gallery, the Queensland Museum, and the State Library of

441

Queensland. One evening Robin was attending a performance in the spectacular Queensland Performing Arts Complex, which he also designed, when he overheard the conversation of the couple seated in front of him. The lady was gushing over the design of the building and, in particular, the comfort of her seat. Robin leaned forward and said something like, "Thanks, I designed it." The woman continued gushing, saying that she had never met a seat designer before! Thereafter, Nick referred to his dad as "the famous Australian seat designer." The four of us had dinner with Nick's Mom and Dad, and they were delightful.

Memories of the Kids

Linda's Memories

Sean (age 6) and Larry Rule (age 11) were staying with us in Fox Mill for the month of July, 1976, when Andrew was born. The nurses were astonished when Jack arrived at Fairfax Hospital with a stair-step set of four boys to pick up me and baby Andrew! So this is why we needed our first station wagon...a brand new brown Chevy! We drove this wagon for many years before selling it and buying the almost-new wagon which affectionately was called the Blue Bomb. Often there were three (or four) boys and a dog in sleeping bags in the back of the station wagon driving to my parents' house at Glebe Harbor for a weekend. One winter was so cold that the creek froze at the Glebe and we all went ice-skating on it...dogs included.

In July of 1994, the five of us were getting dressed for an office party to meet Jack's staff in Melbourne, Australia. Mike had flown in from Korea, where he was stationed. Steve, Andrew, Jack and I had flown from Dulles. Suddenly, Jack and I heard annoyed words of dismay from the other bedrooms. All three guys were dressed in blue dress shirts, khakis, and loafers and unhappy about being triplets! They did survive the evening.

Obviously, Jack Did Not Get the Memo

The 2010s

Floating by Nature's Splendor

In 2008 Jack set up a family hiking and rafting trip to the Grand Canyon for September. This trip included our immediate family plus our new daughter-in-law Stephanie, her dad Carl Warren, our nephew Sean Pendray, and my sister Susan. Mike said he had had enough of desert, heat, and sand in Iraq and begged off. The trip commenced with a fabulous dinner for my 66th birthday at the historic Bright Angel Lodge. (Sharon Warren also joined us for dinner.) The next morning we gathered around 6 a.m. at the south rim of the canyon with our backpacks and boots on and hiking sticks in hand. We turned in our duffle bags containing the supplies that we would need for our 4-night camping trip. These would be carried down by mule to the Wilderness River Adventures rafts, while we hiked The Bright Angel Trail down the canyon to the river near the Phantom Ranch. Our group was basically 22 people and two motorized rafts with crew. Our family group was on one raft, joined by two young Marine fighter pilots, Justin and Brendan, who volunteered to sit on the front of our raft and absorb the waves of 52-degree water that poured in. We had a glorious adventure of rafting, including rapids, camping under the stars, eating good meals prepared by our great crew, and sitting around the fire. After dinner on our first camping night, our guides produced a wonderful birthday cake for me that they had made in a campfire Dutch oven. Our wine supplies were dragged behind the raft in a net, and so were always chilled and ready for dinner. Jack and I brought several gallons of box wine as our contribution, which was met with ridicule from our connoisseur children. The first two nights, our gang consumed all of the fine bottled wine, after which time they developed a fine appreciation for guzzling box wine. We had some amazing hikes in the side canyons...which the crew kept telling me would be easy. I did not find it easy to swing from tree limbs, jump from boulder to boulder, or walk a 2-foot-wide path with canyon wall on one side and drop-off to canyon bottom on the other! The last day we were helicoptered out to the Bar 10 Ranch for our first showers and real flushing toilets in several days. It was good to leave behind OSCAR, the portable toilet provided by the crew and accompanied by flashlights to search for snakes and vermin during night-time visits.

We were now River Rats and had certificates and pins to prove it!

Chucky and the Blue Bomb

Steve and Pete Nordvall, the engineers, were always stumbling onto interesting projects. At the Trumbull garbage dump they found a large doll. Next thing I know, the head of the doll was jammed onto the hood ornament of the Blue Bomb. It was very difficult to remove, so sometimes I left it on to

446

do errands. Then our engineers decide to make some modifications and hook up red lights in Chucky's eyes with a wire running under the hood to the battery. There might have been a switch hanging down near the driver as well. One night I picked Andrew up from his job at Carvel after he closed at 9 p.m. As we drove through quiet little Trumbull, I was pulled over by the police. The policeman seemed surprised to see a soccer mom behind the wheel but politely explained to me that it is illegal to have any type of red lights on the front of a car. Whew! Another time I was introduced to a lady at a meeting. I discovered she lived down the street from Dave Sadler, one of Andrew's best friends. I explained that I often drop Andrew off at Dave's house. "Are you the lady in the blue station wagon with the doll head on the front?"

Jack's Memories

Floating Away Together

On December 22, 2011, Linda, Mike, Sean, Steve, Steph, Andy, and I went down to Glebe Harbor, where Linda's folks had retired near Mount Holly, VA, for a nostalgic couple of days. On the 23rd, we went to the house of our, and the Lawrences', long-time friend, Dave Edwards, for the purpose of dispersing some of Gladdie's ashes in Glebe Creek.

447

Dave's house is about half-way between the two houses that Bob and Glad lived in during their time there. Dave had put up a Christmas tree on his dock for the occasion, and he participated with us. Linda had prepared a modification of Glad's Freedom Plaza memorial program, which we all took turns reading. At the end, Sean led us in the Lord's Prayer. We each had a little baggie of ashes to scatter in the creek, and Linda also supplied each of us a yellow rose, which we all tossed in together. Incredibly, six of the roses immediately floated under the dock and stayed there, but two others broke off and drifted together towards the big house that Bob and Glad built and shared with all of us. Inexplicable, and deeply moving.

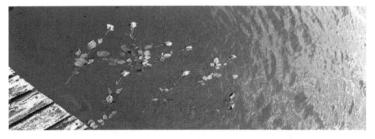

The 2010s

Gladys Rosemary Lawrence
July 28, 1916 ~ September 25, 2011

We celebrate the life of Gladys Rosemary Lawrence. She was a generous, loving and compassionate Wife, Mother, Grandmother, Great Grandmother and Friend.

She is survived by her daughter Linda and her husband Jack Pendray and her daughter Susan and her husband Gordon Harvey. She was blessed with 6 Grandchildren, Michael, Sean, Kelly, Stephen, Megan and Andrew. Her Great Grandchildren, Cheyenne, Georganna, Samantha, Hailey and Jake, were blessed to have had the gift of knowing and loving her. The love they shared with her was magical.

Gladys was born in Harvard, Nebraska. She met and married her husband of 65 years, Robert C. Lawrence, in Lincoln. Bob's career as a geologist kept them on the move. When Bob joined the US Army during World War II, their exciting life together was destined to stay busy. They lived in Japan, Germany and Thailand. She often worked as a secretary wherever they were stationed. Gladys particularly enjoyed working in General MacArthur's headquarters in Tokyo, Japan.

She was a wonderful cook, hostess, and bridge player as well as an avid reader and crossword-puzzle enthusiast. She was active in the DAR and Eastern Star and a Pen Pal to her friends all over the world. Gladys and Bob loved to entertain, to travel in their RV, and to boat and crab on the Chesapeake Bay.

Since moving to Freedom Plaza she was a devoted member of water aerobics, Merry Widows, bridge, dominos, and poker. Thank you to all her wonderful friends who made these last ten years happy ones.

Celebrating the Life of
Gladys R. Lawrence

July 28, 1916 ~ September 25, 2011
Freedom Plaza Auditorium
Monday, October 17, 2011
2:00 p.m.

Receiving Premature Eulogies

To celebrate Thanksgiving of 2019, we had a several-day gathering of over 30 relatives in Wintergreen Resort, VA, where our son Mike lives, and two of my cousins have vacation homes. In the afternoon, after a splendid Thanksgiving luncheon at the Copper Mine restaurant in Wintergreen, we met for a light dinner and (adult) beverages at my cousin Jim (and Kathy) Coleman's house. During the evening, our youngest son, Andy, hushed the crowd and, in celebration of my recent 80th birthday, gave a heartfelt speech honoring and thanking Linda and me for our years of parenting. Our other sons, Steve and Mike, as well as our nephew Sean (our 4th son), followed with similar speeches of their own. More than a few of the attendees, including me, did not have dry eyes at the end.

Most parents never hear such wonderful things said about themselves by their children, as this is usually reserved for their funeral eulogies, but we were blessed to share ours among many of our family. A greater gift is impossible to imagine.

Screwing Things Up

I always had a workbench of some sort wherever we lived, and spent a lot of time fixing things with my tools. As soon as he was big enough to get at them, Steve would grab one of my tools and go around the house "fixing" things. Many of the tools, like his favorite, the screwdriver, were dangerous if he should fall on them, so I was often yelling at him and grabbing a tool away, sending him into a scared crying fit. Eventually, it dawned on me that this was lousy parenting and all I was doing was scaring Steve. So, I found a short flat-head screwdriver and a short phillips-head screwdriver, filed the sharp points off the flat-head and presented them to Steve as his own tools. He would wander around the house trying to unscrew things with his tools, but he was not strong enough to take many things apart, for a while.

Rasping Away

When Andy went through the same tool phase as Steve, I finally found a better answer. I got Andy a half-round wood rasp and a stool so he could sit next to me at my workbench. The two of us would sit for hours, me fiddling with something and Andy rasping away at the 2 by 4's that composed my workbench. By the time he grew out of this phase, I had a nice notch through one of the 2 by 4's.

Unappreciated Success

Being our first-born, Mike had the thankless job of training his parents. By the time Steve came along two years later, we were wiser and more mellow, and Steve could let Mike take most of the heat when we failed at good parenting. Coming four years after Steve, Andy almost had *laissez-faire* parents and got away with things that we would have harshly disciplined Mike for. Mike's parent-training duties did not end until he left home, and he probably would say they continue to this day!

As an example, let's talk about SAT tests. Mike was the first to take these modern-day prerequisites to college entrance. When his scores arrived at school, he came home and proudly announced that he had made 1460 out of a possible 1600. I was disappointed, because, knowing how brilliant Mike is, I expected him to make 1600, or pretty close to that. Instead of congratulating and praising him, I told Mike that he should take the tests again and see if he could do better. At this, Mike's face dropped and he went into his bedroom to get away from me. Stupid me! I now know that 1460 was an exceptional score, since, without ever taking the tests again, Mike was one of the rare National Merit Semi-finalists, and won an even rarer National Merit scholarship to the University of Florida. When Steve and Andrew also came home with semi-finalist-qualifying scores on their SAT tests, I was properly impressed and praising of their achievements. Mike had borne the brunt of my moving slowly up the parental learning curve, and this is just one of many examples.

I now realize that I have the lowest SAT score, 1280, and the lowest IQ in the family, as evidenced by it taking me so long to learn basic parenting skills. I'm still learning.

Electrical Wizard

When Andrew was 2, his favorite plaything was a collection of electrical apparatus. He possessed extension cords, Christmas lights, a wall lamp, and one spinning humidifier. He'd drag these things around, connect them together, find a wall plug, plug them in, and they would always all work. Whenever he got shocked, he'd scream for a while, get comforted, and then go right back at it, rearranging the order of his devices each time. One day, one of the members of our neighborhood Gourmet Group, Tim McInerney, witnessed Andy in action with his traveling electrical show and immediately christened him "Andron," and Tim called him that to his final days.

Défends Toi Même

When Mike was 4 ½ years old, he became eligible for public school in France, in pre-kindergarten. The local elementary school was less than a block from our house in Nanterre, so we enrolled Mike. We had few fears since Mike's first language at that time was French, and he got along well with his French neighborhood playmates. One day, Linda was watching the kids on the teacher-supervised playground, and one kid was hitting Mike. Linda scheduled a meeting with the teacher and the teacher admitted that Mike was bullied by the French kids. When Linda asked her why she didn't stop it, she replied that Mike needed to learn to defend himself. We took Mike out of that school and put him and Steve in a private school of international kids who weren't allowed to bully.

In my opinion, the moral of this story goes deep into the French culture, at least the culture that we found in France in the early '70s. After working with the French for a couple of years, I came to the conclusion that one of the dominant traits of the culture was the attitude that everyone felt he was alone competing against the world. I jokingly said that "French team" was an oxymoron. "Defend yourself" was ingrained into the French from pre-kindergarten on, as we saw with Mike's experience. One of the hardest tasks I had as the general manager of a French company was building teams and positive team spirit, and our moderate success at doing this became one of our major competitive advantages. In defense of the French, it is perfectly understandable that they have a low-trust culture after many instances of occupation and division by foreign powers. As Americans, we can't fully appreciate the consequences of this.

Bike Trickster

Steve was always the best jock in our family, and he loved riding his Mongoose bicycle. I had spent a lot of time on my bike as a kid, but never came close to doing what he could on a bike. For instance, he could balance on his bike at rest forever without falling over. Wheelies, whatever, he could do. We thought it was a great injury-free sport until we heard that Steve and a neighborhood friend were jumping over a picnic table on their bikes. After that, we worried, but never had cause to, thanks to Steve's skill.

Steve and The Bike

A Private Tour of the White House

In January of 1984, we were in the process of moving from Fox Mill Estates in Herndon, Virginia, to Trumbull, Connecticut. One of our neighbors, Tom Wiley, was a Secret Service Agent on President Ronald Reagan's protection team, and he invited us to a private tour of the White House. Tom was our escort and guide and we had quite a tour, which included the grounds, all of the normal visited rooms, and some rarely visited, such as the Oval Office. At one point when we were visiting the grounds, one of the kids walked on the lawn, and Tom rapidly pulled him back while telling us that the lawn had sensors. Of course it would!

At the Door to the Oval Office with Secret Service Agent Tom Wiley

The Oval Office with the Resolute Desk

Steve Likes Steak

While I was at CBIS, we had a large contract with the Australian telephone company, Telstra, which required me to visit Melbourne and Sydney several times a year. On a trip in June of 1994, I decided to take the whole family and make a family vacation out of it. Mike was in the Army in Korea, so he just flew south a while to join us. Thanks to frequent-flier miles, I was able to fly everyone else business class, which, in 1994, was quite a luxurious way to travel. Steve had a steak between New Haven and Chicago, another between Chicago and LA, and two more between LA and Sydney—a four-steak flight—way to go, Steve!

Sailing into the Sunset

We've done several bare-boat sailing trips as family, but the last one is probably the most memorable. In May of 2003, we did our last sail with the four Pendray boys as crew—Mike, Sean, Steve, and Andy. We rented the biggest boat we could afford and got a 46-foot catamaran to take, one-way, from St. Vincent to Grenada, with two-day stopovers at each end. It's impossible to tip over a catamaran that big, so we didn't. It was a wonderful boat, with four staterooms and four heads, two engines, generator, and air conditioning.

The 46-ft Catamaran "Super Nova"

I gave each of the guys a specific job: Mike had the mainsail, Andy had the jib, Steve had the engines, and Sean had the anchor windlass. Being the only non-engineer of the crew, Sean got the windlass because it was a simple matter to push buttons to pay out or bring in the anchor line. Well, maybe not so simple. Turns out the windlass had two broken parts and required someone to guide the chain and line into or out of the windlass, a tricky job putting fingers in peril. Our financial advisor was up to the job and still has all his fingers!

Sean Operates His Anchor Windlass

On the other hand, the captain (me) left something to be desired. We quickly learned that handling the anchor for a large catamaran was difficult, as the bow was very high above the water and working from the trampoline net was problematic. After several embarrassing attempts at setting the anchor in a harbor crowded with other sailboats, a lady on one of the other boats gently yelled over, "It's a lot easier if you take the anchor in and out of the water at the stern (rear) using the built-in swim steps and then walk the line forward." Red-faced, the captain thanked her and downed another Red Stripe beer.

The End of Another Anchor Drill

The Crew Under the Bimini

CHRISTMAS 2012

Hello Out There...With this 42nd edition of this letter, I will have written them for several years more than half of my life, and narrowed my friends down to three who are still willing to receive it. My savings on postage are probably single-handedly responsible for the financial difficulties of the Postal Service...This year's liquid lubricant is one of the best, a bottle of The Dead Arm Shiraz from the d'Arenberg winery in McLaren Vale, Australia. It is from a case of wine that arrived unexpectedly on our doorstep in Nov. In the case were 12 bottles of Australia's finest wines, but no note or card. Linda went to work and found out that it came from one of Jack's past students in Perth, Mike Williams, and should have had a note saying, "To my professor, thanks." Jack was strutting around the house, wine in hand, until Thanksgiving, when his family drank most of what was left...This year really began with an ending. In late Dec., our family gathered on Glebe Creek, near Montross, VA, to spread some of Linda's mom's ashes in the waters near Linda's parents' house, where we all have such fond memories. A wonderful friend of ours, and of the Lawrences, Dave Edwards, even erected a Christmas tree on his dock for the occasion and took the photo...Wow!, this Dead Arm is like drinking candy! Hope I finish before I am finished...January saw the whole famn damily (hereinafter referred to as "damily") in New York to celebrate Steve's big 40. His wife, Stephanie, threw a big bash for him in a NYC restaurant, and we all helped run up the bill in true damily tradition...Feb., March, and April are our stay-in-FL months, when we enjoy watching the news about the ice and snow storms elsewhere. Global warming is nothing new to Floridians. Also during this time, the population of Sarasota doubles and we get to spend time with our "snowbird" friends and other visitors seeking to escape the frigid north. It is also the time when Jack catches up on his repairs around the house. Since he doesn't see so well anymore, nor hear so well, nor have steady hands, he has to call on our capable handyman, Al Higashi, to fix all the things that Jack fixed...Our oldest, Mike, has this horrible job, which he walks to from his apt, which requires him to spend a week every month reviewing the IT security at federal courthouses in all the best cities. He spent a week in Tampa in Feb., so we had him, and his teammates, for dinner...March was like April, more partying with friends, drinking, going to theaters, drinking, eating, (did I say 'drinking"?), etc. The "season" in FL is tough! (Was that a deep sigh of sympathy that I heard?)...The bottle of Dead Arm is now half gone. I'm definitely losing this race...April was fun. One of Jack's high-school-and-beyond friends, Frank Molinari, visited for a week. We all took off for Key West, where we fit in with all the other kooks that abound there. Weird, but lots of fun...Believing that the real estate market had bottomed, Jack bought a condo in Sarasota with what was left of his IRA. Much to our surprise, the market did not immediately re-enter the Great Recession... The "season" ends in May, so we rented a villa on the Med in the south of Spain for three weeks. Naturally, the damily found out and joined us. We were near the "white town" of Mijas, and visited Seville, Rhonda, Granada, and Gibraltar. The "kids" also flew to Barcelona for a few days. Mike's friends, the Schoonmakers, and our neighbors, the Gibsons (on two days' notice!), also joined us. Terrific time was had by all...In June, we took our usual trip to Asheville, NC, but only for two weeks this time. We spent some time with a Realtor, Rick Shearin, looking at houses for sale. We ended up making an offer on a small place, the "cabin," about 15 miles south of Asheville...In July, we met up with some Aussie friends of ours, Dennis and Kay Neil, in San Francisco. They had just spent a month driving around the western U.S. in a 25-foot RV, so, naturally, we rented a minivan and drove them around some more. After a couple of days in San Francisco, we drove to Yosemite, where we stayed in Jack's cousin's cabin nearby. Jens and Jeanie Hanson's cabin is just outside Yosemite, and it was a super place to stay. We then drove to San Simeon to visit Hearst's castle (a quaint little country place!), before going to Carmel for a night (no, we didn't see Eastwood, nor his empty chair). From Carmel, we went to visit our youngest, Andy, in Sunnyvale for two nights...We returned to NC in late July to close on our cabin and get started on the work that needed to be done, staying with Stephanie, in her folks' lake house on Lake Hartwell, GA...Aug. was hot and boring in FL, so we spent most of the month in NC working on the cabin, and it needed lots of work (and still does)... Enough work! Off we went in Sept. to Natchez, MS, to meet up with another of Jack's high-school-and-beyond friends, Inky Philips and his wife, Mary. From there, we drove to College Station to visit our friends, John and Judy Guido. Jack and John went to the Texas A&M vs FL football game, which was the introduction of A&M into the SEC. FL squeaked out a victory, but the A&M folks were great hosts anyway. The Guidos joined us in a trip to New Orleans, where we celebrated Linda's special birthday (it wasn't 60, nor 80, so take a guess). Mike's terrible job had taken him to Baton Rouge that week, so he drove down and joined us for Linda's birthday party...After coming home for a week, we drove to NC, and then on to Northern Virginia for the wedding of long-time friends John Nilsen and Helen Hayward. That was a blast...We spent a lot of Oct. working on the (darn) cabin in NC, with a weekend trip to visit our neighbors' (the Gibsons, from the Spain trip, remember?) cabin near Dawsonville, GA. Dawsonville was having the annual Moonshine Festival that weekend, and Jack got to check that off his bucket list...Early Nov. was a period of mourning for Jack after the election. He is now convinced that democracy will prove to be a non-sustainable form of government, as the takers will always eventually overwhelm the makers and destroy the economy from which they both feed. Cheery thought!...Thanksgiving gave us all a reason to sample, read; drink almost all of, the great wines received from Mike Williams, so we did. The whole damily was here, Mike, Steve and Steph, Andy, Jack's nephew Sean and his girlfriend, Melanie, Linda's niece, Kelly, and her three daughters Cheyenne, Georganna, and Samantha...In Dec., we're off to spend Christmas with Mike in NOVA. The ulterior reason we are going is to attend the party given by Jack's cousins, Jim and Kathy Coleman...Jack had an active year (for a retiree), buying two more places to maintain. For someone who complains about the maintenance on the Sarasota house, he isn't too bright... Linda is about to take over the social life at our church, being chairperson of two committees and serving on others. With her new NC house and travels, she keeps busy (for a retiree)...Mike is still in Reston, VA, walking to his horrible job, except when he is flying off to interesting cities...Steve and Steph are still in NYC. Steve is still at AMEX. They are looking at houses in CT, which would give them more space...Andy is still in CA, in Geek Valley, working for Symantec. He loves it there, except that his damily keeps visiting...The joke this year is on Andy. He came from CA for Thanksgiving for some R&R, or, as the kids call it, "vegging," but it didn't work out quite that way. Jack had discovered that the church's network was in distress, and he pressed Andy into service fixing it. It took most of three days. Now that Andy is gone, the folks at church are depending on Jack, who hasn't a clue, so maybe the joke is really on Jack...Well, the Dead Arm is dead (yes, the whole bottle), and my arm is dead, and my mind is dead, and I need to toddle off and take a nap.

We wish you all a very Merry Christmas and Happy New Year. May 2013 bring peace and prosperity to you, your family, and the world.

The Pendrays

50 Years of Christmas Letters

Books that Changed Me

I have read many books over my life; however, some of them permanently changed how I thought about things. Here is a short list of several that made the most impact.

The New Testament of the Holy Bible—Whether one believes that Jesus Christ was divine, a prophet, an ordinary man, or just a fable, *The New Testament*, in my opinion, is the best guidebook on how to live a life that is enjoyable and fulfilling, while contributing to the general welfare of others and society.

Frames of Mind: The Theory of Multiple Intelligences by Howard E. Gardner—I have always felt that society puts too much emphasis on what we call intelligence, as often measured by the IQ test. In this ground-breaking book, Gardner defines six different categories of "intelligences," which gives more appreciation of the spectrum of innate qualities that people can possess. While this is a more balanced view and solved my concern over the single-focused intelligence issue, it was personally distressing since I realized that I was competitive in only one of the six categories. Rats!

Frogs into Princes: Neuro Linguistic Programming by Richard Bandler and John Grinder—*Where Frames of Mind* deals with different human intelligences, *Frogs into Princes* deals with the different human senses and how their use affects communication. I am surely not among the intended audience for this book on psychology, but I found the underlying analyses of how people use their senses differently to be enlightening and useful in ordinary communication. The main lesson for me was to observe and listen to your interlocutor before trying to communicate effectively, and this book gives you a way to do that. My problem is that it requires concentration and discipline, which I'm short on.

Atlas Shrugged by Ayn Rand—Ayn Rand's classic novel changed me into an economic Libertarian for life and has always helped me keep economics and politics separated in my mind. In a nutshell, if the creators of value are not allowed to keep a larger share of the <u>incremental</u> <u>new</u> value they have created than those who created much less or nothing, they will stop creating. Simply said, those who make the pie bigger deserve to receive a comparatively larger piece of the pie than others. On the other hand, economic politics concerns the distribution of the pie, and society as a whole will only advance if the pie is continually becoming larger. So, the job of the politician is to encourage the value creators to succeed by letting them profit from their new value added, but retain enough of the new value added to increase the distributions received by others. Seems simple, right?

Dress for Success by John T. Molloy—This book appears to be another superficial business book, but the underlying premise and the supporting research on first impressions and appearance is far from trivial. This book is why I wore suits for 40 years, in spite of my real desire to go through life in shorts and flip-flops.

Snakes in Suits by Paul Babiak and Robert D. Hare —This book about psychopaths in the workplace explains a recognizable personality disorder without over-using psychological gobbledygook. It helped me understand, accept, and deal with this type of malevolent individual.

50 Years of Christmas Letters

CHRISTMAS 2013

Hello Out There...Happy Thanksgiving! Well, it's the middle of November and here I sit writing this 43rd edition of this letter. Yes that's a little early, but we're spending December in Australia (Oz, as they call it down there), so I have to get this out early. The bad news is that you're getting the letter anyway. The good news is that it may be short...Preparing for the trip to Oz, I'm sipping one of its best values in wine, Black Opal Cabernet Merlot. It's a very old vintage, 2012. Since I'm getting a late start today, it's already noon, I may have trouble finishing the bottle before my bedtime, which is usually about 4 p.m. when I write this letter...We spent last Christmas in Virginia with Mike, and had Christmas dinner with Jack's Florida relatives, the Coleman Clan (who are mostly now around D.C.). I hope we behaved (I don't remember) and get invited back again this year (hint, hint)....We returned home in January in time for Jack to watch the bowl games. Florida lost and Stanford won, so he wore his Stanford colors after that. This year, he burned his Florida apparel, and ordered more Stanford stuff...Jan. thru March is the social season in Sarasota, because it's actually cool enough to go outside. We

473

all get in our cars and idle along in the congested traffic, while listening to weather reports from places like Minot and Buffalo. It is also the artsy season, so we get the opportunity to sleep through some excellent performances, lectures, ballets, etc. There is no lack of nap inducers for us oldsters here...Our Realtor and good friend from North Carolina Rick Shearin came to visit us to verify that we actually had a house here, based on how difficult it was to get us to purchase something in NC...Most of our old Virginia gang, the notorious Gourmet Group (hereinafter referred to as GG), came through town during the "season," but we didn't have a mass gathering, since we already had one scheduled for Sept. in Rapid City, SD. Where else?...We finished the "season" by having our pool refinished. We heard that green-water-looking pools were out and blue-water-looking pools were in. It turns out that one can change from green to blue for about $6,000, a no-brainer (as in: not having any brain)....In May, the standard heat and humidity returned (there are no people in FL between June and Oct.), so we went from FL to NC to VA to Europe. In Europe, we spent a few days south of Frankfurt with friends from Jack's Stanford days, which were right after the Boer War. Klaus and Karin Pfitzner were very gracious to us jet-lagged travelers and gave us a royal tour of the area. We then trained to Berlin, where we hooked up with our Grand Circle tour group for a bus tour from Berlin to Dresden to Prague to Salzburg to Linz, where we got on a river boat and floated to Vienna, Bratislava, and Budapest. All of these were terrific, but Budapest was fantastic. After we got off the boat, Klaus and Karin (from south of Frankfurt, remember? There will be a test later.) joined us for a couple of days more in

The 2010s

Budapest. Coulda spent a month there…June through Sept. were spent living in the projects south of Asheville. When we bought the little house there, we called it the cabin. Now it is called the money pit, or just "the pit." The projects were to replace the deck, add a screened porch, replace the 100 feet of rotting-railroad-tie retaining walls with block walls, tear out the entire driveway and replace it, repair and expand the walkway and patio, and fix up the interior of the house to be habitable by us and guests. At the end of the summer, we all were exhausted: Jack, Linda, and the checkbook. Not wanting to be left out of living in the projects, several friends dropped by for the experience. They included, Jan Rumberger, Bob and Dot Johnston, John and Helen Nilsen, and Jim and Dee Gutfreund. Fortunately, they did not all arrive at the same time…In Sept. we drove up to Reston, VA, for the 50th wedding anniversary of John and Eileen Giaquinto. I heard it was quite a blast and that I had a good time, but I don't remember…The rest of Sept. was spent traveling with the GG from Rapid City (remember? No? You flunk!) to Salt Lake City on a tour of some of the national parks. The tour was arranged by John Nilsen, who got sick and couldn't make it. We compensated by sending him live photos and videos of us having a good time in all the places he planned for us, while he was in the hospital. See what such good friends we are? Great tour of our incredible parks…In Oct., we had to return to FL so Linda could co-host, with Tom Schwartz, her high-school reunion, at our house! Luckily, the Army's Munich American High School in Germany was small, so Siesta Key was a perfect site for the gathering of 19 attendees. Quantity, small, quality, extremely high, and can they party!...Back to

NC to watch the leaves turn, and finish the projects. Next summer, no more living in the projects, hooray!...Tomorrow, we head for Miami. As usual, we'll stop in Naples both coming and going to visit Don and Beverly Vining. Don is one of Jack's favorite fraternity brothers from his days at UF, right before the Boer War. Anyway, we're off to Miami to attend the wedding of our fourth son (really, Jack's nephew, but don't tell Jack that), Sean, to Melanie Price. It took Sean a while, but it was sure worth the wait, as he has convinced a really super person to be his bride. We're all excited to be there and welcome her as she adds the Pendrays to her family, and we add her to ours...In last year's letter, I mentioned that Jack roped Andy into helping him with the church's WiFi system, thereby ruining Andy's Thanksgiving vacation. Even Andy couldn't solve the entire problem in three days, so Jack had to continue on after Andy left. He ended up installing five routers, three extenders, and three switches on four WiFi networks around the church campus. Talk about having to do some research by a has-been techie. Amazingly, some of it works most of the time...Jack did give up on learning Spanish and plodding (his version of jogging) this year. Seems his brain and his knees are both well over the hill...On the other hand, Linda seems to be just hitting her full stride. Not only did she co-host her high school reunion, live in the projects all summer, and entertain guests in fashion, but she is also a pillar of our church. She is co-chair of the Foyers group, where we meet in homes for dinners and refreshing beverages (yes, the real ones. After all, we are Episcopalians.). She also is one of the team leaders on our homeless support activity and our fair trade market...Mike moved this year. He was evicted by his landlady, Linda's sister, Susan, who decided that it was such a great apartment that she and her husband, Gordon, would move in (which was always their known plan). After exhaustive research (several hours on the Internet), Mike found the perfect place, down the hall. Now, he and his aunt are hall-neighbors. Mike came to Tampa on one of his job's assignments examining federal courthouse IT security, and he invited us to Bern's Steakhouse for dinner. For the uninitiated, one has to drive at least a Rolls Royce to have the valet park your car close at Bern's. Could this be the passing of the baton where we eat free and they pay? I like it!...Steve and his wife, Stephanie, made the big move from a dinky apt in New York City to an actual house in Darien, CT. Only a five-minute walk from the train station to NYC, it is a prime location. Being a short sale, and after many weeks of Stephanie's work, they got it at a great price, but had lots of work to do. We hear that Stephanie has painted OUR guest room lavender. As a house-warming present, Jack gave Steve his tap-and-die set, a piece of any engineer's soul. Steve can now tap and die to his heart's content, and maybe someday he'll even explain to Jack how to use it...Andy continues to flourish in California's Silicon Valley. Having survived several iterations of layoffs during Symantec's re-structuring, he finally got tired of it all, lifted his head from the trenches, and found a great new job. He now works for HyTrust, a Silicon Valley start-up where he can make a meaningful contribution. Between his new job, his volunteer work at the local animal shelter, and his social life, Andy is not bored...Did I promise a short letter? I lied. Well, the Black Opal is almost empty after all, and it's almost 4 p.m., so good-night...Normally, we take a hop, skip, and jump approach going to Australia, but this time it's straight (via Beijing and Bangkok!) to Perth, and straight back (via Singapore and Beijing!). So, as we pack to take the plane to Oz, sing along with us: "We're off to see the wizards, the wonderful wizards of Oz, etc." All you wonderful wizards in Oz, be ready, for here we come.

We wish you all a Happy Thanksgiving, a very Merry Christmas, and a Happy New Year. May 2014 bring peace and prosperity to you, your family, and the world.

The Pendrays

Joe Carey, Steve, Stephanie, Jack, Sean, Melanie, Linda, Ken Barrett, Andy, and Mike at Melanie and Sean's wedding reception, The Rusty Pelican on Virginia Key, Miami, FL

CHRISTMAS 2014

Hello Out There...Here it is, December 6th, at 9 o'clock in the morning, as I sit down to write the 44th edition of the annual Pendray Pageant (def.: Pageant - An elaborate public dramatic presentation that usually depicts a historical or traditional event. Fitting, huh?) Last year, I promised you a short letter, and I lied. Blame it on last year's Black Opal Cabernet Merlot. At 9 o'clock in the morning, champagne seems appropriate, so absolutely no promises this year, just lots of lies. Being produced in the U.S., my "champagne" is actually a Chandon *methode traditionnelle* California Brut Classic. Since champagne, and its imposters, always go straight to my head, fasten your seat belts for a wild ride. I better type fast, as I will probably be in bed by noon...First flute finished, it's good!... When I left you off last year in an early Christmas letter, I said that we were on our way to Australia. What I left out was that it was to be a very bittersweet trip. While it is always a joy to visit with our wonderful friends down under, two of Jack's

479

dearest friends in Perth had both contracted brain cancer and we wanted to visit with them while we could. On our arrival, we discovered that they were two doors apart in the hospice unit of the hospital. Since they did not know one another, Jack had the opportunity of introducing them and their families to each other. The ward nurses were puzzled trying to figure out who this Yank was that flew in from the U.S. to introduce their Australian patients and families to each other. Sadly, they both have since left this phase of their existence. David Plowman, who, as head of the MBA programs at the University of Western Australia, hired Jack, and Dennis Neil, a fellow engineer, sailing partner, church member, and travelling companion, were dear friends and valuable persons whom the world will miss almost as much as Jack does…We returned on Dec. 23rd to Mike's place in Reston, Virginia, where we celebrated a jet-lagged, fuzzy Christmas, joined by most of our far-flung family, photo enclosed. Jack's cousins, the Coleman Clan, did invite us back for their terrific Christmas dinner, where we all ate and drank too much. Great fun!…Second flute finished, even better!…In Jan., we returned to Sarasota for the winter. We've decided to sell the waterfront house and start the process of simplifying our lives by moving into something less demanding, albeit still in Sarasota. Jack decided to try and sell it himself on Zillow. Nada, zilch, nothing. The good thing was that Jack had to go around and fix anything in the house that he should have fixed a long time ago, so that kept him out of trouble for the

the summer. From there, we drove up to Fairfax, VA, for the "immortalization" of Alan and Sally Merten when George Mason University named the admin building after them. A fitting recognition of their many successful years building GMU into a leading national university...In July, we spent two weeks back in Sarasota supporting the local medical and dental practitioners. Seems like all of the dental work we had done as kids is now ready to be replaced. Not sure what the dentists will do when the fluoride generations retire, but our generation should enable them all to retire early and wealthy...In August, Sean, Melanie, and Sophia came to NC for a visit. What a cute and precious child! Girls are different, even Pendray girls!...Fourth flute finished, woo hoo!...In Sept., we joined some Aussie friends in a trek across some of the hot spots of America. Yes, we went from St. Paul, to Fargo, to Jamestown, to Bismarck, to Minot, and to East Glacier. Jack had extolled the pleasures of train travel in the U.S. to John & Rosemary Pearman and Fay Drayton, and they made the mistake of believing him. Turns out that Amtrak is a national disgrace. Our trains were 3 to 6 hours late, with missed connections. Something to do with lots of oil trains in North Dakota. Glacier National Park, the beautiful aspens in fall color, and terrific friends saved the day, and we all had a great time...Ending the train ride in Seattle, we had dinner with Jack's brother, Keith, to celebrate his wife's, Renee's, birthday. She was too sick with the flu to join us, so we ate enough for her, too...From Seattle, we flew to San Francisco winter...Winter in Sarasota is difficult. Sometimes, it gets cold enough that we even have to close the windows! Also, many of our friends come to town and we have to party. Some members of our Gourmet Group from Virginia even come for months, and that really requires partying. Don't even mention the snowbirds that come and party for the whole winter. Yes, winter in Sarasota is difficult, one has to know how to party to survive...In Feb., Jack gave up and listed the house with a real real estate agent. This led to a contract in which we traded our house; lock, stock, and furnishings, for a condo; lock, stock, and furnishings, plus some cash. Unfortunately, or maybe fortunately, the other party decided that this was a crazy deal and backed out, so we are still here and on the market...Third flute finished, the best!...In March, we made a trip to Miami to see Jack's nephew's new baby. Sean and Melanie had a baby girl, Sophia Kate, on Mar 14th. The first member of the next generation, and a girl, unheard of in Pendray-land! Now, they are expecting a boy in 2015...In April, we went to Williamsburg, VA, for Linda's induction into the Old Guard at William & Mary. Since this honor is reserved for the 50th alumni reunion, it has more to do with old than with guarding. However, we did manage to guard the bars and food lines very assiduously...May saw us in Connecticut to celebrate the 7th anniversary of Steve and Stephanie's wedding with dinner at our favorite restaurant up there, Le Chateau, in South Salem, NY. Saw lots of old friends and had a great time...In June, we took the house off the market and went to Asheville, NC, for and spent three days with Andy in Sunnyvale. The money moving around in Silicon Valley was palpable...October was spectacular in the mountains around Asheville. Jan Rumberger, one of Jack's friends and past business partners, and Mike joined us for the fall colors. Mike and Jan wanted to do a Bar B Q restaurant comparison, so we ate Bar B Q every day. Not a bad thing...Thanksgiving was in FL and everyone attended, except Stephanie who had to stay in CT to care for the dog. Poor Owen got his tail caught in a door at day care and lost an inch or so of it, and he needed lots of TLC from Steph. Mike, Steve, Andy and his girlfriend, Krystal Wang, Sean, Melanie, and Sophia, Cheyenne (Linda's grandniece) and her boyfriend, Cheyne, were all here for, perhaps, our last Thanksgiving in this house...Not sure where we will spend Christmas this year, but everyone has to be somewhere...Fifth flute finished, feeling good!...Between the house being for sale and the cabin in NC, Jack keeps busy fixing the things he breaks while fixing things...Linda keeps busy organizing activities at church, running two houses, and keeping Jack out of trouble...Mike is still in Reston, VA. He has changed jobs within his company, and no longer travels all over the country. His company did move its offices, so he can no longer walk to work, poor Mike...Steve, Steph, and Owen are doing well in Darien, CT. The puppy in the photo is now almost 90 pounds of frolicking fun, and he is eagerly awaiting twin human siblings, a girl and a boy, to arrive early in the New Year!... Andrew is doing well in Silicon Valley. He is driving a new

Audi S6, so some of that wealth must have trickled down to him…The joke this year is on Steve. After living in midtown Manhattan for many years, he and Steph moved to Darien, CT. This year, Steve took a job that is two blocks from his old apartment in New York. So, now he commutes to where he used to live. Go figure!…Sixth flute finished, bed time!

We wish you all a Blessed Christmas and a Happy New Year. May there be peace on earth!

The Pendrays

her sister's wedding, and Sophia's and Luke's baptisms on Dec. 6th...After the twins' baptisms in May, we were sick of traveling, so we flew to Paris for two days, Istanbul for three days, and Tuscany for two weeks. We stopped in Paris for old times' sake and to visit one of Jack's high school fraternity brothers, Dave Taylor, and his wife, Yori, and also Mike and Steve's baby-sitter from the early '70s, Maryse Poullaouec, and her husband, Dominique. In Istanbul, we were hosted by one of Jack's friends from his grad school days at Stanford, Fikret Keskinel, and his wife, Ayhan. We were treated like sultans by the Keskinels, and introduced to the delights of this wonderful city. Next was Bucine in Tuscany, Italy. Our oldest son, Mike, rented a small 9-bedroom villa there and invited all the extended family and some of his friends to visit. We thought that was a good idea, so we invited some of our friends too. Another of Jack's high school fraternity brothers, Paul Huck, and his wife, Donna, from Coral Gables, shared four of our delightful 14 days there with us. The Hucks also joined us for a couple of days in NC at the end of Sept., and we retaliated by staying with them in Dec....In Oct., we flew to Reston, VA, for the memorial service of one of our almost-40-years-old Gourmet Group, Eloise Vincent, one of the kindest, most unpredictable, and truest Christians the world has ever known. I wonder what she could be doing in heaven, as there are no needy folks to help up there. A toast of bubbly to Eloise!...On Oct. 10, our youngest son, Andrew, proposed to Krystal Wang, and she accepted! We are thrilled at the prospect of having her as a daughter-in-law. Krystal was born in China and moved to Texas at the age of two. She loves dogs, motorcycles, and going shooting with the guys. Talk about fitting in with our family!...Also in Oct., we sold our house on Siesta Key for the third time, and this time it actually closed, on Oct. 30. Since we had plans for a family Thanksgiving in the house, the buyers agreed to let us stay until Dec. 4, so you're getting the last family picture taken on that dock...Bubbling right along here...Linda's Munich American High School held a reunion in San Antonio (Munich, San Antonio, same thing) from Nov. 8 to 12. Great friends, great time...We had 22 family for Thanksgiving dinner. The next night, some McInerneys and Nilsens, from the Gourmet Group, joined to make a group of 30 for pizza by the pool. The last three houseguests left on Monday, Nov. 30, and the movers arrived Tuesday morning. Typical insane Pendray planning. Oh, we also closed on our new house on Nov. 24...We wanted a smaller house to simplify our lifestyle to match our advancing years, so we bought a fixer-upper that will keep us busy for a few years. So much for simplifying. We thought about going away for Christmas, but then realized that we would be leaving a house full of contractors. Not a good idea, so here we'll stay. Jack is pushing for Christmas dinner at Cracker Barrel, the traditional grits and fried okra...Out of bubbly, gotta go (if I can stand up).

I'll not finish this year with a joke, but rather with a remembrance. Leaving the house on Siesta Key after 16 years was difficult, but it's time to start simplifying things. We leave the house behind, but the memories of family, friends, pets, celebrations, parties, and, yes, trying times that were shared in that house will live on with us. That is the real blessing that we treasure. Please come to Sarasota and help us add to that treasure of memories in our new home.

HAVE A VERY MERRY CHRISTMAS AND A SPECTACULAR 2016!

The Pendrays

50 Years of Christmas Letters

CHRISTMAS 2016

Hello Out There...Run for cover! Here comes the 46th edition of the annual Pendray Pulp (def: Pulp - a magazine or book printed on cheap paper and often dealing with sensational material (or, at least, worthless material, ed.)) ...Predator...No, that is not my nickname (that I know of), but the brand of old vine red zinfandel wine that is charging my battery as I write this; zap, zap. Where do I get the knowledge to find such good wine values as Predator? From the same place I get most of my knowledge nowadays, from my kids. Thanks Steve & Steph for this wine tip...We moved into our new home in Sarasota on Dec. 29 and spent most of Jan. shopping on Craig's List. You see, the buyer of our old house also wanted our bedroom and office furniture, so we furnished our new bedrooms and office from Craig's List. Now we can say, "Interiors by Craig." We met some very nice folks in the process, and ended up with better furniture than we have ever had, at **25%** of the cost. Long live the Internet!...In between Craig shopping visits, we flew up to CT to celebrate the birthdays of Steve and the grandkids, Brooke and Robbie. It was a warm visit, but cold outside. Long live FL...Charging along nicely on my second glass of Predator; zap, zap. I better write faster, or I'll be finished before the letter...In Feb., Jack joined two high-school/college buddies, Inky Philips and Frank Molinari, for a few days at Mole's place in AZ. These old frat boys did a lot of drinking (two beers) and raised hell, until soon after sunset. No friends like old friends...To escape the new "fixer upper" house, Linda and Jack took a cruise from Santiago, around Cape Horn, to Buenos Aires. Pretty cool (pun intended)...In March, we joined some other members of our infamous Virginia Gourmet Group (GG) for a weekend in Florida's "Disneyworld for Adults," otherwise known as The Villages. Always a good time with the GG, and no one was injured by speeding golf carts... Things slowed down a little when Jack was diagnosed with prostate cancer and had the offending organ removed, so April was a quiet month of recuperation...Start third glass; zap, zap...Not being able to do much while recovering from his prostatectomy, Jack decided to have his long-delayed left shoulder rotator cuff repair, thereby completely incapacitating himself. He did, it worked, so May was really quiet...June is wedding month, so Linda's grandniece, Cheyenne, married Cheyne Hammond on

Siesta Beach. Perfect day, perfect couple, perfect wedding. So now Cheyenne and Cheyne are chez Hammond...After the wedding, we took off for Asheville, fleeing from the FL summer. Jack got to spend the 4th of July weekend in Mission Hospital in Asheville, where his kidney stone went septic and he went into septic shock. He does not recommend this as the best way to celebrate the 4th of July...More Predator! zap, azp...At the end of July, our youngest son, Andrew, married Krystal Wang at Gardener Ranch in Carmel Valley, CA. Just about all of our family members attended, thereby producing the enclosed photo, which can also serve as an eye test in facial recognition. The Pendrays met the Wangs, which resulted in a lovefest and fabulous wedding and party...Not having had a hurricane in FL for almost 15 years, we decided to take our portable generator to Steve and Stephanie in CT in Aug. Naturally, we caused FL to be hit by several hurricanes in 2016, including a Level 5. We apologize. Anyway, we got to spend some time with the grandkids in CT, which is justification enough...I'm getting fully charged, azp, pza...In Sept., we headed to Coral Gables for the 4th reunion of Ching Tang, Jack's high school fraternity. Quite a blast, but the gang is thinning out...We returned to NC in time to welcome friends from Australia, Chris and Chris Lawson-Smith and Kay Neil. We showed them the NC mountains and shared a few bottles of wine... Oct. was the month of our 50th wedding anniversary, so we rented a big house west of Asheville and invited the family to come see the fall foliage. They came from afar: Jack's brother, Keith, and his wife Renee came from Seattle, Andrew and Krystal came from San Jose, Sean and Melanie from Miami, Steve and Stephanie from Darien, Susan and Gordon from their summer place in Michigan, Mike from Reston, and we drove all 30 minutes from our place in NC. We had 13 adults, 4 toddlers, and 1 Labrador for most of a week. A wonderful celebration of the results of our union 50 years ago…After the festivities, Andy and Krystal stayed on another two days for a taste of Asheville, both wine and beer…I won't mention the election in Nov. to half of you, but to the rest I say, yippee. Although I voted for Trump while holding my nose, I feel that the life of the American experiment in democratic government has been extended, surprising me and most others. Our oldest, Mike, is the only one I know who saw Trump's victory coming…Mike, Sean, Melanie, Sophia (almost 3), and Luke (almost 2) joined us for Thanksgiving. Sean and Melanie slipped off for two days to watch FSU thrash UF, leaving Linda, Jack, & Mike to watch the toddlers. Since we had them outnumbered 3 adults to 2 toddlers, we all survived and had fun…We're off to Virginia to spend Christmas with Mike and Linda's sister, Susan, and her husband, Gordon, then back to FL for the winter…Having spent the year taking care of a recuperating Jack in addition to her usual activities, Linda is hoping for a new year in which there are no bored, whining, stubborn, or needy patients in the house (Ahem)...The Predator has destroyed me (Ah ha, that's why they call it that!), so I'll finish while I can still see.

This year the joke is on Jack. After having ranted and railed for years against what he calls "The Sarasota Conversation," where the old folks sit around and try to one-up each other with tales of illnesses, aches, pains, doctors, hospitals, etc., he finally gets it. Having had a hernia repair, prostatectomy, rotator cuff repair, and a bout of septic shock all within a twelve-month period, he can now more than hold his own in The Sarasota Conversation.

WE WISH YOU AND YOURS A VERY MERRY CHRISTMAS AND A TERRIFIC 2017!

The Pendrays

The Pendray family members at Krystal and Andy's wedding—Gardener Ranch, Carmel Valley, CA

CHRISTMAS 2017

Hello Out There…Here it is, darn! The 47th edition of the Pendray punishment for people of purposelessness. (People with purpose have already sent this to the circular file cabinet.) Due to popular demand and death threats, it is in a brave new format, with fewer words and more integrated pictures (hooray, the crowd roars!) Having updated from Word 1994 to Word 2016, I should be able to do this…Inspiration this year is provided by a bottle of Tomás Buendia Tempranillo from somewhere in Spain. I have no idea where it came from or how it got here, but it has a screw top, so I could get it open… In Jan., we went to CT to celebrate birthdays with Steve, Brooke, and Robbie. For some unknown reason, Stephanie picked Oct. for her birthday, thus avoiding a January fourfecta. (I think I just invented a word.) There should be a picture of the Connecticut Pendrays somewhere around here…

In Feb., we hosted Joan & Gene Gildea and Kathy & Tim McInerney for a week of sun and fun in Sarasota. Since the Gildeas have many times provided us with a B&B in Darien, this was a fun way to say thanks...In March, we visited Legoland with the Miami Pendrays: Sean, Melanie, Sophia, and Luke. Being with the kids reminded us why young folks have kids and grandfolks just watch. We also visited long-time (rather than old) friends from our CT days, Nancy & Gus Serra, on Marco Island (known as Collier City to old

Floridians like Jack)...The Tempranillo, whatever that is, isn't bad...Apr. was quiet, just visited with friends, old and new... in May, Linda's sister, Susan, visited in FL before we pushed off early for NC. We had to get there early so we could drive to Virginia to catch a plane to Paris, where we met up with Donna & Paul Huck to go to Normandy for a week, followed by 2 days in the Loire Valley and 3 days in Paris. Paul and Jack go back to Jr. High days, but Paul still speaks to Jack, amazing!

In Normandy, our babysitter from our days in France had us all over for a light 5-course lunch. Thanks to Maryse & Dominique Poullaouec, we saved money by not having to eat for a couple of days after that. The highlight of the trip occurred on the U.S. Memorial Day, May 29th, at the U.S. Cemetery in Brittany, where two American flags fly over thousands of American, and some German, war dead. The cemetery superintendent, Bruce Malone, asked us to help him lower and fold the flags. The guys did one and the gals the other. See if you can find the photos of it. Paul and Jack, the tough old vets, both had tears in their eyes.

Dinner in Paris with Jack's patient French boss from long ago, Michel Fievet, and his wife Franceline, was a great way to end the trip...Coming back from France in June, we set out on a "mooch tour," sponging off Kathy & Ken Homa in Maryland, the Gildeas in Darien, and Eileen & John Giaquinto in Delaware. Mooching doesn't get any better. At the end of June, Sean, Melanie, and the kids joined us for a long weekend in NC...In July, we came back to FL for a week over the 4th. Too damned hot, so we rapidly went back to NC. Jack, the 4th generation Floridian, is now officially a Snowbird...Tempranillo, whatever that is, is pretty good... Aug. was quiet, if you don't count the visit to NC of Judy & John Guido, a trip to Virginia for the 50th anniversary of Ellen & Jim Mullen, and a trip to Russia with Judy & Ted Copland. For the latter, we took a Viking cruise from Moscow to St. Petersburg, with an extension to Helsinki. For us old Cold War veterans, it was quite a surprise to see that Russian cities are just like ours with persistent traffic jams, chic women everywhere, and great stores full of stuff. The progress since they abandoned Communism is remarkable. Somewhere in this letter, you may find a photo of the four of us in front of some church, somewhere in Russia, or Finland, or Estonia, wherever…

In Sept., we drove up to Charlottesville, VA, for the wedding of Jack's cousin's daughter, Courtney Coleman. The Wintergreen area up there was perfect, and has changed a lot in only 45 years...Tempranillo, whatever that is, is great!...Oct. took us to Boulder, CO, for Linda's reunion for the Munich American High School. This terrific group celebrates reunions all over the country. From there, we went to see our new granddaughter in San Jose, CA. Krystal & Andrew had Aiden Julian Pendray on Oct. 2nd, the same date that Stephanie had chosen for her birth. There should be a photo of the CA Pendrays around here, including Keizer in the distance.

Yes, Julian is also Jack's middle name, and he is honored to share it with Aiden…In Nov., we got back to Sarasota and began our annual round of doctor visits. Doctor visits are the main social events for Sarasotans. Party on! …The Miami Pendrays and Mike, from Virginia, joined us for Thanksgiving. Marvelous weather and lots of pool time. If I'm lucky, there should be a photo…

Tempranillo, whatever that is, sucks. The bottle's run dry!...We plan on going to VA again to spend Christmas with our oldest, Mike, and Linda's sister, Susan, and her husband, Gordon…This year the joke is on Steve and Steph. They love the area where they live, but couldn't survive in their little house. So, after years of extensive research, they found the perfect house, catty-corner across the street. They bought it and will be moving in about now. All jokes should end so well.

WE WISH YOU AND YOURS A BLESSED CHRISTMAS AND A HAPPY 2018!

The Pendrays

The Times, They Are A-Changing

Being born in 1939, I am in the middle of the Silent Generation, 1928 to 1945, also called the Lucky Generation, a more accurate name, in my opinion. Lucky because we were preceded and protected by the Greatest Generation, our parents, and also because we were allowed to finish schooling before the unrest of the following Baby Boomer Generation hit. We are a small generation in numbers, and we quietly rode the wave of security and prosperity created by the Greatest Generation. We also adopted their culture of family-based morals and values.

It is often said that the rate of cultural change accelerates with advances in technology. Lord knows I've seen significant technological change in my life, and even contributed a tiny part to that. However, when viewed in the grand sweep of thousands of years of human existence, the societal and cultural change in America in my 80 years puts technological evolution to shame. Here are some examples that have caught my attention.

Changing Parental Roles

Excuse me if I oversimplify, but I'm not qualified to write a treatise on this subject, only to make a point or two from my experience. In my day, parental roles were simple: the man was the provider and the head of the household and the woman was the nurturer and ran the household. In a sense, husband and wife lived different lives, the man's life was outside the house and the woman's life was inside. Families adjusted their needs to stay within the means the provider produced, often on a pay-as-you-go basis. Individual wants beyond the family's means were left to the individual to provide for as best he or she could. Children ran relatively free and were left to learn many of the lessons of life through experiences, both good and bad. When the school authorities reported that a child needed discipline, it was usually rendered with few questions.

It seems to me that little of this family culture remains today, some for the better and some for the worse. Role sharing is the new norm, varying on a sliding scale from the above classic model to a complete role reversal, with 50/50 often being the goal. Mathematically easy to express; not so easy to do. Even though the level of means provided by parents has increased with the increase of our standard of living and even with two providers in the home, it seems that the family wants (notice that I did not say needs) frequently exceed the means, leading to debt, no savings cushion, and financial stress. Children are often pampered, hovered over, and protected from life experiences that may be painful, sometimes leading to adults who are ill prepared for the realities of independent living.

Don't mistake me; I think the sliding scale is a great idea. Every parent and every family is unique and should be encouraged to build the family environment that is best for them, with no dictated roles. If done right, it can be a win/win solution that optimizes the contributions of both parents and the resulting nurturing and learning of the children. Nevertheless, I am concerned the new flexibility could yield an unbalanced shifting of responsibilities onto one parent, but that can be a problem in any model. I'm sure it's not easy to find that perfect and fair balance.

Role Models

I was once asked if I tried to be a role model for my family or business associates. My response is no. I don't think one can try to be a role model without being a hypocrite, playing a role. If some have seen me as a positive role model, I'm sure there will be as many, if not more, who consider me a good example of what *not* to do. Looking back on my life, I would join the not-to-do group. In life, mistakes weigh much heavier than things done right.

Segregation in My Life

Being born and raised in the American South in the '40s and '50s, I lived a segregated life in a segregated culture, in both Chattanooga and Miami. It was part of the culture, in the woodwork, un-questioned, un-noticed, and, in hindsight, un-acceptable. In those days, there were three restrooms: men, ladies, and colored. There were two water fountains: white and colored. Two sections on the bus: front and back. Perhaps worst of all, two sets of schools: well-funded and not. I was neither a segregationist nor an integrationist. Frankly, I didn't dwell on it because that's just the way it was. I do recall that I thought segregation was pretty stupid due to the terrific loss of opportunity for so many folks to make their best contributions to society and the economy.

I am a proud southerner from a southern family with roots that go back to the Civil War, but I'm glad we lost that war. I don't believe any of my ancestors held slaves, but that was probably for economic reasons rather than moral ones. My mother and grandmother were both big bigots, but somehow that never rubbed off on me or my brothers. In fact, my brothers and I made fun of them over it. Not being black, or any other minority unless you consider Irish Catholic a minority, as they did in Chattanooga in 1944, I will never be able to experience, or even truly empathize with, the discriminated-against people of our country. I can only imagine, but that is nothing like experiencing.

In my opinion, it will never be possible to declare total victory in the fight against racism and prejudice, not as long as human beings are involved. However, I would like to recognize and celebrate the incredible progress and achievements that have been made in the USA in my lifetime. Progress in civilization moves at a snail's pace, usually taking many generations to see noticeable change. In comparison, the changing of our culture in terms of minority discrimination and attitude over the last 60 years has been at light speed. In particular, I'm proud of the South. It is amazing to me to see that the whole tone of the old South has changed, and not superficially, but based on reflection, recognition, and understanding. Prejudice holds up poorly under the bright light of examination, and I believe that most southerners were receptive to such examination. I don't feel we were coerced, but rather enlightened, thanks in large part to the peaceful guidance of Dr. Martin Luther King.

I will feel better when every American is able to compete on a level playing field and is provided the resources and opportunity to succeed, prosper, and contribute to the best of his or her ability. Then we will have answered my criticisms of both the economic stupidity and the immorality of discrimination.

Passing the Morals Down

Whuff, this is a tough one. I have no idea how to pass morals down in a world where everyone is connected to everyone and the home is mostly a place to eat and sleep. I have no idea how a parent can even know what is going on at the other end of the communications device in a child's hand providing access to the world: the beautiful and the ugly, the good and the evil. That's a scary thought to me. We are a technology family, so our sons were early users. One day, our nine-year old son, who is now well past 40, came up from his dial-up connected computer in the basement and asked me what an alternate lifestyle was. I went and looked at the blog he was on and saw it was an adult gay blog. I read the conversation and was relieved when I saw that, when they discovered he was nine, the bloggers had responsibly told him to please leave the blog. I could only imagine what could have transpired if the bloggers had been criminals, scammers, or other malevolent types. I can't imagine the risks that children face today, nor how to prepare them for it, but try one must, and starting at an early age.

I am proud to say that I believe that our three sons are highly moral people who add value to society. Yes, we dragged them to our Episcopal church every Sunday, tried to set a good example, complimented them when earned, disciplined them when they erred, and practiced "contrived deprivation"—a Jack Pendray special form of modern parenting. Let me explain.

Throughout history one of the main purposes of parenting has been to provide for the physical needs of children—food, shelter, clothing, etc.— and it has been a struggle to meet these needs adequately. In the past, most children have been more or less deprived of the resources to fully meet their legitimate needs. In my opinion, some such deprivation can be good life experience and build moral character if appreciated properly. Now, it seems to me that sometime in the late 1950s the affluence of the average American household crossed over the line to where parents could finally provide for all of the legitimate physical needs of their children without sacrifice. In fact, it became easier to provide for the needs and wants of children than it was to disappoint and resist the constant badgering that children can produce. Consequently, many in our society coddled their way into having entitled progeny who did not fully understand the need for restraint nor have any life experiences of deprivation from which to learn. Therefore, I developed my approach of contrived deprivation, or saying no even when it was much easier to say yes. The answer was often, "It's OK for you to have that, but you need to acquire it honestly on your own, or live without it." I call it contrived because one has to choose the right opportunities to practice deprivation yielding a positive lesson. Another thing easier said than done.

CHRISTMAS 2018

Hello Out There...Here it is, the 48th edition of the Pendray Page. To save trees, postage, and effort, many of you received this letter via email. Those of you who received an actual piece of paper via snail mail, please email us your email address in order to receive future copies. (Did you see that? A simple way to unsubscribe from this spam!)... It has been said that a picture is worth a thousand words, so consider this as having been spared 8,000 words (Oh, Lord, no!)...This year's insipiration (misspelling intentional, cute huh?) is provided by a fine Kiwi from New Zealand named Kim Crawford and his merry band of sauvignon blanc producers...January, we went to Darien to celebrate the Jan. birthdays of Steve and the twins, Brooke and Robbie, in their new house. Somewhere around here should be a photo of Steve and Stephanie and family...

Feb., March, April, & May were mostly quiet times in FL. At their ages, Jack and his child-bride, Linda, spend most of their time in Sarasota visiting doctors, and having the "Sarasota conversation" (talking about visiting doctors) with other Sarasotans...June saw our return to Asheville to hide from the scorcher of a summer in Sarasota. It was even hot in the mountains of NC, reaching 80 on several occasions!...Our new dog, Champ, really enjoyed NC, but he wasn't interested in the deer. Linda says it was because the deer do not have people with them, as all people in NC seem to carry dog treats in their pockets...

(Nice stuff, thanks Kim Crawford)...July took us to MD and CT to visit our neighborhood gang from our days in CT: the Hammers, the Homas, and the Jaffes. The Steins also joined the party in Trumbull. Lots of wine, fun, wine, laughter, and wine...In Aug., our oldest, Mike, joined us as we visited Jack's cousins, Jim Coleman and Barbara Grimsley, with their spouses Kathy and Charles, in Wintergreen Resort, VA. Mike really liked their two vacation houses there, so he up and bought one a half-block away. He moved there in October, and now works from home in Wintergreen. Nice life, telecommuting...And then things got busy, strike that, crazy...We drove to Chattanooga in August to visit Jack's stepsister, Betty Pendleton. We had a great time, but Jack couldn't get over how much Chattanooga had changed since he was a kid there only 73 years ago. Jack ages poorly...Mid-August,

Ted and Judy Copland escaped the FL heat with us for a few days...At the end of Aug., Andy and Krystal's nanny had to take an abrupt leave, so we went to San Jose to try to fill her shoes. We were marginally adequate, whew. We were welcomed into the splendid home of our cherished friends, John and Cindy de Santis. A picture of us with Andy, Krystal, and our granddaughter, Aiden, taken in the de Santis yard should be lurking around here somewhere. Aiden is 1, always smiling, and into everything...

In early Sept., Jack's cousin, Barbara Grimsley, and her husband, Charles, visited us for a few days, followed by John and Judy Guido. The cool NC mountains are like a friend magnet in the summer, and we love it...(Kim Crawford is doing the job, feeling good.)...In mid Sept., we started our planned trip out west. We re-visited Andy & Krystal (no nanny duties this time) in San Jose, and Jack's brother, Keith Hoeller, in Seattle. You should find a photo of us with Keith and his wife Renee dining in Seattle.

We then met Mike, Linda's sister, Susan, and Susan's husband, Gordon, in Victoria BC, Canada, where a branch of the Pendray clan had settled. When we arrived in Victoria, our dear friend from Australia, Fay Drayton, was waiting for us. She happened to be in Victoria on a tour from Perth. Small world...We strolled along Pendray Street (all of two blocks long), stayed in the Pendray suite at the Pendray Inn, and had high tea in the Pendray Restaurant. Proof of this is in the photos.

From Victoria, we ferried to Vancouver for a night, then took the Rocky Mountaineer train to Jasper, via Whistler. A terrific two-day train trip. It being Canada, we had a foot of snow fall on our way to Jasper, which covered the trees, beautiful. From Jasper, we bus toured to Lake Louise, Banff, and Calgary. There's a photo of us in Jasper, or Lake Louise, wherever. A terrific trip...

In Oct., we returned to Darien for another visit with Steve & Steph, and stopped by Wintergreen to see Mike in his new house...We welcomed our last friends of the season, Jan Rumberger and Kathy Vary. Fun, food, & great wine...Nov took us home to Sarasota for a round of doctor visits and Sarasota conversations. Mike, Jack's nephew, Sean, and his family, Melanie, Sophia, and Luke, joined us for Thanksgiving in Sarasota. Nice and warm with lots of pool time and too much good food. Sean and Jack sported their school colors prior to Florida's thumping of FSU for the first time in many years, Go Gators...

We're going to spend Christmas in CT with the almost 4-year-old twins. Should be a treat...This year the joke is on Linda. We contacted Labrador Rescue to get another dog. Linda was very clear that she wanted a small, female, yellow Lab. Take another look at our black, male, 80+ pound Lab. You take what you can get, and we love Champ dearly…(Cim Krawfrd is done, and so am I.)

We wish you all a Blessed Christmas and Happy and Prosperous New Year.

The Pendrays

50 Years of Christmas Letters

My Loves

I wish to say a few comments about the very personal thing called love. I have had the good fortune to have been in real love four times. As you become old and realize that your future is behind you, i.e., the great events of life are in the past, past loves can be a confusing memory. Are you still in love with those past loves? What would life be like if the past paths taken would have been different? Did you make the right choices? In my case, I pondered these questions during the COVID-19 sequestration and came to some fairly clear conclusions.

- Love is not limited, as there is an infinite supply available to each person. One does not have to displace love for one person in order to love another.

- Regrets and desires for "do-overs" are misplaced. Let the past rest, forgetting the hurts while cherishing the fond memories.

- The people you loved in the past no longer exist. They have moved on, evolved, and changed. In my case, I know that all four of my loves have led fulfilling lives, prospered, and have loved and been loved by people of value.

- I love the memories of having loved the women I loved and the times we shared. Each was the right person for me at the right time in my life. I am a much better person because of the impact of each of them on my life. I hope they feel somewhat the same.

College was better for me than high school, girl-wise. My first year, I had no dates and was a full-time engineering student and frat boy: a geek who partied. I think it was during the summer between my freshman and sophomore years that I went back to a high school party given by Tallet, a girls' club at Gables High, and saw Jane, the girl I consider to have been my first girlfriend. She had joined Tallet while I was away at UF, so I didn't know her. I clearly remember seeing her seated across the room, a gorgeous blond-headed ray of sunshine with a killer smile. Being a "college man," I mustered the confidence and courage to ask her out, and we dated way beyond my normal two-date threshold. Due to my lack of communication ability with women, I don't know if she considered me to be her boyfriend, but I felt that I finally had a girlfriend, and what a catch she was! She was bright, patient, straightforward, caring, and fun to be with. She was my first serious love, and she did wonders for me. She gave me much needed self-esteem. I thought, if this wonderful person could think that I was OK, then maybe I was OK. I'm not sure how it ended, perhaps the distance separation was too far, perhaps I ran away as usual, perhaps she moved on to better options; nevertheless, I did move forward with a new-found confidence that I was OK in the eyes of at least one exceptional girl.

When I was living on Le Jeune Road and a freshman at the U of F, I had a neighbor, Bud Trammell, who lived across the street on Bargello Ave and he was in the 11th grade at Gables High. I was visiting him one day and saw a portrait photo of his girlfriend who was in the 10th grade at Gables. I remember thinking what a stunning, attractive, and happy looking girl she was. Two years later, in my junior year at UF, I finally met this girl, who was then a senior at Gables High. Kathy became my second true love. Kathy was a very sharp free spirit who enjoyed people and life. I was a bit of a straight-laced, stodgy, and judgmental person. Kathy taught me, by example, to be happy and enjoy life. We had a great time for most of a year, and kept in touch for several years after. She moved to Boston, I went to Palo Alto, and she met a better person in Boston, to whom she has been married for 56 years. I am a better, and happier, person because of my time with Kathy. Her happiness was infectious.

I was a 4 ½-year engineering graduate at UF. Upon graduation on February 3, 1962, I received orders from the USAF to go to Stanford, beginning in June, to learn about data processing. The Nuclear Engineering department at UF gave me a 4-month research assistant job working on the UF reactor to tide me over until June, so I was a practicing nuclear engineer for all of four months. I moved into the Sigma Nu house and worked a forty-hour week with no exams or pressure, a great time. Karen was finishing her senior year at Gainesville, and she gave me a second chance. You see, the prior year I had asked Karen to the Sigma Nu weekend, a big deal, and she had accepted. Well, I put on quite a show: got drunk, jumped into the fish pond at the fraternity house, threw up, and passed out. Someone else had to take Karen home, and I avoided her thereafter in embarrassed disgrace. As I said, she gave me a second chance, and I did better. Karen was my third true love. She was beautiful (the UF Homecoming Queen), smart, refined, gentle, patient, and caring. She was an adult, and treated me as an adult, which I tried to become. Karen was the first, and only, girl to ever wear my fraternity pin. She taught me that I could trust a woman. I'm sure we could have had a good life together, which we discussed, but I went off to Stanford, and the separation was fatal to our relationship. I never saw her again, even though my son and her son were Sigma Nu's together at UF. She has since left this world, which makes it a lesser place for all of us. From Karen I learned trust, kindness, consideration, and adult responsibility.

After Stanford, the Air Force assigned me to the USAF HQ Data Services Center in the Pentagon. Initially, I shared an apartment with another Stanford USAF computer scientist, Alan Merten, in

Annandale, Virginia. Alan and I lived in an area of garden apartments where we quickly noticed that there were four attractive girls in another of the buildings close by. The problem was that every time we saw them in the parking lot, they were moving heavy stuff, or had guys with them, or had some other unappealing thing going on, all of which we avoided. So, one day we just waltzed up to their door and knocked. Some guy answered the door...awkward! We stammered around a bit and he called one of the girls to whom we introduced ourselves as being their neighbors. We were invited in, introductions were made, and the girls' dates started showing up to take them out...awkward! Anyway, it turned out that the guy who opened the door, Kerry Byrd, was dating Linda's sister, and he was just visiting. Kerry kinda took us under his wing and we became good friends. Alan and I were smart enough by now to know that girls talk to girls and there was no way we could ever date more than one of these girls. So, since we had no television and the girls did, Al and I would go watch television at the girls' apartment and observe events in order to decide who we would like to ask out. Actually, for me it was never a question, I fell for the ravishing redhead, Linda. She was beautiful (Virginia College Queen '64), very intelligent (Phi Beta Kappa), poised and personable (President of her Chi Omega sorority), and fun, but too damned popular. I could never get a date with her! Finally, in desperation, I schemed with one of her roommates to pick Linda up at the airport in place of said roommate. When Linda got off her plane, I was there and said something like, "I know you're not busy tonight, so let's go to a party." She agreed, and that was the beginning of my pinnacle true love, number 4. The party was a New Year's Day party at a USAF officer's house. We must have had a really good time with plenty of adult beverages, because we drove home in January with the top of my Corvair convertible down. We thought we were really cool!

It's been 54 years of happy and faithful marriage now, and I can say that I'm not only in love with the girl in the memories of our courtship and marriage but also in love with the young woman who bore and wisely nurtured and raised our three terrific sons, in love with the patient companion who stood me up when I fell down, in love with the supporter who applauded my infrequent successes, in love with the person who is respected and appreciated by so many friends, in love with the grandmother that our grandchildren ask for, and in love with the woman who gracefully shares with me the trials and tribulations of aging.

My penchant for being lucky in the big things was again demonstrated by the good fortune of having Linda as my life's partner, the biggest stroke of unmerited good luck I ever had.

Dabney Ragland, Penny Guerin, Ellen Brohard, Susan Lawrence Byrd, Linda, Jack, Tom Pendray, Kerry Byrd, Al Merten, Dick Abbott—St. Andrew's Episcopal Church, Arlington, VA

50 Years of Christmas Letters

CHRISTMAS 2019

Hello Out There...Here it is, the 49th edition of the Pendray Page. As we used to say in the Pentagon, burn before reading!...So many people have told me to "stop whining" that I will not use wine as my motivation this year, but rather a concoction of 50% Bailey's and 50% Kahlua introduced to us by our son, Andrew. We call it a Bahlua, but some of our friends in Sarasota call it a Pendray, of which we are terribly proud. You see, it is the perfect drink for folks our age; enough alcohol for a good <u>buzz</u> balanced by enough caffeine to keep us awake to enjoy it... buzz...Author's note: We saw so many wonderful friends this year that their names would fill the letter, but they are too important to not mention so a separate page is attached giving the Cast of

Characters...Jan. thru mid Apr., we were in Sarasota doing Sarasota things, e.g., doctor visits, dentist visits, physical therapy, comparing illnesses and doctors as to who had the biggest and bestest (the "Sarasota conversation"), eating out, naps, etc. In between medical experiences and Sarasota Conversations, we squeezed in some lecture series, house maintenance, shows, and dinners with friends. And don't forget church, as Sarasota is called "God's waiting room" for a good reason. We did spend time with some winter visitors (the other reason Sarasota exists) who you will find listed in The Cast of Characters...buzz (refill Bahlua)...In the middle of April, the craziness began. We drove to Asheville, NC, to list our house for sale with a Realtor friend. We also drove our dog, Champ, to summer camp in Highlands, NC. Since we had such a hectic travel schedule coming up, we had to find a place where Champ could stay for 3 months. Fortunately, the lady who had found and fostered Champ out of the Miami dog pound offered to keep him while we traveled, so he had a summer of cool climate, waterfalls, outdoor music concerts, and winery visits. We weren't sure he would come back to us, but he came back very happy and a bit spoiled. He has since trained us to meet his new, higher expectations... The travels started in May with a 14-day re-positioning cruise from Tampa to Amsterdam with two couples of our infamous Gourmet Group from our days in VA in the '70s. Still fun to be with them....From Amsterdam, we trained to Paris where we rented an apartment near the Eiffel Tower for two weeks. While in Paris, we flew down to Valencia to spend a delightful two days with Sarasota friends who have moved there. Valencia was a surprisingly delightful mix of the modern with the charm and history of Spain. The purpose of the visit to Paris was to re-connect with some of the friends and work associates from our days there in the early '70s. We had dinner with our babysitter and her family, close friends to this day, and Jack managed to locate ten of his work associates who were willing to join us for lunches and dinners. Several even came from distant parts of France, and all of them had a "Jack story" from 50 years ago. Some of the stories were even positive! Frankly, these folks are why we enjoyed our 5 years in France so much, and Jack says they also represent the apogee of his business career in terms of work associates, job enjoyment, and personal satisfaction. Jack left Paris with a large smile, and a tear in his eye...buzz (refill)...Jun 2nd we trained to London and had dinner with our relatives from Derby. Pendrays are everywhere! Home to Sarasota for a few days and then fly to Wintergreen, VA, for Jack's cousin's daughter's, Emily Grimsley's, wedding. Steve, Stephanie, and the twins also came to the wedding, one of three visits they made to Wintergreen this year. We flew back home and soon had to drive back to Wintergreen and on to Northern Virginia for a funeral. The heart and soul of the Gourmet Group, Tim McInerney, joined his Lord, leaving a saddened and incomplete world without him. Hundreds came to the services to honor and mourn Tim, and Jack was honored and weeping as a pallbearer...buzz (refill)...We went to CA to house sit our friends' house and visit our West Coast branch, Andy, Krystal, and Aiden...The last half of July was dedicated to getting the NC house in shape to close on its sale on the 31st. We also collected our dog, Champ, from the fantastic summer camp and its terrific operators. We got back a happy, trusting, and affectionate dog, who now liked getting on the furniture!...In Aug, we also closed on the sale of our investment condo in Sarasota, leaving us with only the house in Sarasota. Old folks need simpler lives. We now summer with our oldest, Mike, in Wintergreen VA, and Linda and Jack piddle around with "improving" Mike's house as much as Mike can stand for...In Oct., we flew from VA back to CA for another brief house sit, followed by a drive to Sonoma for a reunion of Linda's Munich American High School class. Tall tales of Munich in the '60s abounded, sprinkled with a few Sarasota conversations (even in ever-young CA!). We returned to VA, picked up Champ, and drove home to FL where Jack celebrated his 80th birthday. Sean, Melanie, and their kids drove over for the festivities...buzz (refill)...We drove back to VA for Thanksgiving, where we were joined by 30 of Jack's relatives from his Mother's side. Never before have so many Condon descendants gathered in such harmony and had so much fun...We intend to have a quiet Christmas in Sarasota, and stay put for a while...I hereby promise that next year will be simpler, and the 2020 Christmas letter will be much shorter & less confusing (yeah, bet on that one)...buzz (no refills left)...This year the letter will not finish with a joke, but rather with a serious, but joyous, reflection. Jack is weary of watching loved ones precede him in passing into the next phase of our existence, so he declared that our travels were now part of a joyful victory lap celebrating our life together. Not the victory of competitions won, nor of riches gathered, nor of educational credentials garnered, nor of status symbols collected, nor of bragging rights flaunted. While there have been modest amounts of these over the years, the true victory is the enormous love amassed. The nurturing, perpetual love of immediate family, the intimate, irreplaceable love of extended family, the lifelong, profound love of school-days friends, the accidental, fortuitous love of neighbors and work associates, and the assuring, spiritual love communicated through religion. In these, we unabashedly declare and celebrate victory worthy of a victory lap, and you, the recipients of this letter, are included among the loved ones we celebrate, thanks!

The 2010s

We wish you all a Blessed Christmas and Happy and Prosperous New Year full of life's little victories.

The Pendrays

The Cast of Characters

(In order of appearance)

January thru mid April:

We visited with: Tom Bisker & Rich Swastek, Shari Sadler, Ted & Judy Copland, John & Judy Guido, Susan Breese Bowers, Dick & Barbara Abbott, John & Eileen Giaquinto, John & Helen Nilsen, Michele Burnette, Alan & Sally Merten, Sean & Melanie Pendray, Gus & Nancy Serra, and Mike & Gree Jones.

Late April in NC:

Rick Shearin (our friend and Realtor), Sara & Jarrod Wooster (the wonderful dog spoilers)

May:

On cruise: John & Judy Guido, Jim & Helen Manning
In Valenica: Tom Bisker and Rich Swastek
In Paris:
Maryse & Dominique Poullaouec & their daughters Anne Gael & Marie with Jean Fauquier
Jacques Bentz, Philippe Loutrel, Vincent Tixier
Therese & Jacques Bentz

Catherine de Verdiere, Philippe Loutrel, Olivia du Jeu, Richard du Jeu, Francois de Verdiere, Maud du Jeu, Linda, Jack

Georges & Liliane Attard, Jacques Bentz, Philippe Loutrel
Jean-Yves Leclerc
Georges Attard, Vincent Tixier

Francoise Tixier, Sylvie Gouraud, Vincent Tixier, Georges Attard, Raymond Maugey, Henri Gouraud, Jack, Philippe Loutrel, Patricia Maugey, Linda, Jean-Loup Perrin (by telephone)

Richard & Maud du Jeu, Vincent & Francoise Tixier

June:

In London: Kim & Marion Pendray

Barbara & Charles Grimsley & their daughter Emily's wedding

Kathy McInerney & her family & friends at Tim's services

July:

House sit for John & Cindy de Santis

50 Years of Christmas Letters

October in Sonoma:
  David Allen, Stan Dewey & Ann Goldman, Walt & Ferne
  Mizell, Skip Morris, Toby & Julie Teorey, Sharon Tiller
  & Lowell Bergman, Sheila Warnock
November Thanksgiving in Wintergreen:
  Jim & Kathy Coleman & their children Courtney
  (with Ryan), Matthew (with Kaitlin), Patrick & Tim;
  Barbara & Charles Grimsley & their daughter Sara;
  Jens & Jeanie Hansen & their daughters Rachel &
  Jennifer; Susan Harvey; Keith & Renee Hoeller; Andy
  & Krystal Pendray & their daughter Aiden; Mike
  Pendray; Sean & Melanie Pendray with their children
  Sophia & Luke; Steve & Stephanie Pendray with
  their twins Brooke & Robbie

In Memoriam: Tim McInerney, Aleta Prebianca, Phil
Scheffsky, Bob Shaw. They are greatly missed.

The 2010s

Some Photo Ops

Linda, Jack, Krystal, Aiden, Andy

Champ, Jack, Linda, Mike

Steve, Jack, Brooke, Robbie, Linda, Stephanie

Sophia, Linda, Jack, Luke, Sean, Melanie

CHRISTMAS 2020

Hello Out There...Here it is, the not-coveted Covid chronicle cringely (not a real word) collected that no one is waiting for, the 50th edition of the Pendray Page. Last year, I promised a much simpler and quieter 2020, but I am not responsible for Covid, I swear...Pickings are slim this year for alcoholic inspiration, as I drank everything we had months ago while sequestered, right before the divorce and electric shock treatments. Nevertheless, since they have let me out, I found a store this morning that had not been stripped clean and negotiated a deal where I only paid $125 for a box of indeterminate red wine, my favorite. As it is now noon, there is still some wine remaining to accompany me on this virtual ride through the year of Covidtime. And away we go...Locked down in Sarasota, followed by locked down in Wintergreen with Mike, followed by locked downed in Sarasota, again. Well, that about covers our activities for the year...Oh, wait a minute, I forgot to mention all of our travels that were canceled and all the refund credits that we have accumulated with the airlines, cruise lines, and hotels. If we can ever travel again, we should have a full year of pre-paid vacations, assuming we can get there before the travel companies all go bankrupt...We did have many new experiences this year, like going to our church services in the living room in our pajamas, watching Netflix series that were rated as being the 167th most-liked show, learning how to use Zoom to visit our progenies' homes to witness the shell-shocked parents trying to school the grandkids who are under the tables or climbing the walls, having the weather report as the most encouraging thing on TV, receiving seven emails a day from companies that we never heard of telling us how they are changing their way of doing business just to keep us safe, and watching U.S. politicians blame each other for the virus which started 12,000 miles away... Actually, Jan, Feb, and most of Mar were fun months. In Jan, Linda's sister, Susan, and her husband, Gordon joined us for a week or so to help us celebrate Mike's 50th birthday at Ruth's Chris in Sarasota. Oh, we also let Mike fly down and participate, too. Big of us, huh?...In Feb, we slipped away for a weekend in Miami to visit Sean, Melanie, Sophia, and Luke. We got there before Covid, so the household was relatively sane. Great fun. There's a photo around here somewhere of their graduation from virtual school...

Jack sold his 2008 Audi A4. This hot little red beast of a car with 255 h.p. was replaced by a very little white Honda Fit with 128 h.p. and pedal assist, but with current safety features. Since the seats are bigger than shrinking Jack, he is not visible when driving, so the neighbors think we have a new self-driving car...Joan and Gene Gildea escaped from CT for a few days in Feb to share some of our warm sunshine...In early Mar, John Morse, a friend since Jack's days in Palo Alto in 1962-1964, and a private pilot, made his last flight: to Heaven. He is deeply missed by us and many others...Mar started just like Jan and Feb, with dinners out, attending performances, visiting friends – and then the world stopped for Covid...In Apr, Jack learned to Zoom, purchased a subscription, and became a Zoom host. As a host, he can mute anyone in his Zoom meetings, a power he has sought his entire life. Consequently, his Zoom meetings have few, if any, attendees. Our grandchildren are all relatively young and probably believe we live in an iPad, and that they can turn us off by pushing a red button on a screen. I hope they aren't too disappointed when they next see us *in vivo* and find out we aren't that easy to get rid of....To fill our very empty days during Covidtime, "The Boys" bought a subscription to StoryWorth.com for us to use to tell our life stories. Now the family is capable of seeing pages and pages and pages of stuff just like this Christmas letter. We call that payback...On May 21st, our lifelong friend since his and Jack's grad school days at Stanford, Alan Merten, moved on to his reward, leaving his family, our family, the academic world family, and the world in general much less enjoyable and enlightened. After the sadness diminishes, we will always have the stories to re-tell, and the warm memories of having shared his life...At the end of May, we drove to Wintergreen VA to spend the summer with Mike. (See the photo of us with Mike and Champ. Champ is the one with black hair.)

We spent one night on the road, where Linda used a whole container of sani-wipes to disinfect every square inch of our motel room. Traveling is less fun than it used to be...Jun slipped by unnoticed, but we had a very festive 4th of July: we hung out the flag, whoopee!...On July 12th, one of Jack's Ching Tang high school fraternity brothers and lifelong friend, John Landry, died in Sarasota. John was a star at Gables High, a star at the Univ of Georgia, a star in life, and he is now a star in the firmament making the night sky a little brighter; however, earth is lonely...We flew to Sarasota on basically empty planes at the end of July to go to all the doctors appointments that had been postponed due to Covid. We got there just in time for the resurgence of the disease in Florida, but we did both get haircuts! Linda can put away the cereal bowl that she used to cut Jack's hair...Steve, Stephanie, Robbie, and Brooke spent the summer hiding from Covid on Lake Hartwell in GA, but we got a photo of them in CT in their Covid-inspired wardrobe. In August we did get to spend an hour with them at a rest stop on I-81, properly masked and distanced!...

After canceling two trips to CA to visit Andy, Krystal, and Aiden, we gave up, with hopes to go in 2021. They sent us a nice photo of their family enjoying San Jose's hottest summer on record, sunglasses and all...

This year's joke is on Jack. (He's still an easy target!) At the end of 2019, he turned 80 and received an epochal birthday present, hearing aids. Big spender that he is, he went straight to Costco and got their Kirkland specials. (Linda got some too, but only to make Jack feel better.)

After years of dreading this symbol of old age, he loves them! Turns out that he can connect his aids to his iPhone by Bluetooth, which gives him access to his phone calls and the 1,800 oldie/goldie tunes he has stored on his phone. Better yet, with his tiny in-the-ear-canal speakers, no one hears what he is listening to. Best yet (is that an expression?), the aids sense when he is listening to music and push the sounds through his equalizer algorithm, which amplifies frequencies where needed. Jack is now hearing musical instruments and background singers that he hasn't heard in many years, and is loving music again. So, between talking on the phone and listening to music, he is now the loony old man who, while walking his dog, alternates between talking to himself and showing his creaky moves while bopping along to unheard music. The neighbors now really keep their distance, politely citing social distancing requirements.

So ends a half-century of Christmas letters. Fifty years of family, friends, fortune, failure, futures, fatalities, and, most of all, fantastic good luck and fun. In the immortal words of my favorite

554

philosopher, Dr. Seuss: "Don't cry because it's over, smile because it happened."

We wish you all a Blessed Christmas and Happy and Prosperous New Year full of effective vaccines and therapeutics.

The Pendrays

50 Years of Christmas Letters